Tropical Revelations

By David Nash

Tropical Revelations
By David Nash

For Michelle, who inspired this story and the author.

Published by Amnesia Castle Publishing
Copyright © 2007 David Nash
David Nash photo by Lisa McCracken
Layout and design by Firman Design Works, Kansas City, MO
ISBN: 978-0-6152-0488-8

www.amnesiacastle.com
davidnash@amnesiacastle.com

Tropical Revelations

By David Nash

CHAPTER ONE

It was the first summer of the new millennium and I had been living out of my boat on one of the smaller islands that made up the group called Bimini. The weather was perfect for the most part and there were few tourists who came to the small town where I was moored in the harbor and other than the few hookers who worked in the two bars there were few eligible new women that happened to come to the island. I was retired but had done so at a young age. When I was just past fifty I had taken a chance and gotten lucky when I sold some stock on a fluke when it soared very high and I cashed out at just the right time. My luck bought me a very respectable sailboat and enough money when it was invested the interest from it would keep me from working and I would be able to live nicely. I was very comfortable to say the least and enjoyed sailing from place to place, mooring where I wished and staying until I felt a change of scenery was necessary. I had been to this island several times in the last two years and I was well known to the boys in the harbor there. The small town consisted of a hotel and two bars where I kept up my chess game and some decent conversation with the owners and some of the island regulars who were educated and had come to the island to get away from different things in their lives.

Most of the tourists who came to the island were brought by the sea planes that landed there morning and afternoon or the once a day ferry from the larger island

1

which would usually bring supplies for the hotels, bars and the few residents who would order hard to get items from the mainland. Some of the residents were quite well to do and their tastes for hard to get foods and clothing was mostly what was ordered. I bought my food staples from the local store but mostly fed myself by spear fishing and cooking my catch on the propane grill that hung from the after rail of my yacht. I enjoyed having cocktails and cooking after a few afternoon drinks and I loved the solitude my boat gave me. I also had occasional requests to take visitors sailing for a morning or afternoon. These requests would usually come from my friends that bartended or my friend who ran the hotel. I was usually opposed to taking my boat out for hire but if the money was right and the people looked intelligent I would accept the charter and take whoever sailing for a few hours. This was especially done if there were women who were in the party and looked like they might look good in a bikini lying on the aft cushions or the foredeck. The extra money just went to my bar bill or my tab at the store. I was far from broke but it just gave me more and I did like to sail.

It was early that May when the afternoon plane landed and taxied to the big float by the pier to unload its passengers. I watched the passengers disembark with the rest of the drinkers who were in the bar. This was typical as all of us were interested in whoever came to the island. There were two couples of middle age and a young girl in her late twenties who looked good from a distance. I assumed she was with one or both of the couples and went back to my drink and chess game as they walked the long pier to the shore. They disappeared to the hotel and I put my mind back to what was happening to the chessmen on the board. I was being severely beaten by my friend and wasn't enjoying the game very much. My friend had been a great chess player at one time in his life but years of alcohol abuse had dulled his game except for occasional moments of brilliance that would come to him. When these moments occurred he would play like the nationally ranked player he used to be and was very hard to take a few pieces from let alone beat his game. This was one of those times and he was killing me with his moves. The game was his five moves later and I ordered him another drink for his winning and a beer for myself. I sat back looking at the water from my chair and thought about going to grill the rest of the Flounder I'd bagged with my Hawaiian sling that morning. I finished my beer and headed towards my boat stopping at the beach on the way and diving into the crystal clear water. When I had cooled off I got out and began dripping dry while I walked along headed to the pier. I stopped at the freshwater shower on the end of the pier and rinsed off before continuing to my boat and the meal I'd been planning in my head for the last hour. I dried myself off when I got to the boat and I gathered the things I would need for cooking and took them to the cockpit table where I set them out and started the grill. I went below for the fish and opening another beer I went back up to the cockpit to put my dinner on the fire. I sat down and surveyed the beach seeing the girl who had gotten off of the sea plane that afternoon. She was stripping off her shirt to reveal an outstanding body barely covered by a small bikini. I smiled when I looked at her and watched as she went into the water and began to swim. In another minute I turned my attention to the grill and using the tongs turned the Flounder over to get the other side done. It was ready to eat in another minute and I put it onto the plate along with the tomatoes and pasta that were left over from the morning and the night before. While the fish cooled some I went below to get the open bottle of white wine also left over from the night before. As I opened it I sat down and pouring myself a glass full of the cold dry Bordeaux I began to eat and looked again at the beach where the girl was now drying off and preparing to lie down to catch the last of the afternoon sun rays. I watched her as I ate until one of the charter fishing boats distracted me and I looked in the other direction down the pier. They were hanging up a pretty respectable catch from their day on the water and I thought of what would be cooking at the hotel restaurant in a few hours. They had some very respectable King Mackerel and I knew they would taste great after Will the chef got to them. Will had been a chef on the mainland in Miami for a number of years but came to the island two years before and wouldn't say much about his past. The island was such a place where no one pried into anyone's past and the locals just let people be as they wanted as long as there were no problems. There were several people who lived on the island who insisted on more anonymity and the locals gave them their desire. There was a sculptor who lived there six months out of the year and from the work I saw of his I considered him to be very good. I thought he must have a good career on the mainland but never spoke to him about his work. We only talked about the weather or sometimes minor things in the local newspaper that was brought from the big island. I let him be what he wanted as did the rest of the drinking crowd. There were others on the island from different places and they were treated with the same respect. I finished my meal after noticing the girl was gone from the beach and took my dishes to the galley to clean and picked up the book I'd been reading for a few days. When I got tired of my book I turned on the television that worked through the magic of satellites and watched while scrolling through the number of channels that I paid each month for the privilege of receiving. There was nothing of interest on so I went to the bar for another drink before going to bed.

I woke up the next morning and after putting the coffee on I drank two cups and headed for the beach with my mask and fins and spear gun. There were always plenty of fish off of the beach and I hunted until I saw a respectable white trout and nailed it to the sand below me. I hauled it in and began to kick my way into the beach with my catch. When the water became shallow I took off my fins and started up the beach with my fresh catch. I noticed the girl from the day before lying on the sand and she noticed me coming out of the water. As our eyes met she smiled at me and I nodded to her as I turned to head for the pier to rinse off and clean my catch in the weathered wooden troughs which were there for that purpose. When the trout was clean I went to my boat and started the grill. I ate it when it was done and washed the meal down with coffee reheated from earlier that morning. I finished breakfast and got my book out to relax by reading in the shade of the dodger. The morning air was still cool and there was a nice five knot breeze blowing that pleased me.

I had been there for about an hour when I heard footsteps and a voice said, "Hi there, the owner of the hotel said you take people sailing sometimes."

I looked up and seeing the girl from the beach said, "Sometimes, it depends on who and how many."

She said, "Well I'm the who and also the how many. I'm here by myself and I'd like to go sailing."

I said, "OK have you ever done any sailing?"

She said, "Yes I have. I've done plenty on the mainland. I can say that I can handle a boat."

I said, "All right a little help is always good. When would you like to go?"

She said, "This afternoon before cocktail hour. How much do you charge?"

I said, "A hundred an hour is what I usually charge unless it's a long sail."

She said, "What if I help with the boat and bring the refreshments and some snacks?"

I said, "Well that would be different. How about one-fifty for two hours and change?"

She said, "That sounds good. Can we leave at three?"

I said, "Three it is. Meet me here at the boat."

She said, "I'll be here at three. See you then."

She nodded her head at me and walked off down the pier towards the beach. I thought about the deal and it was good. Not great but she was stunning and had a great body. Slim with beautiful light blond hair and deep blue eyes that I'm sure could be seen from across the street. She was a great looking woman and I wondered why she was on this island and not at some fancy resort in the Bahamas or somewhere else. To each his own I thought and went back to my book after watching two of the charter fishing boats leave the dock taking tourists out for their days fishing. I thought about ice and decided I would get extra for the cooler at two to keep my customer's refreshments out of my refrigerator and separate from my own supplies.

I put my book down just before noon and turned on the TV for the 12 o'clock news. There was nothing good about it so I watched for awhile and then went to the bar for my first beer of the day and a roast beef sandwich that Ben the daytime bartender sliced for those who were hungry. Ben had become my friend in the last few months and he made a hell of a sandwich. He liked to make his own brown mustard and it was excellent. That and some salt and pepper made for a sandwich that was to die for and they only served them once a week. When the roast beef was gone so were the sandwiches. I had learned to get there early on Tuesdays having been left out on too many occasions when they had run through the beef. I was talking to Ben about different things between his slicing beef and serving drinks at the bar. I finished my meal, signed my tab and went back to the boat to check on fuel and water, clean towels and the basic shape of the stateroom and head I usually gave my customers to use for changing and personal hygiene. I put clean towels in the head and replenished the toilet paper after doing a quick cleanup so it would smell clean and nice. I then filled the fresh water tanks so we'd have plenty. When I finished it was getting on towards two so I headed down the pier to the store get a bag of ice for my customer. I was back to the boat shortly and left the ice in the shade where it would stay until my customer showed. She was there in a short time and was carrying two shopping bags with her. She brought beer, good wine and plenty of snacks to eat. I smiled inside at the snacks as I knew I probably wouldn't be hungry that night if the snacks were good. I helped her ice the beer and wine and stowed the snacks in the galley. The cooler was left in the cockpit for accessibility.

When it was all done I said, "Are you ready to go?"

She said, "Quite ready thanks. What would you like me to do?"

I said, "Go up to the bow and untie the forward lines and put them onto the pilings."

She headed forward as I started the diesel and I watched as she took the lines from the cleats and placed them onto the pilings so they wouldn't hang in the water. When she got back to the cockpit she sat down and I tossed the stern and spring lines onto the dock to port and starboard. I looked both ways in the harbor and seeing that no boats were moving pushed the throttle forward and eased my sloop out of her slip. When we were clear I spun the wheel to port and we headed for the entrance to the harbor staying to the starboard side in case any other boats might be coming in. We passed the entrance and ran out a couple of hundred yards.

I turned the boat to the wind and said, "Do you know how to keep the boat pointed to the wind?"

She said, "I sure do, are we raising sail?"

I said, "That's it just keep her into the wind."

She said, "Do you need help with the winches?"

I said, "Sure if you know how. I'll raise the mainsail first, the winch has two gears, port is high gear and starboard is low gear for when the sail gets heavy."

She nodded that she understood and I went forward to remove the gaskets from the sail that lashed it to the boom. She saw when I was finished and holding the helm with her foot she reached for the winch and began to crank the big sail up the mast while I made sure it wasn't catching anything on the rigging. When it was all of the way up I headed for the jib and released the roller reefing on the jib. It began to unfurl and my guest was already cranking it out and in with the other winch. I got back to the cockpit and took the helm letting the boat fall off of the wind. The sails filled with air as we fell off and she did a good job of setting the jib while I set the main the way I liked it. We were sailing nicely in another minute and as I steered she sat on the cushions on the high side of the boat.

I looked at her and she smiled and said, "This is a very beautiful boat."

I said, "Thank you very much."

She said, "What kind is she?"

I said, "She's a Beneteau 473 with a few additions to her."

She said, "For instance?"

I said, "I had her built without the normal mast and roller mainsail rigging. Roller mains can get caught when you're rolling them up and that's no good when there's a squall coming down on you and you're by yourself."

She said, "What else?"

I said, "I gave her stronger rigging and a little bigger mast. She'll make about two or three knots better than the boats from the factory."

She smiled and said, "Anything else?"

I smiled back and said, "A little extra flotation and larger freshwater and fuel capacity."

She said, "It sounds like you enjoy sailing blue water."

I said, "I do at that but I also like staying places I like until I want the scenery to change."

She said, "Like here?"

I said, "Yep I like it here just fine. It's just about right for me."

She said, "It's nice here. I've only been here since yesterday but I like it already."

I said, "I know. I saw you get off of the plane yesterday."

She said, "I guess people coming and going on the island are a pretty big topic of conversation."

I said, "Not really. We do notice who comes and goes but the island tends to leave people alone."

She said, "Can I get you a beer?"

I said, "I'd love one thanks."

She reached for the cooler and handed me a cold frosty brown bottle. I said, "Thanks very much. Would you like to take the helm for awhile?"

She said, "Yes I would. Is there anything I should know?"

I said, "Just how to sail," making her laugh. "Just keep her pointed like she is and feel free to harden up or fall off to see how she's running."

She did as I'd said and putting the sloop nicely on the wind said, "What's your name?"

I said, "I'm David Nash and yours?"

She said, "I'm Michelle Murphy. What's the name of your boat?"

I said, "She's the Amnesia Castle."

Michelle said, "Amnesia Castle? That's an interesting name for a boat. How did you come to name her that?"

I said, "It's the name of a boat I remember from a book I read when I was a kid. I've always liked the name and sometimes I can't remember the place I was the day before so I guess she gives me Amnesia."

Michelle said, "Sailing from place to place must be wonderful. I'd like to do that someday."

I said, "Never too soon or too late. It took a long time to arrange an early retirement so I could do this."

She said, "So you're retired? You look too young for retirement."

I said, "I just got lucky. My dot com stocks were good to me."

She said, "I should think so."

I said, "What about you? We don't get many young people here for vacations. I would think you'd head for one of the big resorts in the other islands."

She said, "Can we not talk about me being here please? I'd just like to say that I'm here on vacation and leave it like that."

I said, "Sure you can. I didn't mean to pry."

She said, "No problem I started it by asking all of the questions first," she reached her empty bottle towards me saying, "May I have another beer please?"

I got her another beer from the cooler and after it was open I handed it to her. I noticed she indeed was a good sailor and let her have the helm as much as she wished.

She sailed the boat for another half hour and said, "Would you mind taking the helm back I want to get some sun?"

I said, "Not a problem," and took the wheel from her. She went below and came back in a couple of minutes wearing a very small bikini. She smiled and telling me to help myself to the beer she lay on the cockpit cushions in the sun and put her head on her lovely arms.

I kept the boat on the wind and her in the sun for another hour and when I noticed she was beginning to burn I gently nudged her saying,

"Michelle, you're beginning to burn some and it's time to head back to the harbor."

She raised her head saying, "Thank you for getting me up sleeping in the sun is wonderful."

She reached for the cooler and asking where the corkscrew was she headed below to open the bottle. She took awhile coming back with a tin of very decent caviar and a plate full of sliced cheese and assorted crackers. She poured me a glass of wine and we munched as the sun headed towards the horizon. When we finished the plate she went below and came back with more wine as well. I smiled at her saying thanks and she sat eating and drinking in the cockpit while I sailed the boat.

We finished the second plate and the bottle of wine as the harbor grew in the distance. She went below and came up again saying she put the trash in the basket and it pleased me that she wasn't a mess to the boat as some of my customers could be and often were. I thanked her as we turned the boat into the wind and furled the sails. When we were done I started the diesel and turned my sloop towards the harbor. The charter boats were in and we pulled near my slip and I backed the Castle into place while she went for the bow lines without being asked.

When we were tied up she reached into her bag and produced a wad of bills and after counting off the correct amount handed them to me and said, "Thank you that was wonderful. Can we sail again tomorrow?"

I said, "Same deal?"

She said, "Yes the same deal. Is there anything you'd particularly like for snacks?"

I said, "No get what you want. I'm happy with almost anything and thanks for what you brought today. The caviar was delicious."

Michelle smiled and left the boat heading for the hotel that was in town. I went about cleaning the boat and dealing with the trash that was left while I thought about what I might like to drink at the bar when I got there. I finished all that needed to be done and headed off of the pier to the bar. I walked inside and took the stool I usually occupied.

Harry the evening bartender walked up behind the bar and said, "Dave what'll you have?"

I said, "Scotch please two rocks."

Harry went to fetch my cocktail and on his return said, "Charter this afternoon?"

I said, "Yep and a nice one at that."

He said, "I saw her come off the boat. Damn pretty girl what's she doing here?"

I said, "Just on a vacation I guess. She likes to go sailing and chartered me again tomorrow afternoon."

Harry said, "Nice. Where's she from"

I said, "The states is all I know and I didn't ask questions."

Harry said, "Nice of you, maybe she'll be in here tonight."

I said, "Maybe, I don't know. I've got a book to read so I'm not staying around late tonight. If she comes in fine. She's a nice girl so don't let the regulars mess with her just for me. She's chartered me again tomorrow and you know how much I like to get paid for sailing around."

Harry smiled and went to get me another cocktail which I finished just as the sun was going down. I walked back to my boat enjoying the evening as I walked along to the pier.

I was halfway to the boat on the pier when I saw Michelle sitting on one of the pilings seemingly enjoying the evening I walked up next to her and before I got to her said, "Hi there nice evening huh?"

Michelle turned her face towards mine and I could see in the dim light she was crying. I said, "Hey are you all right?"

She said, "No I'm not but thanks for asking."

I said, "Anything I can do?"

She said, "No thanks. I just need to be left alone please."

I said, "OK but if you need anything you know where my boat is."

Michelle smiled a weak smile at me and I walked away from her and went to the boat where I lay on the cushions and wondered what might be troubling this nice girl. I read for awhile and woke up several hours later finding from my watch that it was after midnight and I was chilled from the damp night air. I looked to the piling where Michelle had been sitting earlier and she was gone. I dropped myself down the companionway and headed for my stateroom and the comfort of my bed.

The next thing I knew it was past dawn and the intense light from the day was streaming in my portholes and through the skylights of the main salon. I started the coffee and decided to go into town for bacon and eggs. I went to the hotel and walked up to the buffet where I loaded a plate with what I wanted and went to sit at a table. I was halfway through my meal when Michelle came into the dining room and noticing me gave me a small wave and went to fill her plate at the buffet. I went back to eating and noticed out of the corner of my eye that she sat a table on the other side off the room and had started eating. I finished my breakfast and left without bothering her heading for the bar to see about a game of chess. Ben was there setting up and put the chessboard and men onto the bar when he saw me come in the door. I set the pieces up in their places and made the first move. Ben walked up and moving one piece walked back down the bar leaving me to make the next move. This went on until the game became more complex and Ben sat behind the other side of the board to think about what he was doing.

We each made a few more moves when he said, "Dave what about that girl who you took sailing with you yesterday?"

I said, "What about her?"

Ben said, "She was here last night when I was in and was drinking pretty heavily. Some of the guys started to hit on her and she didn't like it very much."

I said, "I don't think I'd like it either from that bunch."

Ben said, "No doubt. The boys gave her a ration until Harry came and told them to leave her alone. She left right after that. Harry said you told him to look after her. What's the deal?"

I said, "No deal. She chartered the Castle yesterday and again today. I was just looking out for my customer."

Ben said, "Oh I just wondered if something worth talking about was up."

I said, "Nothing's up. I thought she was nice and she's here by herself so I told Harry to watch out for her. You know how the rummy's in here can get."

Ben grunted his acknowledgement and moved a piece on the board. We spoke no more of the incident or the girl and I took Ben's queen from him a few moves later and the game shortly after that. I headed back to the boat after that and proceeded to relax until it was time for lunch. After lunch I checked on the diesel and the generator and at two I went to get a bag of ice from the store for my afternoon charter.

I got back to my boat with the ice for the afternoon and placed it in the shade as I had done the day before. Michelle showed up at the Castle just before three and we iced the beer and wine she brought with her.

When the cooler was packed she said, "Should I get the bow lines?"

I said, "Sure I'm ready to go."

She went forward to deal with the lines and I tended to the ones aft. I started the diesel and we moved out of the slip as we had the day before. When we cleared the harbor entrance we raised the sails and ran south on a tight reach for quite awhile. Michelle had said little so far so I stayed quiet and waited for her to start any conversation.

After awhile she said, "Mind if I take the helm?"

I stepped aside and said, "Not at all. Would you care for something to drink?"

She said, "Yes I'd like a beer please."

I got up and took two from the cooler in the cockpit. I opened them and handed one to her. She put the bottle to her lovely lips and after taking a long drink said,

"Thanks for last night."

I said, "For what?"

She said, "For telling the bartender to look out for me. That was very nice of you."

I said, "Not at all. I know how some of the fellows in the bar can get. I was just looking out for my customer."

She said, "I appreciate it anyway. I should know better than to get that drunk in a strange bar. I've always attracted too much attention like that."

I said, "Well you're an attractive woman. The guys get out of hand when there's a single woman around. We don't get many on the island."

She said, "I can understand that. I don't like to cause problems. I came here to be by myself and take some time out."

I said, "This is a good place for it. The guys will leave you alone from now on. If they don't Harry will cut them off at the bar and that's their worst nightmare."

Michelle laughed and said, "I'm sure that it is. They probably wouldn't have much to do except for the bar."

I said, "You're right about that. They're all good men but not exactly intellectual types."

Michelle laughed again and said, "What about you? Where were you last night?"

I said, "Reading here on the boat and being an intellectual type."

Michelle said, "So you're an intellectual."

I said, "Not really. I've had a lot of education but I don't consider myself an intellectual. I just like to read books when there's nothing on TV."

Michelle finished her beer and motioned for another one. I supplied what she gestured for and got another one for myself.

She said, "Is it all right if we go about soon? I'd like to put the boat on the wind for awhile."

I said, "Sure, do you want to stay with the helm?"

She said, "Yes if it's all right."

I said, "Not a problem. I'll handle the sails. Just let me know when you're going to go about."

She said, "How about now?"

I got up and went to the winches and said, "Ready about."

She said, "Hard alee," and spun the wheel.

I let the sails out a little to help them come around to the new tack and as I cranked in the jib she tended to the winch for the mainsail bringing it in smartly. She held the boat to the new tack nicely and the Castle heeled over some as she hardened up on the wind. I cleated the jib and main sheets and sat back down. She said, "You're a good sailor. That was a nice tack."

I said, "Thanks you're not bad yourself."

She said, "Where did you learn to sail?"

I said, "On the Gulf Coast of Mississippi when I was a kid. My family sailed so I learned with my dad yelling at me."

Michelle laughed and said, "Oh I know about that. We must have had the same father. I learned the same way. You don't speak like you're from the south. How did that happen?"

I said, "I started my travels when I was in my early teens. Nothing like a lot of sailing to get your mind right ".

She said, "Did you sail all over the world?"

I said, "I did at that. I've always liked the water and sailing from place to place. I've covered a lot of ocean in my life

She said, "Nice way to live your life; hey are you hungry?"

I said, "I could eat. Do you want me to take the helm?"

Michelle said, "Yes, let me go below and make some snacks."

I took the helm from her and she was back in a few minutes with a tray of canapés and an open bottle of wine with glasses from the galley. She offered me the tray and I extended it to her as she sat to starboard on the cushions. She took the tray and after taking some for herself she offered it back to me. I scooped up a few and started to eat.

They were excellent and I said, "There are great. Thank you very much."

She said, "You're welcome," as she began to take her shirt off and get some sun. She ate her share and handing me the tray she lay down on the cushions and fell asleep. I sailed the boat drinking wine and eating canapés while she slept. I kept the boat on the wind for a long time letting her sleep until the sun began to get low and I knew we should be getting back to the island. I woke her up and watched as she stretched in the afternoon sunlight.

She said, "You let me sleep for a long time."

I said, "You looked peaceful and seemed to be enjoying you nap."

She said, "I was thank you. I haven't been sleeping well lately and the rest that I got yesterday and today was the best I've had in a long time."

I said, "Do you want the helm back?"

She said, "Yes please."

I said, "Sail as we did yesterday and come up into the wind about where we did before so we can furl the sails."

Michelle nodded her understanding and held the boat on a good course.

When we were about a half mile from the harbor she put the boat into the wind and I went forward to flake the main onto the boom while she rolled up the jib onto its roller reefing. When it was all tight I started the diesel and pointed the boat to the harbor entrance.

We backed the Castle into her slip and tied her up. Michelle sat onto the cushions and said, "Mind if I finish my wine here on the boat?"

I said, "Not at all. Is there any left for me?"

She smiled and poured me another glass. I sat across from her and she said, "David can we sail again tomorrow?"

I said, "Sure I'm not busy. Do you want to go at the same time?"

She said, "Yes but are there any places we can sail and spend the night? I'd love to spend the night in a lagoon someplace."

I said, "There are some great places close by. Excellent lagoon living if I do say so. Lots of fish to spear and good sunsets to watch below the yardarm."

She said, "Do you have any diving gear?"

I said, "Yes I have a couple of tanks and all of the other things. Do you dive?"

She said, "I was certified years ago but I never kept it up. I'll be all right as long as it's not deep."

I said, "This is another charter I suppose?"

Michelle said, "Absolutely, what will it cost?"

I said, "Well you've been good with the boat and the food make me an offer."

She said, "How about four hundred and I'll buy the food".

I said, "Ok throw in the refilling of the scuba tanks and you've got a deal."

She said, "Deal, can we go after lunch?"

I said, "Ok is one o'clock all right with you?"

She said, "That sounds great. Will the store deliver the groceries and the booze?"

I said, "They will, don't forget to buy plenty of ice."

Michelle stood up and after shaking my hand stepped up onto the pier and walked off to the hotel. I finished putting the boat away and when I was done I walked to the bar where Harry was setting up for the evening. I walked up to the end of the bar and taking my usual stool motioned to him.

He said, "Scotch?"

I said, "Not today, how about a gin and tonic?"

Harry scooped ice into a glass and said,

"What about that girl who you took sailing?"

I took my drink from him and said, "Nothing about it. I heard you kept the boys off of her last night thanks."

Harry said, "No problem she was shooting pool and they got too touchy feely with her because she was drunk. She's not a bad pool player."

I said, "Thanks anyway she's a nice girl. Good sailor too. She's chartered me two days in a row and again tomorrow."

Harry said, "Good enough will you be able to pay your tab soon?"

I said, "I'll pay it now if you want. You know I just run it up to aggravate you."

Harry said, "You do at that. Want another Gin?'

I said, "You bet thanks."

Harry poured another drink for me and after putting it in front of me turned to wait on three new customers who had come into the bar. I drank my drink watching the pier from the ocean side of the bar and noticed Michelle headed for the beach with her towel. She peeled to her bikini and I watched as she walked to the water. I finished my drink and nodding to Harry walked to the pier and the Castle that I boarded and went into the galley to prepare something for dinner. I was still pretty full from the afternoon snacks and decided to eat light. I opened a can of soup and heated it in the microwave. When it was hot I took it to the cockpit and ate while I read my book. At some point after I finished eating I lay back on the cushions and fell asleep.

I was nudged awake sometime later and as I was opening my eyes a voice was saying, "David don't you want to go below to your bunk?"

Michelle was there and I said, "What time is it?"

She said, "Almost ten. Do you sleep here in the cockpit very much?"

I said, "Not much but I do sometimes and wake up damp from the humidity. I go below after that. Thanks for waking me up."

She said, "Not at all. I was out for a walk on the pier and I saw you lying there and I thought you might like to go below. I'm headed back to the hotel now to get some sleep."

I said, "No bar tonight?"

She said, "No not tonight. I was embarrassing enough last night."

Michelle smiled and stepped off of the boat and I stretched before going below and climbing into my bunk and finishing the sleeping I had started.

I woke with the sun the next morning and after coffee I made myself some eggs and took them to the cockpit to watch the very early morning. After cleaning my breakfast mess I checked on the scuba gear and my regular supplies I kept to see if there would be anything that was needed for the trip to the lagoon. Everything was ok so I headed to the beach for a swim when I was drying off I saw the charter fishing boats heading out and the morning sea plane coming in with the day's passengers There was nothing unusual about the tourists who got off of the sea plane and they passed me while I was showering in the fresh water that was on the pier. I headed to the bar dripping wet and went in to see Ben. He was there behind the bar and I ordered a coke while he went through the motions of stocking the place for the day. I mentioned I was headed to one of the lagoons that were close for an overnight with my customer and he smiled when I told him.

He said, "Overnight huh. You two getting along that well?"

I said, "Nothing like that at all. She's just a customer and shame on you anyway."

Ben smiled and said, "Well you have to admit she's great looking."

I said, "I know she's great looking but she's also young enough to be my daughter."

Ben said, "But still old enough to be your thrill."

I said, "I know, I know. Look there will be enough talk around here when we get back from the lagoon. There's no sense in starting any rumors early. They'll be flying by tomorrow night when we get back."

Ben said, "There will be talk tomorrow. If you don't come back should I send out a search party or should I let you have a honeymoon for a few days?"

I said, "Search party please and knock off the commentary. She's nothing but a customer."

I finished my coke and saw that the grocer was heading to the boat with a couple of boxes of food and some ice. I called to him as he passed the bar and went to help him carry the provisions for the day. We got it to the boat and he helped me bring it below where I tipped him and started to store the items we brought. It was eleven by the time I was done and I made a sandwich for lunch. I filled the water tanks and checked the fuel status. I always liked to have full tanks when I went overnight and made a mental note to fill up at the fuel dock before we left the harbor. Michelle showed up just before lunch and stepped onto the boat knocking at the companionway while I was below.

She said, "Did the groceries get here?"

I said, "Yes they did. Come on down."

She came down the companionway steps with a suitcase and said, "Oh good. I was hoping we wouldn't have to wait for them."

I said, "Are you ready to leave?"

She said, Sure just let me put my bag into the stateroom."

She put her case into the stateroom and we both went to the cockpit. Michelle headed for the bow lines and I took care of the stern. I motored us to the fuel dock and we loosely tied the boat. I stayed by the fuel inlet to supervise the filling of the tanks and she went below to put her things away. When the tanks were full I signed for the fuel and we motored out of the harbor and continued until we had enough sea room to raise sail. Michelle did her job as well as she had done the two days before and we were sailing nicely on a course of 110 degrees west south west. The day was fantastic and the Castle was doing great in the fifteen-knot breeze that was blowing.

Michelle went below and came back wearing her bikini and said. "Can I have the helm?"

I said, "Sure, just keep her on 110 degrees."

She stepped behind the wheel and I backed off to give her room to steer.

I took my shirt off to get some sun and she said, "How old are you David?"

I said, "Fifty-two last November'.

She said, "You really look good for fifty-two. I think sailing agrees with you."

I said, "Thanks but I think that it's just genes. My dad stayed slim and trim for his whole life lucky for me."

She said, "It is lucky. I take after my mother but I have some friends who constantly have to watch their weight. I think some of them have been on a diet since they were thirteen or so."

I said, "Well you look very nice yourself. You're lucky."

She said, "Where are we sailing?"

I said, "We're headed for Brewster cove. We'll be there in about three hours if we don't lose the wind. There's never any other boats there and there's a nice beach you can sleep on if you want."

She said, "Good diving?"

I said, "Great diving. Lots of good fish to eat and lobster in the rocks. Do you like lobster?"

She said, "Do I like lobster? Do Barnacles grow on pilings?"

I laughed and said, "I'll teach you how to get them out of their holes. We'll boil a pair for dinner tonight."

Michelle said, "That would be great. David, why aren't you married or with someone."

I said, "I was married once. I liked being married pretty well. It lasted a couple of years. I think she didn't like the work that boats take. Anyway I woke up one morning and she was gone."

She said, "Oh I'm sorry."

I said, "Don't be, that was years ago and it did hurt for awhile but I've gotten over it."

She said, "I'm sorry for all of the questions. It's not fair for me to ask things about you and not to offer anything about myself. I just can't talk about myself right now. I have a good reason and maybe sometime I'll be able to tell you about myself."

I said, "It doesn't matter. You're the client and I don't mind questions about myself and one of these days you'll tell me what you want?"

Just then the GPS beeped and told us it was time to make a course change.

Michelle said, "What should I do?"

I said, "Just look at the GPS screen. There will be a compass heading and the screen will show you a line to follow when you hit that heading. Just follow the road. I'll get the sails."

Michelle pointed the boat north north east and followed the GPS map on the screen.

I adjusted the sails and Michelle said,

"David would you like some lunch?"

I answered in the affirmative and when I took the wheel from her she headed below. She was back in a few minutes with sandwiches and sodas and I was pleased that they were good. Thin sliced rare roast beef was always one of my favorites and the salt air made the sandwiches taste great. We finished our lunch and telling Michelle to take the helm I headed below to get the dishes out of the way. They were washed in a few minutes and I heard Michelle call below to me.

She said, "David there's an island on the horizon!"

I went up the companion way and looked forward. Brewster cove was in front of us a few miles away and right on the money. I took the helm from her and steered for the cove. A half mile out we doused the sails and I started the diesel. I knew the cove well and headed for the deep part of the inlet. The depth finder was telling me we had plenty of water below the keel and I guided my sloop into the cove. When we were in the middle I spun the wheel to port and came up into the wind. I handed the helm to Michelle. I adjusted the throttle of the diesel and she held her stationary while I went forward to drop the anchor and let out the rode. As the anchor went down I signaled for her to cut the diesel. She did so and as the Castle fell back I let out the rode until we had enough length to swing from.

I cleated the line after wrapping it around the winch and went back to the cockpit and said, "We're here."

Michelle said, "I think so. Is there anything you want me to do?"

I said, "Just enjoy yourself. I want to go for a swim. How about you?"

Michelle said nothing and began to take her shorts off. I lost my shirt and bailed over the starboard side of the boat. I went down into the clear water and as I looked towards the boat I saw her below the surface on the port side of the keel. I swam under water to where she was surfacing and came up next to her in the water. She said,

"This is wonderful."

I said, "I'm glad that you like it."

Michelle smiled a beautiful smile at me and I went back under the boat to the other side. When I got to the surface she was right there next to me and still smiling. I swam to the swim platform and hauled myself up and out of the water. She stayed in the clear water and as I dried myself in the sun she swam around the boat. I watched enjoy herself until the fresh breeze got the best of me and I fell asleep on the cushions in the cockpit.

Michelle woke me about an hour later by saying, "David, what about those lobster you mentioned for dinner?"

I lifted my head from the cushion and said, "Let's go get some now."

I got up and went below to the storeroom where I kept the three scuba tanks that were on board. I handed her one of the tanks and after picking one up myself grabbed up the mesh bag that held the masks, fins and snorkels. I followed her up the companionway to the cockpit where she began to adjust the harness of the tank she'd been given. We worked at the tanks for a few minutes and Michelle followed my lead by putting on a T shirt before swinging her tank onto her shoulder and putting her arms through the straps.

I put my tank on and said, "Feel comfortable?"

She said, "Yes it feels good."

I reached behind her head and turned on her air valve. She put her regulator on and took a few breaths. She nodded and reached for the other mask and after putting it on she sat on the rail for her fins as I did. I nodded to her when mine were on and gestured over the side and behind me with my thumb when I was done. I went backwards over the side into the water and I could see her hit the water on the other side of the boat. I swam to her under the boat and we met about ten feet down. She nodded that all was OK so I motioned towards the rock ledges at the edge of the lagoon. I swam and she followed me. As we got to the rocks I started to look for holes where lobster might like to spend their days. When I found one I reached in and feeling the back of a good sized one grabbed it by the shell behind the head and pulled it out. Michelle looked pleased at me when I turned and showed her the two-pound lobster. I put it into the mesh bag that was hanging from my waist and went for another hole. I repeated the process again while she watched and drew my hand out holding another sea bug. She swam to the next hole and stuck her hand inside. She was brave and came up with one of the delicacies as I went to the next hole. We had four when we got back to the boat and I hung the bag to the ladder while I took my tank off and climbed out on the swim platform. I reached for my tank that she handed to me and pulled it up. I put it into the cockpit and went to get hers that she was already taking off.

I pulled it up as well and by the time I placed it with the other she was pulling herself up the ladder she said, "David that was fantastic. I've never seen that done before. Thank you so much for showing me how to do it."

I said, "No problem it's my pleasure."

Michelle was down to just her bikini in another second and we sat to dry on the cushions. When the gear was dry I began to haul it to the storeroom to get it out of our way and she helped with the chore.

I was finishing putting things in their places when she said, "David would you like a cocktail?"

I said, "Yes please."

She said, "What would you like?"

I said, "How about some Gin and tonic?"

She said, "Gin and tonic coming up."

I heard ice clinking into glass as I lashed the tanks in their place. I came out of the storeroom as she was finishing the mixing and was handed a full glass when she turned to me in the galley. I turned to the companionway as she reached for the cheese and crackers that had come from the grocers that morning. She piled them onto a plate and was right behind me through the companionway. I folded out the cockpit table and she put the plate down before she sat on the cushions across from me.

She smiled at me and said, "David this is just wonderful. It's much better than I hoped for. You really have picked a lovely retirement for yourself."

I said, "Thanks, I think so too. What do you think you might do when you get older and want to retire?"

She said, "I have no idea but this is definitely giving me some."

I said, "Well maybe if you start working on it now it will come true."

She said, "That's a long time off perhaps things will go that way."

Michelle looked to the horizon and I sat quietly in the shade until she spoke. She said, "What do you have to do on the boat tonight?"

I said, "I have a deck of cards and Trivial Pursuit if you care for that. I have satellite TV and a stack of films on DVD. You can E mail or surf the web if you'd like. Other than that there are some books and I have a radio set we can just about talk to Mars on."

"She said, "Wow! You certainly are prepared. Can we use the radio later. I've never done that before. Where can we talk to?"

I said, "Not exactly Mars but it will reach a couple of thousand miles when the atmosphere is right."

She said, "Is it like ham radio?"

I said, "Just like it. It's called single side band. The after stay for the mast is the antenna."

She said, "Do you have friends all over who you regularly speak to?"

I said, "I do at that. A couple of friends on the island and lots of others further south in the Caribbean who are usually on the air at night. Sometimes at sea I talk to ships who will answer my CQ."

She asked, "What's a CQ?"

I said, "We use those letters when we just want to speak to anybody who wants to talk as well. It's an international code."

She said, "That sounds like great fun when can we start?"

I said, "After dinner when it gets dark. The signal goes much further when it gets dark."

She said, "Great, can I get you another drink?"

I said, "By all means. Tell me when you get hungry and we'll start to cook dinner."

Michelle left the cockpit taking our glasses with her and was back in a minute with refreshed drinks. She sat back down and once again turned her attention to the horizon and the setting sun and the clouds that were being nicely backlit this evening by the sun. I put my feet up onto the cushions and relaxed as the sun began to sink below the horizon.

When it was down she said, "David, I'm hungry, can we cook dinner?"

I said, "Right away. I'm hungry too. I'll make the lobster if you'll do the veggies and the salad."

I went down the companionway and came up with the big pot from the store-room I used for boiling shrimp and lobster. I filled it with sea water and took it back below where I added a couple of boxes of boiling spices that were used on the Gulf Coast. I lit the stove and she began to get out the things she bought for the trip. She chopped and I opened one of the cold bottles of white wine she brought. It was of good heritage and I was pleased to know she had some sense about wine.

The salad was done in minutes and she began to boil some broccoli that would go well with the lobster. As the broccoli was done it was time for the lobster and I dumped the live bugs into the boiling water. They were done in seven minutes and I hauled the pot to the sink to drain and she began to set the table in the cockpit. I brought the lobster and the wine up and we sat opposite each other and began to crack and rip at the shells before us. We peeled and ate without saying much and after it was all done we lay back stuffed on the cushions. I folded the blue dodger back so we could see the stars while we digested our food.

We had kicked back for about an hour when Michelle stirred and said, "That was about the best meal I've ever had. Thank you very much."

I said, "Thank you. You helped make it wonderful."

She stood up and collecting things from the table headed below and started in on the dishes and the trash while I cleared the rest and washed the table in the cockpit. It was all done in thirty minutes or so and we poured some whisky for after dinner and went back to the cockpit and the cool gentle breeze that was wafting around the boat.

I said, "Want to try the radio?"

Michelle said, "Yes please."

We went below where the air was thicker and as we went down I started the generator for the radio and turned the air conditioning on to cool the main salon.

She said, "My god, you have air conditioning. I should have known. You have everything else."

I said, "It's necessary. It really gets hot further south and I don't like to be uncomfortable. Who should we talk to first?"

She said, "Let's try some of your friends south of here."

I agreed and in another ten minutes I was speaking to a friend who lived on his boat in Martinique. Michelle listened while we talked about the weather and mutual friends who stayed in various places in the Windward Islands. I let Michelle talk to my friend and she seemed to enjoy the magic of SSB radio. I reached another friend in the Virgin Islands and the conversation was about the same as the first.

I spoke to two others and while Michelle was getting out another bottle of wine and a beer for me I heard a call from Dennis at the fuel dock where we'd sailed from I answered back and he came on and said, "David is everything OK?"

I pressed the mike button and said, "Sure Dennis what's up?"

He said, "You've got that girl on your boat don't you?"

I said, "That's affirmative."

He said, "Look a couple of guys got off of the afternoon plane and started asking a lot of questions about her around town."

I said into the mike, "So what?"

He said, "These guys are on a mission. They're not dressed for the islands and they seem pretty dangerous. They've already been through her hotel room and they're really pushy and intimidating when they ask about her."

I looked up at Michelle who glanced at me with a look of despair on her face. I said into the mike, "What did you tell them?"

He said, "I told them she chartered you and the Castle for a few days of sailing. I didn't tell them I knew when you'd be back."

I said, "Wait ten and call me again."

He said, "Will do."

I turned to Michelle, who had tears in her eyes and said, "Is there anything you want to tell me?"

She said, "Yes I suppose I have to now."

CHAPTER TWO

I said to Michelle, "Speak to me and break the suspense."

Michelle looked at me and said with teary eyes, "Those men who are looking for me work for my ex-boyfriend. I left him in the middle of the night a couple of weeks ago and I thought I did a good job of covering my tracks. I guessed they'd find me but I thought it would take longer than this."

I said, "So why the cloak and dagger?"

Michelle said, "It's because of my boyfriend. He was OK when I started going out with him but he became really controlling and I was afraid to leave him. He's really rich and I'm sure he makes a lot of his money illegally. I can't prove it because it because he hides it so well. There were always very quiet meetings with sleazy guys who had foreign accents. I wasn't allowed to ask about them."

I said, "What about going to the cops."

She said, "He said he'd kill me if I left him. He was really scary. I mean he gave me everything I wanted except a life. He wouldn't let me have friends and barely let me talk to my family. When I did he stayed in the room and listened to the conversation."

I said, "Well that's no good. You have a right to do what you want."

She said, "I think so too. I thought I had it made you know, finding a rich guy with all kinds of money. It just turned into something else I couldn't get away from."

I said, "What do you want to do about this?"

She said, "I guess I'll have to go back home with his goons."

I said, "That might not be necessary."

She said, "What do you mean?"

I said, "I could take you to one of the other islands and you could go somewhere else."

She said, "They'd just find me again. I really don't know how to disappear and I'm afraid of what he'll do to me when they get me home."

I said, "Where's home?"

She said, "Newport Beach in Southern California."

I said, "You don't sound like you want to go back."

She started to cry harder saying, "I don't want to go home. I don't want to go back there ever. David I'm so scared."

I said, "Look you're safe for now. They have no idea where you are and people are hard to find out here. How'd you like to get lost?"

She said, "Are you serious. Do you think I could disappear?"

I said, "Sure, the drug dealers do it all of the time out here. It's a big ocean."

She said, "How could I do it?"

I said, "We'll think of something. Pour me another drink while we wait for the fuel dock to call back."

Michelle poured us each another drink and I waited for the radio to squawk back at us. It did in a few minutes.

I picked up the mike and said, "Amnesia Castle, go ahead Dennis."

Dennis said, "What's up?"

I said, "Dennis when those guys come back tell them she chartered me to take her to the big Island. I'll be gone for another 24 hours. You don't need to know anything else."

Dennis said, "David are you sure about this."

I said, "Yep I'll tell you all about it sometime. I'll be back day after tomorrow in the early morning at just before dawn. Everything is OK and I'm in no danger."

I signed off and turned to Michelle saying, "Want to stay here for another day?"

Michelle said, "David what are you going to do? I don't want you to get into trouble. Those guys can be mean."

I said, "Not to worry. So can I when I want to be. Right now I want you to relax and don't worry. I have a plan to get you out of here."

Michelle said, "You'd better tell me how. I'm very afraid you'll get hurt and I'm not worth that."

I said, "Believe me you're very much worth that and I'm not going to get hurt and neither are you. Want to go sailing with me? This is the exciting part of my retirement."

Michelle said, "David why are you doing this. You barely know me."

I said, "Yes but I'm a good judge of character and I happen to like your company."

Michelle said, "What do you plan on doing?"

I said, "We're going to stay here for another day and enjoy things. Tomorrow night we're going back to the island. I'll arrange a few things with Dennis and we'll hide you until those guys are gone."

She said, "How will they go away."

I said, "I think when they are convinced you're not on the island they'll take the first plane out to look for your tracks. Then we'll leave for points south. There are about ten thousand places to hide down there and I have some pretty outrageous friends who I know will help us."

Michelle moved to where I was leaning against the galley counter and hugged me hard.

She said, "David I'm so scared do you think that this will really work?"

I gave her a good hug back and said, "It'll work. I've got to be smarter than those goons and I'll bet I have friends who know your ex. I've met some pretty underground people down here in the islands."

Michelle hugged me again and said, "I guess I don't have much to lose. At least I'll have a great story to tell in a few years."

I said, "Time for bed. This has been hard for you. Let's get some sleep."

Michelle headed for her stateroom and I went to mine thinking about my plan for getting her back to the island and hiding her until the goons were gone.

We woke up the next day and enjoyed the day in the lagoon. We ate dinner after spearing fish and went to bed early. At midnight we hoisted anchor and sailed out of the lagoon heading back to the island. It was just getting light out when we motored into the harbor and saw Dennis standing on the pier. Dennis was there to help me tie up the boat and stood watch waiting for the guys who were hunting Michelle. He signaled me at about six that they were coming out of the hotel. I had Michelle ready with her scuba tank on and she slipped over the side with her belongings and headed for the spot I told her about under the pier where she could wait on the sand until I came to get her.

I was straightening the boat up when they walked up to me saying, "Are you Nash?"

I said, "I am, what can I do for you?"

The biggest of them said, "Where's the girl who chartered your boat?"

I said, "Who cares? I dropped her on the big island yesterday. She said something about getting a plane to the mainland."

The other said, "Where'd she go?"

I said, "Beats me. After I get paid I don't really care what my customers do."

The bigger one said, "Mind if we look on your boat?"

I said, "Yes I do. Who the hell are you anyway?"

This was answered by the big one grabbing me and holding on tight while the other headed down below. I complained loudly and told the goon who went below that he'd better not scratch my decks with his street shoes.

The other laughed and said, "Send us a bill old man and shut up before I put you overboard."

The goon who went below came up saying, "No sign of her and none of her things are down there."

I said, "Satisfied? I told you I dropped her on the big island yesterday. Why the grief?"

The big one said, "None of your business old man."

The other guy turned me loose and they headed for the hotel. They were back at the pier in an hour suitcases in hand and headed for the float where the morning seaplane was getting ready to leave. They climbed into the plane and the pilot started the engine. I watched while I worked and when the plane was out of sight I put on the other scuba tank and after going over the side swam to where Michelle was waiting under the pier. I came up under the pier and she was there in the dim light. She turned on her tank when she saw me and I motioned for her to follow me back to the boat. Dennis was there when we hit the surface and helped us onto the boat.

We took our tanks off and I said, "Michelle I think we need to get some supplies from the store."

Dennis said, "David where are you going?"

I said, "We're going for a long sail. If anybody asks I'm headed for the Greek Islands via Bermuda."

Dennis smiled and said, "You two send me an Email from time to time."

I said we would and went to the grocery while Michelle put her things away on the boat.

The groceries were delivered an hour later and Michelle and I put them away. Then we went to the fuel dock and filled our tanks. I called the bar and the hotel from the dock and after finding what my tabs were I left cash for them with Dennis.

Michelle and I motored out of the harbor fifteen minutes later and when we were clear of the channel we raised sail and pointed the Amnesia Castle south on a loose reach.

I was standing to the helm and Michelle said, "David you're going to a lot of trouble for me. Why are you doing this?"

I laughed and said, "I've always wanted to help a damsel in distress and I guess you're her. This is exciting. How does it feel?"

Michelle said, "Exciting yes but I'm still scared."

I set the self steering gear and said,

"Come below with me."

She followed and I took her to my stateroom where I opened the closet. I reached underneath and turned the secret lock that held the back closed. The clothes swung out of the way and the boat's arsenal came into view.

Michelle said, "David my god, you're a one man army! Do you know how to use all of this?"

I said, "Sure I do. I'll teach you as well. We can't go out on the ocean and let the Jamaican pirates get us."

Michelle said, "What are all of these guns?"

I said, "Let's see we've got two fully automatic M-16's. A couple of HK-91's, a 70mm grenade launcher, night vision goggles and a stack of handguns that range from Walther PPK's to 9 millimeter's to forty caliber Smith and Wesson semi automatics. Do you think we have enough?"

She said, "What about ammunition?"

I said, "About a thousand rounds for each weapon. We can get more when we stop in Key West."

Michelle said, "We're going to Key West?"

I said, "Yep, there's a great restaurant there that I want to take you to and you need some more wardrobe. I like to go to nice places when I travel."

Michelle said, "My god! I've hitched a ride with James Bond!"

I said, "One of my heroes. By the way do you have any money with you?"

Michelle said, "Yes I've got about twenty grand in my suitcase. Why?"

I said, "Get some out. You never paid for your last charter and don't worry about this one. It's on me."

Michelle smiled and hugged me as I closed and locked the closet after taking a 9mm pistol out and handing it to her.

I said, "Here you might feel better with this under your pillow. Just don't shoot me by mistake in the middle of the night."

I showed her how the weapon was armed and where the safety was.

She smiled and said, "Thank you David. I want you to know I'm not afraid any more. I have a deep feeling you'll protect me no matter what."

We went to our respective state rooms and I changed clothes in mine to go back to the cockpit and sail the Castle through the night. The weather was good and there was nothing showing on the weather satellite screen except for good smooth sailing. I stayed near the helm in case anything should happen and woke up as the sun was coming over the horizon.

An hour later Michelle came through the companionway and seeing me there said, "David have you been here all night?"

I said, "All night long. I usually sleep in the cockpit in case of trouble."

She said, "You should have had me help."

I said, "You can help tonight. Last night I thought it was important you get a good nights rest."

Michelle said, "Thank you I did need a good sleep. Yesterday was a very stressful day."

I said, "Now that you're up you could put on some coffee and watch the helm while I get a shower and some clean clothes on if you would."

She said, "Yes I certainly will. If you need some sleep please get some. I can handle the boat."

I said, "We're going to change course in a couple of hours. I'll get some sleep after that".

She said, "Will that be the course for Key West?"

I said, "Not exactly. They might be watching for us there so I thought we'd put in at one of the keys just north of Key West. I have a friend who has a small marina on Sugarloaf Key. We'll leave the boat there and drive to Key West to get supplies just to be safe. If they're smart they already know you didn't leave the big island by plane."

Michelle nodded her head and stood to the helm. I headed for the shower and changed my clothes. Michelle had coffee and rolls waiting for me when I came up the companionway. I was pleased to sit and enjoy the morning sipping coffee and eating fresh breakfast rolls.

At one point Michelle asked, "David when will we get to Sugarloaf Key?"

I said, "Probably early tomorrow morning if the wind holds for us. I think we'll have good wind all of the way there from what I've seen on the weather."

We settled into the rest of the morning and the GPS let us know when we got to where we would turn North North West for the run to our destination. When we had gone about and the sails were set I headed for the couch in the main salon to sleep while Michelle got a book from the shelf and went back to the cockpit to keep us on course.

I slept until four and woke to find all was well with the boat.

Michelle had kept us on our course perfectly and the seas were perfect for how the boat was pointing. I came up to the cockpit and said, "All well?"

She said, "Everything is fine and I love being out here. It's like a dream come true except for the guys who are looking for me."

I said, "I'm glad you're having a good sail. Not everyone enjoys being out in the blue water. Are you ready for some snacks?"

Michelle said she was so I went below and got the biscuits and some prepared meat from the 'fridge. We snacked on these until I felt like having a beer and went to get one for each of us.

Michelle said, "What will tonight be like?"

I said, "We'll sail like this pretty much through the night. I'm rested so if you can sleep until after midnight and then take the helm for awhile I can get a nap before we get to the key. It would be good to have both of us awake when we get into the harbor."

Michelle went to her bunk at eight and I sailed the boat into the night guided by the GPS. She came back on deck at one and I went to the salon for a nap. She woke me at five saying she could see lights on the horizon. I went to the cockpit and found we were right on track for Sugarloaf Key. In two more hours we were motoring into the harbor there and tying up at one of the most outside slips.

My friend was there and as he helped us tie up he said, "David, it's good to see you. You usually call ahead but this is a pleasant surprise."

I said, "It's good to see you too Chaz. We've got a story to tell you."

Chaz said, "I'll bet. Where did you get this lovely lady?"

I said, "In Bimini where I E-mailed you from. We've got trouble and we need your help."

Chaz said, "Sure thing. Is it bad?"

I said, "It might be if we get caught."

Chaz said, "Nash what have you been up to?"

I said, "Nothing bad but Michelle here has some people from her past looking for her. They're not nice and I thought I'd help her avoid the situation if you know what I mean."

Chaz said, "What do you need? I'm always willing to help."

I said, "We need to borrow your car for a couple of days first off. Then while we're gone I need you to change the paint, name and numbers on the Castle. I'll need paperwork to match as well. I'm going to get some new identification made for us while we're in Key West and I'll call you when I know what our new names are."

Chaz said, "Sounds pretty heavy."

I said, "It is and it isn't. We just need to be anonymous for awhile."

Chaz said, "Consider it done. I suppose if anyone asks about you two I don't know anything about you?"

I said, "That would be good. We need to move fast so can I use your car?"

Chaz took out a set of keys and handed them to me. I hugged him and said thanks. He told us to be careful and we both said we would as we drove from the boatyard onto the highway.

We changed clothes below before leaving and Michelle dressed as good as she had clothes for and I put on a pair of long linen slacks and a nice shirt to blend in with the tourists. We drove into the town of Key West and I cruised the harbor looking for signs of the goons who were looking for us on the island. I saw none of them so I drove to the shopping area downtown. I took Michelle into one of the stores on the street and told her to get what she'd need to be fancy and whatever she might need for the boat. She was good about shopping and I thought she made nice choices. It was almost noon by then so we walked to the restaurant I liked with Michelle wearing a new pair of pants and a nice blouse to go with it. I walked up to the restaurant and opened the door letting Michelle enter first.

Xavier the matre'd looked for a second and then realizing it was me said, "Mr. Nash, what are you doing here?"

I said, "We just came in for lunch Xavier. I'd like to introduce you to Michelle Murphy. Michelle is traveling with me for awhile."

Xavier said, "I'm pleased to meet you. Let me get you a table."

We were seated in seconds and Xavier brought us our menus. He went back to his station and we perused the menus that were brought. Our waiter came up and Michelle ordered first. I liked her choices and told the waiter to double what she'd asked for.

He went away and Michelle sat back and said, "David this is unbelievable. Here we are on the lam and you're acting like you've done this before. How's that?"

I said, "I haven't done this before but I've seen a lot of movies and read a lot of books. I said I have some outrageous friends down here and Chaz is one of them. Let's have a nice lunch before we have to get serious about things."

Our appetizers were delivered to the table and the food was every bit as good as I remembered it to be. Our main courses and salads came next and I could see Michelle was enjoying her meal.

I said, "Pretty good huh?"

Michelle said, "Excellent. The lamb is as good as I've ever had it. What are we going to do next?"

I said, "You're headed for a beauty parlor for some color and a new do. You're too obvious with that white hair of yours."

Michelle said, "OK I'm just following you. What are you going to do while I'm getting my re-make?"

I said, "I have to get our paperwork changed. I'll need to have yours with me and you'll have to stop by for a new photo when you get out of the parlor."

Michelle nodded and we sat back to enjoy our lunch. We had key Lime pie for desert and when we were done I mentioned to Xavier that he never saw us and he nodded that he understood. I got the car and dropped Michelle at a decent beauty parlor along the street and continued to a part of town which I knew was full of illegal activities. I parked a block up the street and walked to an old warehouse my old friend owned.

The guard at the door asked harshly, "What do you want?"

I said, "David Nash to see Hector Vera."

He looked at me and spoke into his sleeve. He nodded a minute later and I heard the electric bolt on the big sliding door click open. The door slid back and I walked inside. I was greeted by a loud voice from the office at the other end of the warehouse.

It said, "Nash! You son of a bitch! What in the hell are you doing here?"

By this time Hector was on his feet in the doorway reaching for me with his huge arms. There were stacks and boxes of different sorts of weapons of war all around him and in his office.

He crushed me with a hug and I said, "Hector I've got trouble."

He said, "With whom? Tell me and I'll kill them."

I said, "I'm not really sure. I'm helping a girl to escape her boyfriend in L.A. but I'm not really sure who is after us."

Hector held up a piece of paper with Michelle's photograph on it and said, "Is this her?"

I said, "That's her. Who's the boyfriend?"

Hector said, "An L.A. cowboy named Peter Wise that thinks he's connected. He's connected but not like some. What did she do?"

I said, "She left him after years of abuse. I'm getting her away from him but I need a favor from you."

Hector said, "Anything you want. What can I do for you?"

I said, "New passports with our pictures and names on them. Anything else will be gravy."

Hector said, "When do you need them?"

I said, "48 hours if possible."

Hector smiled at me and said, "Piece of cake. Will you two stay the night? It's my wife's birthday and we're having a fiesta. Where's your girl?"

I said, "At the beauty parlor getting her hair dyed and cut. We'll need pictures for the new paperwork."

Hector said, "No problem Nash. When will she be done there?"

I said, "About another hour and a half."

Hector said, "I'll send Carlos for her. Let's get drunk you old bastard."

I had to smile as Hector pulled a bottle of Tequila from his desk and poured two glasses for us.

He squeezed a lime into each and handing me one said, "Salute."

I answered "Salute" and downed my drink in one gulp as he did. Hector poured another one for each of us and we launched into conversation about the old days.

I asked, "So Hector where's our old friend Mr. X these days?"

Hector said, "He's around the islands but you'll have to ask everywhere to find him. I can give you the names of some people who know where to look."

I said, "Is he as important as he used to be?"

Hector smiled and said, "Even more so. Why, what do you want him for?"

I said, "I want to hit this guy Wise where it hurts. I want to shut off his supply until he leaves the girl alone. X can do it if anyone can."

Hector said, "He's the one all right. Does he still owe you that favor?"

I said, "Yes he does owe me and it's a good thing too. I like this girl and I want her left alone."

Hector poured more Tequila and said, "Nash I'll be glad to help you destroy this filthy pig. We'll make him so dry he'll be hanging out on the corner to score for himself. Ha,ha,ha,ha!"

I laughed with my old friend and after a number of Tequila shots he called in Carlos to tell him to take the little car to go and fetch Michelle. I called ahead so she wouldn't get freaked out by being picked up by a stranger. I sat drinking with

Hector until Michelle and Carlos walked in the door. Michelle was apprehensive by the look on her face and I couldn't blame her with all of the weapons that were stacked everywhere.

Hector walked up to her and said, "Mucho gusto I'm Hector Vera. Look you're a famous girl," Hector held up her photo on the flyer.

Michelle looked at her photograph and said, "Oh my god!"

Hector said, "Not to worry missy. Nash and I will take care of Mr. Wise for you. Do you know how lucky you are to have Nash looking after you?"

Michelle said, "I'm beginning to."

I said, "Before we get too drunk we have to figure out what our new names will be."

Hector said, "Is Chaz working on that for you?"

I said, "Of course but just for the boat."

Hector said, "Good then it'll be done properly. Why don't you become Donald Hedberg and missy you can be Mrs. Anita Hedberg?"

I said, "Sounds good to me. OK with you Michelle?"

Michelle nodded and said, "Where did you come up with those names?"

Hector laughed and said, "My stock broker and his wife in New York! Ha,ha,ha,ha! I'll call Chaz and tell him the new names for you."

Hector made the call for us and after speaking for a few moments then said, "Business is done for the day let's go to the casa."

A few words to Carlos in Spanish was all it took for us to leave and we walked out into the sunlight and the waiting limousine which would take us to Hector's home. We climbed into the limo and sat back on the plush seats.

I said, "Hector it seems life has been good to you."

Hector said, "Life is good. As long as the navy and the drug dealers keep fighting with each other I'll be rich."

I said, "It's still like it was?"

Hector said, "Even more so now that the drug dealers are fighting each other. I get to supply both sides. Ha,ha,ha,ha."

We drove through the streets of Key West smoothly stopping at the traffic lights and sightseeing. I looked out of the back window and saw one of the goons from the island who was after Michelle.

I said, "Hector, that vato in the cheap suit. He's one of the ones who bothered us on the island!"

Hector said to his driver, "Pull over."

The driver pulled to the curb and Hector pushed buttons on his cell phone while he watched the man. A minute later he gave instructions in Spanish to someone.

He flipped his phone closed when he was done and said, "Maybe we'll see him tomorrow morning. I don't like strangers on my island."

We drove on through the streets until we came to a gated community that looked 100% exclusive. The driver pressed a button and the gate to it swung open. I looked at Michelle who was wide eyed at what was happening but staying very quiet. We stopped in front of a big house on the bay which had catering trucks and florists vans parked nearby and I could see a tent that was erected in the side yard that led to the water. The driver stopped the car and we all got out and followed Hector to the side of the house where the tent was. There were at least a dozen people moving about obviously making the last minute preparations for the event which was to take place in the evening. A large and very beautiful Hispanic girl yelled and ran to where we were.

She reached us and hugging Hector said, "Daddy thank you, thank you for coming home early. Does it all look OK? Please say it does. I've been screaming at the caterers for hours so it will be perfect when Mama gets here."

Hector said, "Linda it's beautiful. You've done a great job, just fantastic, just fantastic. Do you remember Nash from years ago? This is his girlfriend Michelle They'll be with us at the party tonight."

Linda looked at me and said, "You're the Nash I knew as a child? I can't believe it. This is a miracle."

I extended my hand and said, "Linda you're all grown up. You're beautiful. Are you married? How many children do you have?"

She hugged me and said, "Married with three children. We're all well except for me. If I don't get this party going I'll be dead from my heart tonight."

She shook Michelle's hand and said, "Excuse me but I have to have my father for a minute won't you please go to the bar and sample some of the Tequila and wine for tonight?"

Linda took Hector's huge arm and walked him off to something obviously very important for the evening. Michelle and I walked to the bar and gave our order to the bartender.

When we had our drinks in hand Michelle looked at me hard and said, "David just who in the hell are you! You didn't learn this from movies and television at all. My god! New numbers for the boat and new identification for us! Arms dealers getting flyers that have my photograph on them! Hector knew my ex's name when I walked in the door. You didn't even know that. How do you know these people and they all treat you like royalty? David what is going on?"

I said, "Michelle, I told you I would help you and that's what I'm doing. All of these people are friends of mine from years ago. I was lucky enough to help Hector with a great favor and he's been my friend ever since. It's the same with Chaz. There will be other old friends of mine you'll meet as we sail south. You're in the best of hands and absolutely one hundred per cent safe. These people will make sure no harm will come to you in the near future and probably for the whole of your life."

Michelle said, "But David you've known me for three days. Why are you doing this?"

I said, "Well let's just say that I liked you from the start. You were fun to be with and you're a good sailor and I liked the way you look. I do like you as a blond better than the dark red though."

Michelle sipped her drink and said, "David did you really? Do you have a crush on me?"

I said, "That might be a good way to describe it," I sipped my drink looking at Michelle, who said, "You're doing all of this for me because of a crush? I don't believe it. I liked you from when I saw you coming out of the water with your fish on the island but I never thought you'd be interested in me."

I said, "I guess all we have to do now is evade the bad guys and get to know each other."

Michelle said, "David, thank you for helping me."

I said, "My pleasure."

Michelle said, "Does my hair really look OK?"

I said, "Yes they did a good job. You look just great."

Hector was back by this time and asked if there was anything we wanted. We asked him about our things in Chaz's car and he said he would have the car driven to us so we could get our things for the party that evening. The three of us all sat around a table drinking and watching Hector's daughter Linda rush around telling the help what to do and putting the finishing touches her mother's party. A man came up and spoke with Hector after awhile. Hector announced that our things were being taken to our room and asked if we'd like to go and rest before the party. We agreed and Hector took us to the room that was to be ours himself. He opened the door for us and hugged me again.

He said, "Nash it's great to see you and missy don't you worry about a thing. Nash always makes everything all right."

Hector went back to his daughter Linda and Michelle and I walked into the room that was ours. It was really beautiful and furnished from what looked like the best money could buy. Our things were on the bed and Michelle went to unpack her new purchases.

She said, "David, can I shower first?"

I said, "Of course you can. I need to lie down. Hector has made me very drunk this afternoon. Wake me when you get dressed."

I lay down on the bed and was out before the shower started to run. I slept hard and was awakened by Michelle just before seven.

I felt her hand on my shoulder and she said, "David it's time for you to get up and get ready. The party starts in forty-five minutes."

I lifted my head and it stung immediately from all of the Tequila. I said, "Ouch my head hurts. I'm not used to slamming down shots of Tequila in the afternoon anymore."

Michelle said, "What can I get you?"

I said, "I desperately need a cold beer."

Michelle said, "Get into the shower and I'll go get you one."

I stood up and took off my clothes and headed for the shower. The water felt good and as I soaped myself Michelle handed a ice cold beer over the clouded shower door saying,

"Nothing like a cold beer in the shower."

I said, "Thank you very much," and continued my shower. When the beer was almost gone I felt a hundred per-cent better. I finished my beer while drying off and called to Michelle,

"Michelle will you bring me my clothes. I forgot to bring them in here."

The bathroom door opened a minute later and Michelle's arm handed me the clothes I would wear that night.

I said, "Thank you."

I dressed and went into the bedroom and Michelle was sitting before the vanity putting on makeup.

She turned to me and said, "How do I look Mr. Hedberg?"

I said, "Anita you look tremendous. Makeup and your face belong together."

Michelle laughed and said, "It does help but I hate wearing the stuff. I'd much rather have a nice tan on my face."

I said, "I would like you that way too. It's a good thing because when we leave here we'll be living on our own private tanning salon."

Michelle said, "You look nice too. Let's go to the party."

We walked together down the hall and staircase and went through the living room to the side yard where the tent was.

We had just stepped onto the grass when Hector spotted us and called out loudly, "Nash! You and missy come here!"

We walked to where Hector was standing with his daughter and wife together. His wife Maria said, "Nash! You look as young as ever! This is a miracle and on my birthday too. Where have you been all of these years you bad boy!"

I said, "Hello Maria. I've been living in hell with the dragons of course. Where else would I be?"

Everyone laughed at the exchange and I said, "Maria this is my friend Michelle. She and I are traveling together."

The two shook hands and Maria said, "Nash, when are you going to settle down and have a proper family? Michelle are you going to be the one to tame him. You'd have better luck with the devil."

I said, "Maria cool it! I'm still trying to make a good impression here."

Maria said, "Michelle you have every right to know what you're getting into. Come with me. You and I have to have a drink and a long talk."

Everyone laughed as the two women walked arm in arm to the bar. I turned to

41

Hector and said, "Hector you're a lucky man. It's great to see Maria again. I need to visit more often."

Hector said, "Your friend in the cheap suit will be at the office tomorrow morning. He has an apology for you and Michelle. He did not understand whose boat decks he was scratching with his street shoes."

I said, "He told you that much already?"

Hector said, "Oh and much much more. When he saw the sharks circling the boat this afternoon he became very talkative."

I said, "This is like the old days Hector."

Hector smiled and said, "Actually much better. I come to enjoy things more with age."

We all sat down to dinner together and Maria and Michelle talked through the whole thing. The Mariachis played song after song and we all danced together in front of the band. The Tequila flowed and we drank shot after shot in salute to Maria. The mariachis were playing a slow one when Maria insisted I dance with Michelle. She and I walked to the dance floor where I put my arm around her slim waist and felt her breasts against my chest.

Michelle put her head on my shoulder and before the song was half over she said, "David Nash. You have a past."

I said, "What has Maria been telling you?"

Michelle said, "Nothing. Nothing at all. Just a little story about you saving the lives of eight men including her husband Hector. She compared you to Che Guevera."

I said, "Who's that?"

Michelle said, "Don't play dumb with me Mr. Hedberg. You know good and well who he is and you know good and well that Mr. Hedberg isn't your first alias."

I said, "And who told you that?"

Michelle said, "Your biggest fan that's who. Now will you kiss me or do I have to kiss you first?"

Michelle lifted her beautiful head up and I kissed her on the lips for the first time ever. They were soft and wonderful and I was about to get lost in them when she opened her mouth and used her tongue on mine. I felt it all of the way to my toes and was kissing back when the band quit playing and left us kissing on the dance floor in front of the whole party. We stopped kissing and the crowd broke into applause for us.

Michelle kissed me again and said, "Who are you? Can't you even kiss a girl on the dance floor without making it more romantic than a great story would be? How will I ever forget this if you break my heart?"

We walked back to the table and Michelle and I sat together and Hector toasted his wife and then Michelle and me. Michelle sat quietly smiling at me as she held my hand under the table.

It was getting late and the party began to break up. Michelle and I excused ourselves and Hector hugged us before we left and Maria hugged both of us as well.

We walked upstairs to our room and Michelle said as we climbed the stairs, "David is this the night you're going to make love to me for the first time?"

I said, "Only if you think it will be romantic enough."

Michelle said, "There had better not be any Mariachis in our room."

I said, "And why not?"

Michelle said, "Because I don't want to take my clothes off in front of anyone but you."

CHAPTER THREE

Michelle opened the door and peeked into the dim room playfully checking to see if the mariachis were inside. When she saw we were alone we walked into the room where I was immediately kissed next to the bed. We pulled at each other's clothes until we were naked and fell onto the bed where I learned why I was fighting for this girl.

We woke up the next morning with outstanding hangovers. Both of us were hurting and when there was a knock on the door I said, "Yes?"

A voice said, "Menudo in the kitchen in twenty minutes."

I said, "Thank you," and lay back on the bed as Michelle wrapped herself around me. We got up and without showering went to the kitchen where Maria said, "Welcome the Hedbergs!"

We sat at the table and bowls of the hangover cure were placed in front of us. I reached for the hot sauce and poured it into my bowl. Michelle followed what I did and we felt much better when our bowls were empty.

Michelle and I said our goodbyes to Maria and Linda an hour later and we drove our car to the warehouse where Hector conducted his business.

We walked inside and Hector welcomed us as we got to his office and said, "Michelle I have a present for you."

We went to another part of the warehouse and he pulled back a tarp revealing the man in the cheap suit who had been the reason we left the island. He was sitting in a chair tied at the wrists and ankles and had obviously been worked over by Hector's men.

Michelle took one look at him and started screaming, "Grady you worthless son of a bitch! You bastard! You filthy fuck! You limp dicked bitch! You worthless pussy!"

Michelle was too mad at this point to even scream at him and started kicking the man as hard as she could. I let her go until she was drawing blood in large amounts and then stopped her from doing further damage.

Hector said, "Michelle should we kill him and feed him to the crabs?"

Michelle said, "This piece of shit guarded me for my ex! The bastard kept me from doing everything! He would walk into the shower and look at me for kicks because my ex would let him!"

Michelle broke down completely and started sobbing as she collapsed on the floor. I went to her and picked her up and held her as she sobbed. I felt the years of frustration she had suffered and so did Hector. He was fuming and his eyes were becoming narrow. I remembered what he looked like when he was raging inside and waited for him to explode. A minute later he went off and picking up a sharp bayonet from a pile of weapons swung it at the man who was helplessly tied to the chair cutting his right hand off at the wrist.

He said, "Son of a bitch! Get him fixed up at the hospital and send him back to California with his hand in a jar!"

Hector looked at the man as he was writhing in agony and said, "You tell Peter Wise he's dealing with Hector Vera and David Nash. We're saying leave the girl alone!"

Hector turned from the man and gestured to Carlos to get him out of there and to the hospital. We walked to his office on the opposite side of the building where he picked up the phone and made a call.

He spoke Spanish for a few minutes and hung up saying, "My friend with the camera will be here shortly to take your photographs for your documents," then he said, "Michelle you were right not to have me kill the bastard. Sending him home without a hand is a better message. Now he can tell his Mr. Wise who he's dealing with."

Michelle said, "Thank you Hector but my ex won't stop because of what you did to Grady. He'll just send more men."

Hector said, "If he does they will die. You've just seen me angry but Nash is another story entirely. Maria said she told you about David. Does that scare you?"

Michelle said, "No, David doesn't scare me. I feel safe with him. I want to be out on the ocean where we're safe."

Hector said, "Bambina, as soon as the documents are done you can be back in your boat. Dealing with that filth was my pleasure," then he said, "Nash what do you need for the boat?"

I said, "I've got pretty much what I'll need."

Hector said, "What about some Russian rockets? They're good for aircraft."

I said, "Sure they might come in handy."

Michelle said, "Rockets?"

I said, "RPG's. Rocket propelled grenades. They can be fun. I'll show you."

Hector said, "I'll have Carlos deliver a launcher and a dozen to your boat."

Michelle was much calmer and I said,

"Michelle what would you like to do until the documents get here?"

She said, "I don't know."

Hector said, "Why don't you go shopping. That always calms me down."

Michelle laughed and said, "Shopping? Hector you like to go shopping?"

Hector said, "Sure, I like to look nice and buying a new suit always calms me down."

We all laughed and Michelle said, "OK I'd like to go shopping."

Hector and I laughed and I said, "Hector when should we be back here?"

Hector said, "I'm sending Raoul with you two. I'll call him when the documents get here. David do you want a pistol?"

I said, "Can't hurt. His friend might be around somewhere."

When the new photographs were taken we got into a car with Raoul a few minutes later and headed downtown with Michelle holding my arm in the back seat of the car. We went into a fancy women's store and Michelle began to look at things on the racks while Raoul and I watched.

At one point Michelle came up to me and said into my ear, "David do you like sexy lingerie?"

I said, "Yes very much."

Michelle smiled a sexy smile at me and went further into the store to the lingerie department and picked out things while we stood guard for her. Michelle shopped like a pro that afternoon and we went to several stores. Raoul and I were loaded down with shopping bags and walking towards the car when Raoul's cell phone rang in his pocket. He answered the phone and I assumed our new documents were done. We piled all of Michele's purchases into the trunk of the car and were driven back to the warehouse.

We went inside and found Hector who said as he handed me the package with our new identification inside, "The work is very good. The new computer technology is great for this kind of thing. Michelle are you more relaxed now?"

Michelle said, "Yes thank you, very much so."

Hector said, "Then it's time for you two to get back to your boat. Chaz called an hour ago to say that everything is ready for you to leave."

I said, "Hector thank you very much for everything. Your hospitality has been fantastic as always."

Michelle said, "Yes thank you very much and thank Maria again for telling me all about the new Mr. Hedberg."

Hector laughed and said, "Missy give me a big hug. I want you to know that Nash will take care of you or he'll answer to me personally and I want you to take care of him. It's a difficult job but someone has to do it. Nash, here is a list of our old friends who will lead you to Mr. X. Say hello to them from me and let me know by your sat phone what is happening and if I can do anything more for you two."

We all hugged in the office and after saying too many thanks and goodbyes Michelle and I went to Chaz's car and began the drive back to Sugarloaf Key and my boat.

As we hit the highway and turned north Michelle said, "David you're an amazing man. I never dreamed you could be the person I've just found out about. Will you tell me all about your life sometime?"

I said, "That was a long time ago but I'll do it if you like. It will take a long time as well."

Michelle said, "I've got the time to listen. You can tell me piece by piece while we're sailing to find Mr. X. Where are we going first?"

I said, "South to a lagoon near Andros Island. It's off of the Bahamas. I'm not used to so much excitement anymore and now I need a vacation. How about you? Is a vacation in order?"

Michelle said, "Definitely Mr. Hedberg. I want to work on my tan and get used to not being afraid anymore. I feel so relieved. I've been living in fear for so long I'm a mess. I need to find who I am again."

We drove the way back to the boat with the sun setting to the west. It was almost down when we pulled into the boatyard and Chaz walked up to greet us.

He said "Nash everything is ready. You're all fueled and provisioned."

I said, "Thanks Chaz. What color is the boat?"

He said, "Light blue it's all we had without buying anything new and I didn't want to attract any attention."

I said, "Blue is good. What did you name her?"

Chas said, "Mo Cuishle."

Michelle said, "Mo Cuishle, what does that mean?"

Chaz smiled and said, "It's Gaelic for my darling or my blood."

I said, "Not bad, not bad. Why Gaelic?"

Michelle said, "Yes, why Gaelic?"

Chaz said, "Hell I'm Irish remember? I thought you two might want some Irish luck and from what Carlos brought to the boat I think you might need it."

I said, "Where did you put them?"

Chaz said, "Under the berth in the main salon. They're in the false compartment with your spare ammo."

The three of us walked to the boat with our things and Chaz had two of his crew bring the packages from Michelle's shopping spree to the boat after us. We boarded her and I looked at our new papers that went with the new numbers for the boat. They were perfect and our new port was Martinique. I thanked Chaz for his help and Michelle gave him a big hug. I told him we would be in touch and Hector would fill him in on the details from the last two days. Chaz stepped off of the boat as I started the diesel and helped us untie our mooring lines. We waved goodbye and motored out of the harbor and when we had room to maneuver Michelle and I raised sail and turned south west laying in a course for Andros Island where we would lie in the sun for a few days of rest. I was first to take the helm and Michelle went below to make some drinks for us She came up from the salon with our drinks and a small package. It had her name on it and appeared to be from Hector.

She said, "What do you think this is?"

I said, "I don't know. Open it."

Michelle pulled at the wrapping until it was off and opened the box that was underneath. Inside was a chrome plated; pearl handled .32 caliber semi-automatic pistol.

There was a note with it and Michelle read what it said out loud, "To Michelle for your handbag. Never be without this. David will teach you how to use it and there is ammunition for it with the rockets. You must be safe. With love, Hector."

Michelle said, "David, what else are you going to teach me?"

I looked at her and said, "Everything that I can. We're in this now and we have to be ready. That's why Hector sent you that pistol. From now on we'll be armed at all times when we're in port."

Michelle said, "That sounds exciting. I've never carried a gun before. The way I feel now I'd put a bullet between my ex's eyes if he were here."

I said, "All revved up from kicking the shit out of Grady this morning?"

Michelle said, "Yes I am. It felt great. I've wanted to do that for a long time. He was such a bastard to me. I really hate him."

I drank a sip and said, "I think that you're going to be fine for this adventure we're on. There's nothing like a little hate to make you strong."

Michelle drank and said, "David how did you get into this way of living? You know; your past."

I said, "I was in my teens on the Gulf Coast and had my first boat. It was all of twenty-four feet long and wasn't much. A friend and I got the wise idea to sail to Yucatan and buy some pot to bring back and sell. We made the trip and learned a lot but almost became fish food. It was really naïve of us to go but we made money so we did it again. The second time we did it with less trouble. I got hooked on the adrenaline and the money. I also liked being a soldier of fortune of sorts. I really thought I was the shit back then. There were lots of girls in the islands and we had tons of money. Does that fill you in?"

Michelle said, "How old were you on the first trip?"

I said laughing, "I was fourteen."

Michelle said, "Fourteen! David you were too young to even drive then! You must have been out of your mind!"

I said, "Definitely. I was completely crazy back then. It's really a wonder I'm alive today with all of the close calls I had. Did Maria tell you about me escaping from a Cuban Jail?"

Michelle said, "No she didn't. How old were you?"

I said, "Fifteen."

Michelle said, "Fifteen, oh my god. How did you do it?"

I said, "I got caught by the Cuban navy sailing to close to their coastline. I was towed to the harbor in Havana and put in jail. I had read all about Castro and figured he was a sucker for flattery. When the officials finally got around to talking to me I told them I was there to defect. They told him about it and he wanted to meet the young Yankee defector face to face. I met him and knew enough about him and commie politics to impress him. After dinner I was taken back to my cell and wasn't guarded very closely. I snuck back to my boat in Havana harbor and was gone before they knew it. They're probably still looking for me."

Michelle said, "You had dinner with Fidel Castro when you were fifteen years old?"

I said, "Yep, I sure did. I gave him a good rap about Marks and Lenin and he loved it. He was going to use me for advertising his cause. You know, young American teenager denounces capitalism. It would have made great headlines all over the world."

Michelle said, "David if you had told me this four days ago I would have thought you were making it up."

I said, "I can't blame you for that. My past is a pretty outrageous story."

Michelle said, "Who are we going to find first on the list that Hector gave you?"

I said, "After we have a vacation for a few days we'll sail south to Little Inauga. Garcia lives there."

Michelle cuddled next to me on the cushions while the auto pilot steered the boat.

She sucked on the ice in her glass and said, "Tell me about Garcia."

I said, "Garcia honchos a gun running outfit and works with Hector some-times. Garcia is a good person who knows practically everyone in the Caribbean. Garcia will know something about where to find Mr. X."

Michelle said, "Who is Mr. X."

I said, "I can't tell you that."

She said, "Why not?"

I said, "Because if you knew who he was I'd have to kill you."

Michelle pinched me in the ribs and said, "Mr. Hedberg now you're bullshit-ing me."

I said, "I most certainly am."

Michelle leaned over and kissed me on my neck and said, "David will you make love to me again?"

I said, "Only if you insist."

She said, "I insist. Making love to you last night was wonderful."

I said, "I thought so too."

She put her mouth on mine and I felt her tongue between my lips. I loved the way she kissed and I could feel her taking her shirt off as her tongue worked against mine. We undressed each other and lay together on the cushions in the cockpit. The night was warm and there were ten-thousand stars that we could see. In awhile later there were many, many more.

Michelle and I made love for hours that night in the cockpit of the Mo Cuishle while the auto pilot and the self steering held course for us. Michelle was a wonder-ful lover and seemed starved for attention of her choice. We fell asleep at about three in the morning and stayed together in the cockpit. I wondered where this romance I now had was going and if it was just her reaction to sudden freedom and being attracted to her rescuer. After all she was a beautiful young woman and I was easily old enough to be her father.

The dawn woke us up streaking the clouds that were on the horizon to the west. I was first on my feet and went below to put on the morning coffee and get some rolls baking in the oven. When I got back to the cockpit Michelle was sleeping beautifully on the cushions. I let her sleep until the rolls and the coffee were done and then woke her up with a kiss on her lips. She stretched on the cushions arching her back and interlocking her long arms.

She looked at me and said, "Good morning Mr. Hedberg."

I said, "Good morning Mrs. Hedberg did you sleep well?"

She said, "Better than I have in year's thank you."

She looked to the table and saw the table set with coffee, rolls, jam and butter and said, "Mr. Hedberg you made breakfast for me?"

I said, "Sure, I was awake and you were sleeping very nicely so I didn't want to wake you. I wouldn't count on this kind of treatment every day though Mrs. Hedberg."

Michelle said, "I won't. I think it should be my job to make breakfast for my husband don't you think?"

I said, "I think you can even things out by doing the dishes after breakfast like a good wife."

This made her smile and she said, "You're right. Remember I've only been married for less than twenty-four hours my new husband," then said, "When will we get to the lagoon?"

I said, "Maybe tomorrow morning. The wind as been light all night and we have about two hundred miles to cover."

Michelle said, "How safe are we out here on the water?"

I said, "Pretty safe. I'm not really worried about pirates and privateers but I am a little worried about your ex finding us with the satellites photos that can be down loaded from the internet. They're in almost real time and if they spot us they can figure out where we are going."

She said, "That's right the technology works both ways doesn't it?"

I said, "It does but there are a lot of boats out here and they'll have trouble figuring out which one we are if they find us at all."

She said, "Even if they do it should take them some time to get to us. If we keep moving it will make things hard for them."

I said, "Mrs. Hedberg you're catching on fast. How would you like a shooting lesson after breakfast?"

She said, "Only after I get the dishes done Mr. Hedberg. What about showers?"

I said, "I usually shower here in the cockpit with sea water. It will be good to conserve the fresh water. I do the dishes with salt water as well. There are pumps for the galley and the cockpit. I think you'll like it. It's very good for your skin."

She said, "Is the water that clean?"

I said, "Out here it is but in the harbors no."

We had finished coffee and rolls by this time and together we took the remains to the galley and I showed Mrs. Hedberg how to work the sea water pump for the sink. She washed and I dried and she paid attention to where all of the utensils were stored. We finished our chore and I went and got a towel for her and the bar of soap that was made for showering in sea water.

I handed them to her and said, "Here's a towel and soap so you can get clean."

She said, "Mr. Hedberg aren't you going to join me?"

I said, "I was just giving you a chance for some privacy but if you're inviting me sure I'd love to join you."

Michelle went to the cockpit and I followed her up the companionway steps. We shed our clothes in the cockpit and put them on the cushions. I showed her how to turn on the pump and we wet each other down and took turns washing each other. It was very erotic and we ended up making love in the cockpit when we were clean. I wasn't at all used to having a companion with me but she was completely sexy and I didn't mind her appetite for making love. In fact it was very nice but I worried about being able to keep up with a young virile woman who seemed to be making up for something she had been missing.

We dressed for the day and Michelle decided to keep her clothes in the forward stateroom as it had a bigger bed and closet along with the drawers that were built in and a vanity for her makeup. I always used the after stateroom as it was closer to the helm and navigation station next to the galley. When things were finally put away I went to the closet with the secret compartment and got a selection of weapons out to begin her weapons training. I also took an empty milk jug from the store room and a length of line to attach it to the boat. We went to the stern of the boat and I tied the line to the handle of the milk jug and tossed it over the stern rail letting it out about one-hundred feet. I cleated it off and took one of the M-16s in hand. I showed her how to insert the magazine and lock and load the weapon. I put it to my shoulder and took aim at the milk jug that was trailing us. I squeezed off a few rounds and hit it squarely. I handed the rifle to her and instructed her on the sights. She shot several rounds and came very close to the target. I let her go through the rest of the magazine and she did well enough. If the small milk jug had been the size of a person or a boat she would have done serious damage to what she was aiming at. I complimented her on her newfound skill and took the weapon from her. I placed another magazine in the weapon and showed her how to put it on automatic fire. I aimed at the target and fired a burst. I mentioned to her the brilliance of short bursts of fire and she nodded her head and fired at our target. She was very close again and I again complimented her on her accuracy. I let her run through two more magazines until we were out of bullets. I talked her through the handguns especially the one that was given to her by Hector and she did well with them. We shot all of the ammunition we'd brought to the stern of the boat and I hauled in the milk jug that had been hit many times and was by now barely floating.

I showed her the damage that she'd done and she said, "Mr. Hedberg that was fun. What will we do now?"

I said, "Now you get to learn how to break the weapons down and clean them."

We went to the table in the cockpit and I went to get the cleaning equipment. I showed her how to dismantle and clean each weapon and she listened carefully. As each weapon was cleaned and oiled I let her put them back together by herself and she was very good at remembering what part went where. I supervised and she did all of the work finally reloading the magazines that had been emptied. As she cleaned up the table and put the weapons away except for her .32 and my .40. I was in the galley making lunch and she joined me by making a salad to go with the turkey sandwiches I was making. We took it all to the cockpit where we put it onto the table and ate in the shade of the dodger as we sailed along.

Just as we finished the proximity alarm on the radar went off and she said, "What's that?"

I said, "It's the proximity alarm on the radar. It's telling us there's another boat within ten miles of us."

She said, "Do we have to worry?"

I said, "Most likely not. It's probably another boat like us or a small freighter."

She said, "Oh." And went below coming back with our pistols.

I looked at her and said, "Good idea, better safe than sorry."

I got the binoculars from the port lazerette and scanned the horizon and saw a good sized sloop coming at us from an angle that would cause our courses to cross in about an hour.

Michelle said, "What is it?"

I said, "A pleasure yacht like ours. Probably not a threat to us."

Michelle said, "How can we find out?"

I said, "Let's teach you how to use the VHF radio."

I turned the radio on and picked up the microphone and said into it,

"Hello, hello, hello the pleasure yacht to the north of us. This is the pleasure yacht Mo Cuishle out of Martinique. Come back please."

I released the mike switch and we both listened for a minute. The VHF talked back with a woman's voice.

"Mo Cuishle, Mo Cuishle, Mo Cuishle" This is the pleasure yacht Sea Cloud out of Charleston, North Carolina bound for The Virgin Islands."

I said into the mike, "Nice place. It should be good sailing. We're just island hopping and making our way home. We're the Hedbergs and cruising for the summer."

The radio said, "Our name is Darrow and we're a family of four. We have our children with us. Would you like to trade some red wine for white wine?"

I said, "We'll be alongside as our courses cross. Sure lets swap. Mo Cuishle out."

The radio said, "Roger. Sea Cloud out."

Michelle said, "Great, but we should look them over when they get closer."

I said, "We certainly will."

I held us on our course and Michelle watched the boat through the binoculars.

She watched for awhile and eventually said, "I think they're safe they do have kids aboard."

I said, "Go below and get a bottle of red wine for them."

Michelle went below coming back with a decent bottle of dark red wine.

She said, "This is fun. Does it happen often?"

I said, "Sometimes but for us it's good to be careful."

Another fifteen minutes passed and our two yachts pulled together and we matched speed with them. I noticed Michelle kept her new pistol in the back of her shorts covered with her T shirt. I was pleased she was catching on to the life we were beginning to live and smiled about it. When the boats were sailing close enough we tossed a line to the Sea Cloud and I lashed our bottle of wine to it and they pulled it over. When it was received they lashed theirs to the line and we pulled the line back to us. All of the while their kids were watching from the rail as their parents did the transfer. As our line came back I held up our new bottle of wine and waved to them and they did the same. I fell off of the wind to allow them to sail past us and our encounter was over.

Michelle said, "Mr. Hedberg this is indeed a wonderful way to live. I wish I grew up like this. Those kids on that boat have no idea how lucky they are."

I said. "How did you grow up anyway Mrs. Hedberg?"

She said. "I come from an upper middle class Southern California family. My mother was a housewife who took care of my sister and me. My father was an architect who went to work every day and we all ate dinner together every night. I liked the beach and was good at school. I was a cheerleader because I'm pretty and lost my virginity when I was too young."

I said, "What was too young?"

Michelle smiled and said, "I was thirteen and very developed. The boys were all over me. I fell for a line from an older boy and actually thought he was who I was going to marry. He dumped me for one of my friends six months later and I was heart broken."

I said. "Was it hard being popular?"

She said, "Yes and no. It took me a long time to realize which doors my looks should open. I opened the wrong ones for a long time."

I said, "Like with your ex?"

Michelle said, "Yes that was odd. I met him through some film producers who I was trying to get to help me have a Hollywood career. He said he would help me and I went for it. It took me a whole year to realize he wasn't helping me at all. When I told him I was leaving he went nuts and told me he would kill me if I left him. He made me a prisoner for the next four years. I was always watched and he would get furious with me when I got out of line. He beat me up many times and liked to force me into sex whenever he wanted. I finally got up the nerve to escape."

I said, "How did you do that?"

Michelle said, "Let me get us some drinks and I'll tell you. She went below coming back with a soda for each of us. She handed me mine and lay on her back on the cushions putting her head in my lap in the shade of the dodger.

She sipped her drink and went on, "A year ago I started skimming money from the cash I got when I went shopping for clothes and other things. It was always cash because he had so much of it. I went shopping a lot because he loved to parade me around at fancy parties and spending his money was the only way to get back at the bastard. I skimmed a little over twenty grand before I left. I had wigs because he liked me to wear them when he had sex with me and I used them to help me conceal my identity to get away. I left a couple of hours after he'd gone on a trip and I was being watched by that Grady guy. I dosed his drink with some of that date rape drug. It's a wonder it didn't kill him because I put so much in it. When he was out cold I packed a bag and took a cab to the airport. I got a ticket to New York and then bounced around from city to city so there would be a long trail for him to follow and hopefully lose. I moved around for two weeks always staying in cheap motels that didn't require any identification before I took the plane to the island. I stayed one night in each place and went somewhere else in the morning. I heard about the flight to the island from a guy in a bar who was buying me drinks and it was the first flight that didn't want my identification or name so I thought I was safe. If I would have known they were only a couple of days behind me I would have taken the ferry away from the island the next morning. I thought I was safe so I relaxed and decided to go sailing. That's when I met you."

I sipped my drink and said, "That's some story. I'm glad you decided to go sailing though."

Michelle said, "So am I, meeting you is the best luck I've had in years."

I said, "Michelle what are you thinking about this affair we're having?"

She said, "I think it's wonderful. You're a great lover and I love the way you look. I love your blond hair and blue eyes. You have just the right build and I feel very safe with you. Especially since I've gotten to meet some of your friends."

I said, "Any thoughts about the difference in our ages?"

She smiled and said, "Are you worried about being too old for me?"

I said, "A little. I don't want my heart broken if you should run off in six months with some rich guy who's your age."

Michelle said, "David this is the first time I've ever seen you insecure. Do you really like me that much that you wouldn't want to lose me?"

I said, "Yes, I do. You're what I've always wanted. I've been sailing around by myself for years. I've always wanted someone to travel with but never found anyone."

She said, "I can't believe that. You're everything a girl could want. There must be some really dumb women out there. David you're exactly what I want. I don't care how old you are or what the difference in our age is. I only worry that you might get killed in this adventure. Hector told me to take care of you and that's exactly what I'm going to do. When this is all over I think I'd like to spend the rest of my days sailing the world with you if you don't mind."

Michelle stood up and said, "And I think it's time I made love to you again. After that it will be cocktail time and we can go about making dinner together. Now would you like to take your shorts off or would you like me to do that for you Mr. Hedberg?"

I began to take my shorts off and Michelle pulled her T shirt over her head. She smiled at me as I watched her undress and when she was done she straddled my thighs and began to kiss me deeply. I kissed back and we made love passionately as the boat sailed itself into the afternoon.

The wind held great for us and we sailed with the sun beginning to set to our stern. I made cocktails for us as Michelle let the soft afternoon sun slowly tan her exquisite body by laying nude on the cushions with the dodger out of the way. We watched another sunset and drank our drinks. When the sun was gone Michelle went back to her shorts and T shirt and we went to the galley together to make dinner.

There were plenty of fresh supplies on board and Chaz had put some fine steaks in the 'fridge for us so I got out a pair of them and said, "Mrs. Hedberg how do you like your steak?"

Michelle said, "Medium rare if you please Mr. Hedberg. How do you like your asparagus?"

I said. "Cooked please."

Michelle laughed and said, "And your salad Mr. Hedberg?"

I responded, "Raw please with vinegar and oil."

We made two more drinks and drank them together while we waited for the asparagus to soften in the boiling water. When it was done Michelle started on the salad and I went to the grill on the after rail. Michelle set the table complete with candles and when the steaks were done we sat down to dinner.

We started to eat and I said, "This is our first meal that we've really cooked together. That's nice."

Michelle said, "The first of many," raising her glass to mine, "and to ten thousand more."

I said, "Is there anywhere you would like to stop along the way?"

Michelle said, "Yes if we can. I've always wanted to see the Virgin Islands."

I said, "That's very possible. One of the names on the list is there and I know a great restaurant there. The British side is out unless we drive there."

She said, "Why's that?"

I said, "Because of the weapons we carry. If the Brits find them they'll take them away from us and confiscate the lot. Not to mention giving us hell for having them there in the first place. They don't like weapons very much."

Michelle said, "Then we'll just have to drive there then. I want to hear British accents."

I said, "Then that's what we'll do then."

Michelle said, "When will we get to the lagoon?"

I said, "I think tomorrow morning about nine or ten if the wind holds."

Michelle said, "What would you like to do tonight other than sail the boat?"

I said, "I'm thinking I might like to see a film. We can put it on the screen here in the cockpit. Do you want to split the watch with me?"

Michelle said, "I'll definitely split the watch with you and a film sounds like a good escape for me."

We finished our meal and took the dishes to the sink where we washed and dried them. When we were done I looked around on the satellite and found a film we both were interested in seeing. We lay together in the cockpit watching the film and a little more than halfway through it I noticed Michelle was asleep. I let her sleep and held her in my arms. I fell asleep as well and woke up at two in the morning feeling good and not tired. Michelle was still asleep and I let her be. I went below and got some water to drink and while I was below the proximity alarm went off warning us a ship or yacht was nearby. I went up the companionway and Michelle was just waking up.

She said, "Is something near us?"

I said, "Yes it's the radar alarm."

I killed the cockpit light and reached into the lazarette and pulled out a pair of night vision binoculars. I put them on and scanned the horizon in the direction the blip on the radar screen was. After a minute I saw the ship. It was a small inter-island freighter and would be no trouble to us.

I said to Michelle, "Mrs. Hedberg would you like to handle this one?"

Michelle said, "What should I do?"

I said, "Give them a call on the VHF radio and ask them if they see us."

Michelle turned on the radio and spoke into the mike. She said, "Inter-island freighter this is the pleasure yacht Mo Cuishle"

The radio spoke a minute later saying, "Mo Cuishle this is the freighter Mr. William."

Michelle said into the mike, "Mr. William we are five miles south of you sailing 115 degrees south west do you have us on your radar?"

The radio spoke, "Roger Mo Cuishle we see you. What's your destination?"

Michelle said, "Martinique via a few stops. Have a nice night Mr. William. Mo Cuishle out."

The radio said, "Mr. William out."

I said, "Well done Mrs. Hedberg. Now we know they won't hit us."

Michelle said, "What time is it?"

I said, "It's about two thirty. You fell asleep during the movie."

Michelle said, "Why didn't you wake me up?"

I said, "Because I fell asleep too. I only woke up minutes before the alarm went off"

Michelle said, "Then you go below and get in my bed. I'll take the watch until dawn. Then you can make me breakfast before we make love."

I kissed Michelle good night and went below to her bed where I fell asleep until she woke me just after dawn saying, "Hey where's my breakfast?"

I opened my eyes and Michelle was standing in front of me in the stateroom. I stretched and was kissed when I had finished. I got out of bed and went to the galley where I poured myself a cup of coffee that Michelle hade obviously made for me.

I looked around further and she said, "Never mind making me breakfast. I've already done that. The table is set in the cockpit and it's a beautiful morning. Let's go up and eat."

I went up the companionway and there was a full breakfast waiting. Bacon and eggs with fresh fruit and rolls.

I looked at Michelle and said, "Mrs. Hedberg, you didn't have to do all of this. I was just kidding yesterday about you making breakfast for me."

She said, "Mr. Hedberg cooking for you is a pleasure. I did all of this because I have ulterior motives."

I asked, "And what might those be?"

She said, "I want you rested and strong after breakfast. There's something very important for you to do."

I said. "Which is?"

Michelle said, "Mr. Hedberg after breakfast you have to make love to Mrs. Hedberg again. She insists on it."

I smiled and said, "Well if she insists I suppose I must."

Michelle and I laughed and settled into a wonderful breakfast in the cockpit.

We finished our meal did the dishes and I was pulled by my hand into the stateroom where I was undressed and made love to with more passion than I could really remember. We finished making love and were lying in bed when the radar alarm went off again. I got up to see what was nearby and we were ten miles from our destination. I called to Michelle who came on deck shortly.

I said, "Mrs. Hedberg I think our vacation is about to begin."

CHAPTER FOUR

We anchored just before noon and the lagoon was exactly as I had left it two years before. There were Palm trees on the beach and crystal clear water below us. It was so clear we could see the shadow of the boat on the bottom. The lagoon was thirty feet deep and we could easily see marine life swimming below us. When we were properly anchored I set the air funnel in the front hatch to circulate the breeze through the boat and went to relax on the cushions. Michelle already had her shirt off and was lying back tanning herself in her bikini bottoms.

I said, "Mrs. Hedberg don't you look comfortable."

She raised a finger to her lips and said, "Sushhh. Mrs. Hedberg is on vacation."

I smiled and took the cushions on the shady side of the boat and following her lead I fell asleep in the wonderful cool breeze that was blowing past the cockpit.

We spent four days in that lagoon eating, sleeping and making love constantly. The only work that was done was to spear fish each day and clean the bottom of the Mo Cuishle. Which we did on the morning of the second day.

The morning of the fifth day Michelle said, "Mr. Hedberg let's go and find your friend Garcia."

I said, "OK let's do just that," and got out the charts to plot a course for Little Inagua.

Michelle helped with the plotting and I showed her how to program the way points into The GPS. She proved a quick study and when we were done I motored us out of the lagoon to raise sail and steer south west to our destination. We had four hundred miles to go and had to avoid the treacherous Hogsty reef that had claimed many ships over the years. We took our time sailing and arrived on the sixth day. Michelle was a pleasure to sail with and I loved finally having a companion with me. We motored into a small port on the island that I had been coming to for years having done business with both Garcia and the father. We were noticed right away by the locals and before we had cleaned the decks with fresh water a Jeep pulled up to the entrance of the small harbor. An incredibly sexy Hispanic woman wearing tiny shorts, a .45 caliber automatic and radio on her hip and a tiny bikini top got out of the jeep and walked towards our boat.

I smiled when I saw her and Michelle looked and said, "David look at what's coming. Should I get the guns?"

Before I could speak the woman who was forty feet from us shouted, "Nash is that another woman you're with? I've told you about that before! Now get ready to die Blanco!"

Michelle looked at me with puzzled fright as I stood up and yelled, "Not today you Mexican bitch! You're just going to have to get used to the other women in my life!"

The woman was on the boat by this time and was all over me with hugs and kisses and yelling in Spanish. She wrestled me to the cushions while Michelle looked on with real fright in her eyes.

The woman got up off of me and stood in the cockpit and looking at Michelle said, "You must be the woman who's causing all of the trouble. Mucho gusto, I'm Garcia."

Michelle's face changed from fright to quizzical and she reached out to shake Garcia's hand. Garcia immediately said, "Oh bullshit girl give me a hug. It's about time someone got her hooks into Nash. He's been single for far too long!"

Garcia grabbed Michelle and the two hugged in the cockpit while I watched.

They finally let go of each other and Michelle looked at me with fire in her eyes and said, "God damn it David! You just scared me to death! You son of a bitch! You never said Garcia was a woman!"

Garcia and I were howling with laughter by this time and I said, "I'm sorry Mrs. Hedberg. This is all Hector's doing and you never asked if Garcia was male or female."

Garcia said, "We're both sorry Michelle but it was too good a joke to pass up. This is what you get when Hector loves you."

Michelle said barely keeping a straight face, "It was pretty good at that," then smiling she said, "Bastards I owe both of you one!"

Michelle was hugged again by Garcia and this time she hugged back and Garcia said, "Hell Nash where's your hospitality? Get your Blanco ass below and get us some liquor and make sure you bring the ice. It's getting hot today."

The girls sat down on the cushions and I went below. I came up with the Gin and the tonic and a bucket of ice with three glasses in it.

When I got back to the cockpit the girls were talking and Garcia said, "Now that's what I like to see. A white man waiting on my fine Mexican ass. Nash can you cook any better than you used to? For Michelle's sake I hope so."

I said, "I cook just fine thank you. You never could get used to not having your food so muy caliente most people couldn't eat it."

Garcia said to Michelle, "Nash couldn't seem to get enough peppers into the mole'. I would have kept him for a house boy if he'd been able to cook better."

Michelle said, "Garcia I definitely have to have a talk with you. I want stories."

Garcia said, "Then its stories you'll get. Damn girl, you are beautiful. Hector said you were gorgeous but that was an understatement. How did you get a hold of Nash anyway? He's supposed to be retired."

Michelle said, "I just gave him a sob story and shook my ass at him. He's been following me around ever since."

Garcia cracked up and said, "Nash she's fantastic. Let's finish our drinks and go to the house where it's air conditioned. Michelle if I know Nash you haven't had a freshwater shower since you left the keys. Go below and get some things so you can stay. I have a pool and we dress up for dinner. Bring something nice for Nash too. You don't want him to dress himself."

Michelle went below and came back with a bag of things handing me my pistol before we left the boat. I could see hers was stuffed in the back of her shorts and I liked that she was packing. We walked to Garcia's Jeep and got in. I sat in the back with the luggage and Garcia drove to her home like a maniac on the gravel roads. Her place was just as I remembered it. It had been her fathers thirty years ago but he was gone now. His daughter who hated her first name had taken over the house and her father's gun running business. She was good at operating both and was very connected and rich from her efforts.

We pulled in front of her house and we went inside where we were introduced to her lesbian lover. She was a beautiful blond woman with almost pure white hair whose name was Lene' and looked vaguely familiar to me. She was very friendly and immediately had the help take our bag to our room and bring refreshments to us. We sat in the grand living room waiting for the refreshments to be brought.

I said, "Garcia it's wonderful to see you again."

She said, "Nash it's been years. Where have you been?"

I said, "Sailing everywhere and taking it easy. Retirement has been very nice."

Garcia said, "Nash it's just like you to retire to a yacht. Michelle, Nash used to drive us all crazy moving drugs and guns through the islands on his sailboats. They were so slow it was maddening."

I said, "But it was a good cover and if you remember those wooden boats with no lead paint were invisible to radar."

Garcia said, "That is very true. My father always said you were the smartest man in the business."

I said, "He also said you were the smartest woman in the business."

The refreshments were delivered and poured for us. We drank from what we were given and the cold sangria was excellent.

Michelle asked, "Garcia when did you and David meet for the first time?'

Garcia said, "That was a long time ago. So long ago it was when I wanted a man for a lover. Nash delivered a shipment to my father here on the island. I was thirteen years old when Nash sailed into my life. I fell in love with his blond hair and blue eyes immediately. He of course paid no attention to me at all. It wasn't until I was fifteen and had grown some tits and ass that I got his attention."

I said, "I remember that day. I walked up to this house with your father to have drinks by the pool and you were lying there wearing next to nothing. I could hardly believe you were the same girl from the year before."

Garcia said, "You always were the only man my father ever approved of. I think he hoped we would get married."

I said, "Only man? Anything would have been better than those knucklehead young vatos who you used to run around with."

Garcia said, "That's completely true, my father got so tired of los chevarlos hanging around the house and waiting for me outside. They were like vultures waiting for me. Of course who could blame them? I was totally promiscuous back then. It's no wonder I became a lesbian."

I said, "Garcia how about some of that swimming pool. We're pretty salty sailors here."

Garcia said, "Certainly, Michelle do you want to change? We usually swim naked here but if you want to put on a suit you can."

Michelle said, "Naked is good. I like seeing Mr. Hedberg here naked."

Garcia said, "I love the names that Hector gave you two. It cracked me up the first time I heard it."

Michelle said, "Why's that Garcia?"

Garcia said, "Because Donald Hedberg is my stock broker too!"

We all got up laughing and headed for the pool and the servants brought our refreshments behind us. The pool was half shaded and we put our things in the shade and began to take off our clothes. Michelle was first into the water and Garcia was second. I noticed when Lene' took her clothes off as she had one incredible body. Garcia always had good taste in women I thought as I hopped around on one leg getting my shorts off.

I was just about to dive into the pool when Garcia said, "Nash look at you. You gorgeous man. You've got the same body you had thirty years ago. Michelle you are a very lucky girl."

Michelle said, "I know that now. When I first met him he acted like a retired college professor. I had no idea he was so exciting."

Garcia said while putting her arms around Lene', "Nash what happened to the Amnesia Castle?"

I said, "That's her in the harbor. Chaz renamed her for us when he changed the numbers and re-did the paint. He's the one who named her Mo Cuishle."

Lene' said, "What does that mean?"

Michelle said, "It means my darling or my heart in Gaelic."

Garcia said, "Is Chaz getting sweet on us?"

I said, "Not at all. He's Irish and thought we might need some Irish luck."

Garcia said, "You just might. That man that's looking for my new sister Michelle is putting something into it. You and Hector and Michelle have embarrassed him. I heard he's sent a couple of pros after her and you Mr. Hedberg."

I said, "Where are they?"

Garcia said, "Right now they're in the Dominican trying to find you two. They're not doing very well because me and Hector have got the word out about you. Everyone they ask is either sending them down dead end streets or staying quiet."

Michelle said, "What was the word you put out?"

Garcia said, "That Nash is seriously dangerous and although retired he's very connected still. Besides no one wants me and Hector on their ass. You've seen Hector angry and you don't want to see me when I'm having the PMS or the curse. I can be the biggest bitch on the planet!"

Michelle said, "Garcia, I can be quite a bitch myself and I promised Hector I'd take care of Mr. Hedberg here."

Garcia said, "Michelle are you planning on keeping this dog?"

Michelle said, "I've always been a sucker for strays. What do you think?"

Garcia laughed and said, "He's definitely a stray but one with a good pedigree. You're a very lucky girl and Nash this bitch is way too good for you vato."

Garcia turned Lene' around and kissed her mouth open. Michelle swam to me and did the same.

We swam and played in the pool until we were cool and Garcia said, "OK its siesta time. Let's get out and get some rest. We're having people over to meet the Hedbergs after dinner. Nash there will be a few people from your past here after dinner so be prepared."

We all got out of the pool and toweled off. We put our shorts and shirts back on for the short walk to our room.

Garcia kissed us both as we went into the room and when we closed the door Michelle said, Mr. Hedberg you have the most fantastic friends. I absolutely love Garcia. You have no idea what its like to meet a woman that is so strong. Just being around her gives me so much confidence I just can't believe it."

I said, "She's something all right. I hope the stories about when we were younger didn't bother you."

Michelle said, "Did you ever make love to her?"

I said, "Yes we made love a few times."

Michelle said, "Good, I would have made love to her too. I think she's very sexy and her lover is positively hot."

I said, "Are you going over the fence on me?"

Michelle said, "Never, now come here and let me make love to you. All of us in the pool together have gotten me hot, hot, hot."

With that Michelle led me to the bed where she showed me just how hot she was.

We made love and napped until it was six getting up to shower and dress. Michelle showered first and she was dressed by the time I got out of the shower.

She was finishing with a small amount of makeup when she got up turned to me and said. "How do I look?"

Michelle was wearing a very sexy light cotton dress that was low cut in the front and clung to her perfect ass flaring out to stop just above her knees. She was wearing a sexy black bra that maximized her cleavage showing some of the lace it was made of and she looked fantastic.

I said, "Mrs. Hedberg, you look positively mouthwatering. I've half a mind to put you on the bed and have my way with you."

Michelle said, "You can do that to me later. I think I look sexy too. Wearing my new lingerie has gotten me excited as well. Finish dressing and let's go to dinner."

We went down stairs and Garcia was waiting for us with Lene'.

As soon as we were seen Garcia said, "Chiquita, Chiquita. Where you been so long! Michelle you look fantastic and look at Nash in a linen sports coat. You two make a wonderful couple."

Michelle and I said thanks and sat together on the couch opposite our hostesses. A bartender in a white coat came up and asked us what we wanted to drink. We gave him our orders and started into conversation with Garcia and Lene' who looked fantastic.

I said, "Garcia I suppose Hector told you I have to find our old friend Mr. X."

Garcia said, "He did and it won't be too hard. I speak with him on the sat phone but you know X he won't let anyone know where he is."

I said, "The next name on my list that Hector gave me is Desmond Sparrow in Jamaica."

Garcia said, "That would be what I'd suggest. How long has it been since you've seen Ras Desmond?"

I said, "It has to be ten years now. Hector says he's still in Port Antonio."

Garcia said, "Actually he's in Ocho Rios or rather his home is. Des has gotten richer and now lives with the wealthy in the hills there."

I said, "How did he get richer?"

Garcia laughed and said, "His brother got appointed into that phony government they have there so they leave Des alone now. He's also dealing coca where the big money is."

I said, "Is he still a good person to know about X though?"

Garcia said, "More than ever. I'm sure they speak regularly. I'm also sure Mr. X will hear you are looking for him and find you. Be careful not to shoot too soon 'cause the men might be working for X. Anyway when the word gets to him that this bastard Wise is after you he'll be really pissed."

Michelle said, "Garcia, Mr. Hedberg won't tell me who Mr. X is will you?"

Garcia said, "Honey you don't want to know. If you did we'd have to kill you."

Michelle said, "That's what Mr. Hedberg said too."

Garcia said, "Let's just say that our friend X is the most powerful man in the Caribbean and leave it at that."

We were called to dinner just then and went to sit at Garcia's lavish table. The dinner was a full meal and beautifully presented. A whole chicken was prepared with several kinds of vegetables, Mexican rice, tortillas, salads with cilantro and several bottles of white wine. It was fantastic and we ate until we were stuffed and went back to the living room to have our brandy and wait for the guests to arrive.

Half an hour later cars began to pull up in front of the house and Michelle and I stood in line with Garcia and Lene' to be introduced to the guests. As the house filled a string quartet began to play traditional Mexican tunes and we began to mingle with the guests. Michelle was attracting a lot of attention from the men as well as some of the women and I was proud to be with her.

We were standing together when a couple came up to us and the man who looked familiar said, "Mr. Hedberg I'm Jose Cruz. We used to work together if you remember?"

I said,"Of course I do. How are you Jose? It's been a long time. Are the Cubanos still looking for you?"

Jose said, "Not any more. I paid them off years ago when their government became more understanding."

I said, "What are you doing now?"

Jose said, "I work with Garcia as I did her father. She told me about your problem. All of my friends and contacts are at your disposal if you need them. This is my wife Teresa. Don't bother with introducing this beautiful lady we already know her name."

Michelle said, "Jose did you get one of the flyers too?"

Jose said, "I did and the picture didn't do you justice. You're much more beautiful."

Michelle said, "Thank you Jose."

Jose said. "I don't know if you know it or not but Mr. Hedberg here saved my ass one time."

Michelle said, "How did he do that?"

Jose said, "He picked me up off of my boat after the Federales had shot holes in it and helped me escape. The boat was lost but a few days later we went diving for the cargo and saved a lot of it."

I said, "That's right I cruised by and picked you up just before the feds got there. We disappeared into a fog and lost them."

Jose said, "I have never been so glad to see a sailboat in my life. They couldn't find us in the fog because sailboats make no noise."

Jose leaned towards me and put something into my pocket saying softly into my ear, "Nash here's my sat phone number and E mail. Call if you need anything. All of the Caribbean is going to help the two of you."

We shook hands and Jose hugged Michelle before he walked away from us Michelle took my arm and said,

"Look there's Garcia lets get some drinks and join her."

We went to the bar where Garcia was standing and talking with a bottle of

Tequila in her hand. She was speaking to a man who had come late to the party. We were introduced to him and found the he was the magistrate of the island we were on. He was older and well dressed and was swapping shots of tequila with Garcia. We all spoke together for awhile and he excused himself from our group to the bathroom.

When he had left Garcia said, "Dirty old man he's been trying to get into my pants for years."

We stayed with Garcia sharing her bottle with her until the strings quit playing and the guests started to leave.

We stayed with her saying our goodnights until they were all gone and Garcia said, "That's over let's get naked and get into the hot tub."

Michelle said, "Thanks but not tonight. Mr. Hedberg and I have something important to do."

Garcia said, "By all means go and please don't worry about making noise. My suite is at the other end of the house."

We said good night and Michelle and I walked drunkenly up the stairs to our room. When we were inside and the door was closed I went to the bathroom and when I came out Michelle was standing sexily by the bed wearing only her sexy black bra and thong underwear. I walked to her and she began to kiss me passionately as she took my clothes off so we could play.

The next day was for hangovers and we slept late. Garcia woke us at noon telling us to come down for menudo so we dressed and were in the dining room in thirty minutes. The food helped and the hot salsa burned the alcohol out of our bodies. We spent the afternoon relaxing in the pool with Garcia and Lene'. Michelle stuck close to Garcia asking about my life for the whole of the afternoon. Garcia was patient and answered all of the questions she asked. We stayed in the pool recovering until it was time for dinner and after retiring to our room we dressed up once again for our meal. Dinner that night was small but dressing up was always part of dinner.

The conversation was light and at one point Garcia asked, "What do you want to do tomorrow?"

I said, "Well I have things that need to be done on the boat. Would you mind taking Mrs. Hedberg out to your range and give her a little more weapons training?"

Garcia said, "I'd like nothing better. Does that sound OK with you Mrs. Hedberg?"

Michelle said, "Wonderful! Will you teach me how to shoot RPGs?"

Garcia said, "Anything that you want girl. We're going to have great fun together."

All of us went to the hot tub after dinner and spent the evening listening to great music as we all kissed and played in the tub. Michelle was bonding with Garcia and I liked what I saw happening between the two of them.

We all went to bed early that night and Michelle was again very passionate with me. We loved each other for a long time and finally fell asleep in each other's arms.

Garcia woke us early the next morning and I was given a vehicle to drive to the boat and get the maintenance done that needed to be taken care of. Michelle went with Garcia after I left and I looked forward to seeing her later that afternoon. I finished my chores and went back to the house at three and Lene' was there with cocktails on my arrival. I sat with her by the pool drinking until we heard Garcia's Jeep pull up in front of the house. Lene' rang for more cocktails and the two women came into the house and joined us at the pool in the shade. Michelle was dressed as Garcia was and was wearing a pair of denim shorts and bikini top. She had her pistol in a new holster on her hip and webbing over her shoulders. The webbing was filled with spare magazines for her .32 and there was an UZI 9mm hanging under her left arm with a bag of magazines balancing it on the other side. Behind her right hip was a collapsible baton and a Japanese Oyabun knife for work in close quarters. She was the picture of a very sexy mercenary and I said so when she walked up.

I said, "Mrs. Hedberg you look fabulous. Has Garcia been teaching you how to kill?"

Michelle said, "She certainly has. Look at what she's given me. I have an UZI 9mm and I love it. I feel like I could get into the shit tomorrow and be able to save your ass."

I said, "Garcia get the camera. I want a picture of the two of you. Hector will love them and Michelle's ex just might like to see what he's hunting."

Garcia said, "You bet. Lets go out by the jeep were we look nasty and she can hold the loaded RPG launcher."

We went outside and Lene' took the pictures and one with me in it. I looked forward to getting copies and loved that Garcia was going to send one to Michelle's ex.

When we got back inside I said, "What else did you two do? Garcia have you been hitting on my woman all day?"

Garcia said, "Vato she's been hitting on me. All of the bitches love me and you know it."

Michelle said, "She's right but after she taught me how to use the RPGs and let me blow up a couple of old Jeeps what else could I do. Blowing things up makes me hot and horny."

I laughed and said, "It makes me hot too. Does Garcia still kiss good?"

Michelle said, "Yes she kisses great but it just made me wish you were there. And I have a present for you that's at the boat already."

Garcia was already naked and in the pool with Lene' when Michelle took off her new weapons and her clothes and dove in with them. I followed and we all played in the pool together until it was time to go to our rooms and dress for dinner. I was grabbed and forced into sex the minute the door was closed and it felt great to be the object of Michelle's lust. We had a wonderful dinner that night and watched a movie on the big screen in the living room after desert.

CHAPTER FIVE

W̶e woke up early the next morning and when we were done provisioning the boat and saying goodbye we sailed out of the harbor headed for Jamaica and my old friend Desmond.

As soon as we were at sea Michelle said, "Mr. Hedberg come and look at your present."

I was taken to the under berth weapons locker and when I looked inside there was a case of new fragmentation grenades I said, "Mrs. Hedberg for me? You shouldn't have. It's just what I've always wanted."

Michelle kissed me and after biting my ear said, "Mr. Hedberg I like this. I like the power and it makes me horney as hell. Bring on that bastard of an ex. I'll cut his balls off and feed them to him." We sailed to the west heading for our destination.

Our course took us around the southern tip of Little Inagua and when we cleared the point we sailed almost due west to lay our course through the Windward Passage that separates Cuba from the western tip of Hispaniola or Haiti. Once in the passage we would make a course correction and our heading would be almost perfect southwest to the island of Jamaica. We would cover a distance of almost six hundred miles and would most likely be at sea for a whole week. It took us three days to get to the Windward Passage and I kept us close to the Guantanamo Army and Marine base because the U.S. Navy was always present there and the Cuban patrol boats didn't mess with pleasure boats in the area. We were scrutinized by an American destroyer and the spoke to them over the VHF radio. They were just going through the motions and it didn't hurt to have Michelle sunning herself on the cushions topless. They really just wanted to be within binocular range and there were plenty of them pointed our way.

That was not the case a day later when we were stopped in the middle of the night by the Cuban Navy. I hove the Mo Cuishle to and lit up the boat with the spreader lights and told Michelle to be friendly. I knew what they were looking for and it was an easy bribe. They loved looking at Michelle's breasts in the little bikini top she was wearing and it almost made them forget their mission.

They were looking for what we used to call road tax in the old days which was whisky and hard to get items on the island. They were pleased I knew the game and the whole thing cost us two good steaks and three bottles of decent booze. They were happy and we were happy. We would be able to buy more in Jamaica in two more days anyway so it didn't matter.

We made Port Antonio when I expected and Michelle loved being in a large harbor with fancy amenities. We did our laundry and had several good meals at the local restaurants nearby. On the third day we armed ourselves and went to look for Desmond. I had rented a car and we drove to the old building where he used to conduct his business. It was indeed still his place but I was told he wasn't there. After a phone call was made we were driven to his new residence in Ocho Rios in our car.

The driver pulled up to the gate and I said into the speaker box, "David Nash to see Desmond Sparrow."

The gate swung open and we were driven to the front door of a pretty tacky but huge house that had an ocean view. I thought, "This is just like Des, big and tacky." So much for coca money. The front door opened and Des was in the opening with two beautiful white girls on each side of him.

We got out of the car and I called to him, "Desmond sell me a dime bag on credit!"

Des called back, "Not on your life Nash, you still owe me from da las one!"

Come inside mon it's too hot out here Ras. Come an get out of da sun."

Michelle and I went inside and Des was great as always. We were immediately given beer and offered pot and coca. We took the beer and Des sat with his girls on each side of him who snorted the coca the whole time we were there.

He said, "How you been mon? It good to see you face on da island. De says you got troubles mon how can I an I help?"

I said, "Des we need to find Mr. X. Garcia said you might know where to find him or know what island he's on."

Des said, "I an I already ask dat for you mon. De says he on de isle Puerto Rico from what de tell me mon. I an I be glad to see you get de Wise person. He's no good, no good mon. He burn me two year ago. Now he after dis angel here an dats no good."

I said, "Thanks Des who should we see in Puerto Rico?"

Des said, "You see Enrique Rojas in San Juan. You remember him mon he was wit us for dat big score years ago. He help you. I an I give you his number. Now what you doing for dinner mon?"

I said, "No plans what do you have in mind?"

Des said, "Meet us at nine at my brother's dinner club mon. We eat den we skank all night. Dress up and be packin'. It's nice place but rough sometime."

We sat with Des for a long time and he gave us the name and number for Enrique. Des excused himself to do some business and we were driven in our car back where his man brought us from.

We drove back to the boat and on the way Michelle said, "Your friend Des is something. If I wasn't with you I'm sure he'd be hitting on me."

I said, "You know he would. Des has always liked the girls as you could see from his companions. Are you scared to go to dinner at his brother's club?"

Michelle said, "No not with you and what I learned from Garcia last week."

We relaxed for the rest of the afternoon and went to the club that night. Michelle had her pistol and I had mine in my shoulder holster. We had a great night in a real Jamaican Ska club that was filled with marijuana smoke so thick we both were completely stoned when we got out at the end of the night. I hadn't been stoned for years and Michelle couldn't stop laughing or eating so we walked the streets of Port Antonio for hours waiting for the effects of the pot to wear off. It was late at night when we were in a poor section of town that we shouldn't have been in when three young punks came up and wanted money from us.

They said, "Tourist man give up da money."

Michelle stoned out of her mind reached into her bag and pulled out her .32 and said, "Screw you give up yours to us!"

I pulled my .40 to back her up and they looked with great surprise and turned and ran like hell. Michelle just laughed through the whole thing. I was impressed at my girl and would tell her the next day what she'd done.

We took the car the next day and drove to Port Royal where we got a great hotel room on the beach and stayed for two days lying in the sun and eating from room service before driving back to the boat to make our provisions and set sail for Puerto Rico.

We were six hours out of the Port Antonio harbor and had the boat sailing nicely on a course a little south of due west. The sun was in front of us and I was relaxing in the cockpit when Michelle came up from below.

When I saw her I said, "How did you like Jamaica?"

She said, "Just fine. The beach was great and room service was wonderful. I think I like hotel living."

I said, "Then we'll just have to do some more. I'm sorry Des wasn't as exciting as Hector or Garcia."

Michelle said, "That's all right. I liked that it was another glimpse into your past."

I said, "That old thing. "I've been trying for years to forget all of that stuff."

Michelle said, "That old stuff is what made you the person you are. I think you turned out pretty good for a drug smuggling, gun running, playboy, sailor, soldier of fortune. My Mama told me to stay away from boys like you."

I said, "What did your Daddy tell you?"

Michelle said, "To keep my knees together."

I said, "I guess you didn't pay any attention to them."

She said, "Apparently not. All of the rules went out of the window when I met you it seems. Aren't you lucky?"

I said, "I'm very lucky and I hope it doesn't run out."

Michelle said, "And what did your Mama tell you?"

I said, "To go to college and be a doctor."

Michelle said, "What did your dad tell you?"

I said, "To leave the car alone."

Michelle laughed and said, "So you didn't listen either."

I said, "Nope I never got into the habit of listening to my parents. I guess I'm just a bad boy."

Michelle said, "I do like bad. It seems to be a pattern with me. David what's that?"

I turned and looked at what Michelle was pointing at. From the distance it looked like a low flying plane coming directly at us.

I said, "Battle stations! Get below now!"

We both hit the companionway at full speed and went down. I headed for the weapons closet and Michelle went straight for the rocket launcher. We met back in the main salon. I had one of the M -16s and a bandolier of magazines over my shoulder ready for anything. We held our position in the salon and looked through the skylights in the overhead. The plane went right over us and was only one hundred feet off of the water. As it passed us it banked to the left and made a long turn to come over us again. We watched from below and it made a figure eight and came past again.

The plane repeated this once more and I said to Michelle, "Looks like we've been spotted."

Michelle said, "What do we do now?"

I said, "That was just reconnaissance. They didn't fire on us so they're just finding where we are and seeing what our course is. Whoever it is they will try and figure out our destination."

Michelle said, "What should we do?"

I said, "Nothing right now. They haven't seen us, only the boat. What I wonder is who told them where we were. It had to come from one of Desmond's posse who is out to make some extra money. I'll have to call Des about this."

Michelle said, "Can we change course?"

I said, "We could but they'll be watching from the satellites now. Changing course won't help us much. What do you think we should do?"

Michelle said, "We should stay armed and ready and keep our lights off at night. The satellites can't see us in the dark."

I said, "Are you sure you haven't done this before?"

Michelle said, "Don't tease. That plane made me nervous. What would you do?"

I said, "We should stay armed and ready and keep our lights off at night. The satellites can't see us in the dark. Your answer was the right one."

Michelle said, "Really, it just seemed sensible."

I said, "Most of this cloak and dagger stuff is about being sensible. Want to make love?"

Michelle looked at me and said, "Right now?"

I said, "Sure my adrenaline is up how about yours?"

She said, "Mine's up all right," and put the rocket launcher down on the settee.

I put my rifle down as well and took Michelle into my arms. I reached around her and untied the bikini top she was wearing. We kissed deeply and I felt her hands at the top of my shorts.

She said, "Good idea. I didn't know it at first but it's definitely what I want to do."

We went to the stateroom pulling at each others clothes and we were naked when we got there.

We made love like maniacs for about an hour and when we stopped Michelle said, "Mr. Hedberg can you get them to fly over us again? That was unbelievably great. Will it be this good when the shooting stops?"

I said, "Even better. It's just not good if you're dead."

Michelle and I collected ourselves and went back to the cockpit. We ate lunch a little while later and I adjusted the radar to sound an alarm at its maximum distance which was the horizon. I called Des on the sat phone and he listened to what I told him of our encounter with the plane. He said he would get on his posse and see who might have defected. He was angry and I felt for the person who sold us out as when Des found out who it was that person wouldn't have long to live.

Michelle spent the afternoon scanning the sky with the binoculars and I took our radar reflector in so we would be harder to locate. I adjusted our course to take us further out into the Caribbean Sea to keep us away from land. Anyone that would come for us would have to have a long range boat and that upped the odds for us. We split the watch that night into two hour shifts and we would have to keep a good lookout as we sailed through the night completely blacked out. I turned off the radar when it got dark so our radar signature wouldn't give away our position. We sailed blacked out for two days and Michelle relaxed after the first night. Weapons were at the ready in the cockpit and we sailed our course until we were due south of the city of Ponce on the island of Puerto Rico.

We were a hundred miles from Ponce when I turned the boat north and began to head in to the coast. Getting closer to land meant we would be exposed to greater threat and Michelle became more visibly nervous as we approached landfall. Michelle had the watch from midnight to two that night and I was asleep in the cockpit on the cushions.

At a little after one Michelle woke me up saying, "Get up I hear something."

I hopped up from the cushions and listened for sounds in the distance. There was noise all right and it sounded to me like a big ocean racing "Cigarette" boat was cruising in the distance. These boats were very fast and could easily handle the open ocean. The wind was light and our boat was making very little noise as we sailed along. I picked up the night vision glasses and Michelle took a pair for herself. We scanned the horizon in the direction of the sound and before too long I spotted a fast ocean racer running on the horizon. We were lucky as the moon had set two hours before and that would make us harder to find in the dark.

Michelle asked, "How safe are we?"

I said, "It's fifty-fifty right now. Remember that they have night vision too. Theirs most likely aren't as good as ours but they work well enough."

Michelle said, Why are ours better?"

I said, "Ours are American military issue, the best money can buy. They're not available to the general public."

Michelle said, "How did we get them?"

I said, "How did you get an UZI and a Russian rocket launcher?"

Michelle said, "Oh I forgot," and asked, "What will we do if they get close?"

I said, "You got a kick out of blowing old Jeeps up do you think you can hit a moving target?"

Michelle said, "I'd have to lead them some right?"

I said, "Right you are. I'll be firing at them with the HK-91 and they'll have their heads down. When they get close enough I'll go to the 70mm grenade launcher. You should be shooting at them with an HK or one of the M-16s until they get into range. Stay here and watch them while I go down for more weapons and ammo."

I went below getting what was needed for the cockpit and what Michelle would need as I wanted her to be firing at them from the forward hatch. I took the ordinance to the cockpit with four other items and explained to Michelle what my plan was.

I said, "Here's what we're going to do. I want you standing on the bunk in the forward salon with your waist level with the deck. This will divide their fire. Try not to expose yourself too much but you should have a good view all around. If you shoot rockets at them watch out for the shrouds that hold the mast up and the roller reefing for the jib which will be rolled up to give you a better field of vision and fire. Have your UZI and your pistol with all of your webbing on. Full combat gear including knife and baton. You'll need them if they should somehow get aboard. Any questions?"

Michelle said, "How do I keep from being afraid?"

I said, "Get angry. Remember that's your ex out there on that boat. Remember all of the hell he put you through. This is your chance to blow him away and be free. Act like you think Garcia would act."

Michelle nodded and I went below to the galley coming back with a bottle of black rum. I handed the bottle to Michelle and said, "Take a couple of good pulls off of this and get an attitude. Remember that's your ex in that boat and you want him dead!"

Michelle said, "Mr. Hedberg, you'd better take care of yourself back here."

I said, "You too Mrs. Hedberg. Take no prisoners tonight. Here's something else."

She said, "What's that?"

I said, "A Kevlar bullet proof vest and helmet. I've got one too. Now put it on and get your webbing on and get to your battle station. I'm going to put the dodger down so we can see each other. Remember not to shoot until they do or I tell you too. You never know, it might just be a bunch of rich kids out here playing."

Michelle took another slug off of the black rum and went to where I wanted her. I drank from the rum and went below to get a few beers and put the rum back. When I got back to the cockpit I dressed for battle and watched the other boat through the night vision glasses while I sipped on the beer.

Michelle watched as I did and I noticed she had taken beer to where she was standing halfway out of the forward hatch. We watched for a half of an hour and the Cigarette boat suddenly turned towards us and was coming fast.

I yelled to Michelle, "Here they come! Lock and load!" when the boat was about a hundred yards from us.

They fired a magnesium flare which lit up the sky towards us and I yelled to Michelle, "Shut down your night vision it's time to kick some ass!"

We both opened up on them and I could see our tracers hitting their boat as it came towards us. They fired back and splinters of fiberglass exploded around me. Michelle kept firing and I traded bursts with her and we reloaded one at a time. We were hitting them hard and I fired two 70mm grenades at them missing them both times with the grenades exploding on both sides of the attacking boat. This was a big deterrent to them and they changed course when they saw we were heavily armed. They made a loop and we kept our fire up as they turned to run parallel to us.

When they did I thought "damn rookies that was stupid," I yelled to Michelle, "RPG's and lead them good!"

I had them in my sights and was peppering the sides of the boat and shot for their waterline hoping to make holes in it or light them up with my tracers. Michelle let a rocket go as our decks were exploding from their small arms fire. Her rocket missed and exploded to their stern. I was doing my best to keep them busy and they circled around our stern to come up the other side. I switched to the M-16 and kept up the fire as I heard another rocket leave Michelle's launcher. The rocket crossed the short distance to their boat in a second and I watched it score. The Cigarette boat blew into a thousand pieces and I could see bodies coming apart and flying through the air. The heat from the blast got to us and it was very hot.

When the wave of heat passed us I heard Michelle screaming, "Take that you bastards, you mother fuckers, eat shit and die, you're fucking with the Hedbergs you stupid shits!"

I had to smile at what she was screaming and I watched the fuel from their boat burning on the water as I saw Michelle drop out of the forward hatch. I immediately dumped my gear onto the cushions and headed below after starting the diesel and giving it full throttle. Michelle turned on the main lights in the salon and was breathing hard when I got to her.

I said, "Take the helm and keep her pointed north. Let out the jib and keep the diesel running. We need to get out of the area in case someone saw that explosion. I have to go below now and look for leaks that might sink us."

Michelle grabbed the rum and headed for the cockpit while I grabbed a flashlight and some plugs from the storeroom and headed for the hatches. We were clean except for two holes below the water line aft in the engine compartment. I went to work plugging them and then surveyed the rest of the boat. She was a mess and I was particularly disturbed by the amount of splintered fiberglass around the position where Michelle had been firing from. I closed the hatch and looked at the rig. The mainsail had a hundred or so holes in it and the decks were a mess. There were a lot of holes below but they were all above the waterline. I turned on the lights and went to the cockpit where Michelle was standing to the helm.

I said, "All right?"

She looked at me with tears in her eyes and said, "I'm all right are you?

I said, "I'm good but the boat is a mess. We took a lot of licks from them."

Michelle said, "Jesus Christ that was really something! I never dreamed I could turn into someone like that. I started firing and when their bullets started hitting our boat I got angry. I was really pissed off. I've never been like that in my life. God what a rush."

I said, "You were great. You blew them to pieces. Good girl how do you feel?"

Michelle drank from the bottle and passing it to me said, "I'm still pissed off at them. Will you take the helm so I can sit? My knees are still shaking. This is some feeling. For the first time in my life I feel in control. Before I always felt like a victim one way or another. I can't believe the way I feel now. Is this where Garcia gets her confidence?"

I said, "Most likely but she grew up doing things like this. I've been in some shit with her and she acted the same as you did. She'd be very proud of you."

Michelle said, "I need to talk to her can I use the sat phone?"

I said, "Sure but leave the rum with me. Be sure and tell her everything that happened to us. We need to know who they were and her contacts will be able to tell us that before we get to the island. Tell her we're changing our destination where we'll tie up in Puerto Rico. We'll stop at the boatyard Gonzales owns near Guayamo. We'll be safe there until the holes get patched and the decks get fixed."

I took the rum from her as she went below. I was glad the fight was over but it meant things were getting really serious for us. I steered the boat and waited for Michelle to finish her call. She was back up in the cockpit in half an hour. She moved to me and the spent shell casings on the deck at her feet jingled as she walked over them.

She got to me and putting her arms around me said, "Take off your clothes and make love to me. That's the only thing that will calm me down."

I set the auto pilot and started to undress. By the time I was done Michelle was naked and waiting for me on the cushions to starboard. We grabbed for each other and franticly made love in the cockpit.

When we were done and holding each other she said, "I have to tell you something and it's really important."

I said, "Go ahead, I'm listening."

She went on, "When the fight was on and I was shooting at that boat all I could think of was you. I was seriously afraid you would be killed and I would be without you."

I said, "I was thinking about you as well."

Michelle said, "I know this is crazy but I think I'm in love with you."

I said, "Well that is important. I think I'm in love with you too."

Michelle said, "That's a relief. That makes me feel wonderful."

I said, "Are you sure your feelings aren't part of the relief of having someone rescue you?"

She said, "Actually they are but I didn't think you would risk your life for me if you didn't love me."

I said, "Good point. I don't think I would either. Do you want to keep doing what we're doing and just be in love with each other?"

She said, "I think that would be best but after that firefight I don't think I'll ever be the same."

I said, "Did you tell Garcia all of this?"

She said, "I did and she told me that I should tell you about it."

I hugged her and the two of us lay together on the cushions. We were still there at dawn when the sun broke over the horizon. We got up and began to survey the damage to the boat in the daylight and the damage was more extensive than I thought it would be.

Michelle was amazed at the number of splinters and bullet holes very close to where she was shooting from and at the damage where I had been standing. She said, "I didn't realize I was that close to being killed."

I said, "Well I'm glad you weren't."

She said, "You were pretty close yourself."

I said, "Did you hear cracking sounds by your ears while you were shooting at them?"

She said, "I did what was that?"

I said, "Bullets passing very close to your head. Another inch or so and you wouldn't be here."

Michelle said, "What do you think it's like to be dead?"

I said, "I've always guessed that if you were dead you wouldn't know it."

Michelle said, "I think we should talk about something else. Death is just a little too close for comfort right now."

I had to agree and we sailed silently for quite awhile.

CHAPTER SIX

We motored into the harbor that served Guayamo at about three that afternoon. We went immediately to the part of the harbor where my old friend Gonzales had his boat yard. He was out but we were told he would return soon and we tied up the Mo Cushile and went about cleaning up the damage. There were a few looks from the hands in the yard but no comments. Having known Gonzales for a long time I was well aware of his clientele and boats damaged in the manner that ours was were not uncommon.

We were just finishing up our task when a voice behind me said, "Amigo it looks like you could use some fiberglass work."

I turned around and Gonzales was standing on the dock smiling at me. I said, "Hello Huey it's good to see you."

"Huey said, "From the looks of your boat it looks like you'd be glad to see anyone."

I said, "That's the truth. It got pretty wild out there last night. Can we borrow some resin and bondo?"

He said, "Sure you can. How about some hands that know how to use the stuff?"

I said, "That would be nice. Where will you get them?'

Huey said, "Oh we'll find some eventually. How long do you want to stay?'

I said, "That all depends on Mrs. Hedberg here. She might want to go to the beach for a few days. What do you think honey?"

Michelle said, "That would be nice, I can work on my tan."

Huey said, "Get what you want from the boat and come to my office. I'll have the guys get your boat out of the water so no one will know you're here."

Michelle said, "How will that help?"

Huey said, "No one looks at the name of a boat when it's out of the water. Didn't you know that?"

Huey got on the boat and Michelle went below to pack some of our things we would need when we left the yard. When our bag was packed Huey took us to his office where we sat and were offered cold beer which we accepted. Huey got into his seat behind his desk and we sat on the couch to the left.

He said once the door was closed, "Damn Nash you two kicked some ass last night! I heard all about it this morning when I got here. Your boat's a complete mess. Was it really bad?"

I said, "Nothing that me and the Mrs. couldn't handle. Do you two need an introduction?"

Huey said, "It's not necessary. Shit the whole Caribbean knows who Michelle Murphy is. There are quite a few bad guys looking for you Mrs. Hedberg. How do you like life with Nash so far?"

Michelle said, "It's pretty damn exciting. I can't wait to find out what happens next. This is getting to be some adventure."

Huey said, "Life with Nash was always exciting. Tell me who do you need to see while you're here?"

I said, "We need to find Enrique Rojas. I did some things with him and Des a few years ago. We've got to find Mr. X if he lets us find him."

Huey said, "He'll probably find you when he gets tired of listening to the stories about you two. Rojas will be easy to find he and I are still good friends."

Michelle said, "Who were the guys that we blew up last night?"

Huey said, "They were here from Florida. They paid big money to rent that boat they were in last night. They were working for Wise as you know but he can't get any of the locals to work for him. Garcia and Hector have you two covered ten ways to Sunday. You are pretty safe here now. All of them were on the boat you blew up so you're cool for at least a week here. It will take quite awhile to fix your boat though."

I said. "I knew that. She's really a mess. Just patch her up and make her seaworthy. We might have to leave on short notice. Besides I'm really pissed at Peter Wise for shooting up my boat. I think he should buy me a new one. What do you think?"

Michelle said, "That would be good. How about one that's bigger."

Huey said, "Oh shit Michelle look out for yourself. Nash is definitely pissed off and that's not good. Bad, bad things happen to people who piss him off. I've seen it with my own eyes."

Michelle said, "I've been hearing about it myself."

Huey said, "Nash, Garcia said your girl was good in the fight is that true?"

I said, "It sure is. She was the one that let the RPG loose that ended their midnight cruise. She's got great instinct this one. She was top notch during the fight and not bad after it either."

Michelle said, "You're damn right I was good during and after. Huey I made a promise to take care of Mr. Hedberg here to Hector and I can't break it'."

Huey said, "That's nice of you. As you've seen Nash can't possibly take care of himself. He's needed a keeper for a long, long time."

I said, "Now that is the truth and Mrs. Hedberg here made me a proper breakfast just the other day. It was very nice."

Huey said, "Michelle, Nash used to eat Chocolate Coco Puffs for breakfast and when we were out of milk he'd just pour beer on them. It was something that was really hard to watch."

Michelle said, "Beer on chocolate cereal? Yuck, David you didn't really did you?"

I said, "It's sad but true. I've been told I've become much more civilized since then."

Huey said, "Look it's getting late. Why don't you come to my house and stay? You can find a beach hotel tomorrow."

I said, "Fine, what do you want to do for dinner?"

Huey said, "Well I'm between wives right now but there's a pretty good

Chinese place near my house that we can get take out from. What about that?"

Michelle said, "Yes! Chinese food. I want Chinese take out for dinner. Huey do you have a pool?"

Huey said, "Sorry no pool. My last wife took it with her when she left me but I saved the hot tub though."

We gathered up our things and went with Huey to his car and drove through the streets of Guayamo to the Chinese restaurant to get dinner. We waited in the bar for our food to be prepared and then drove up into the hills to his home.

When we got to Huey's house Michelle took the take out to the kitchen and after I put our bag down we followed her. We sat around the kitchen table and Michelle got out plates and utensils for all of us. The Chinese food was excellent and I remembered how long it had been since I'd had any. We drank beer as we scarfed down our dinner and we were done in record time. After dinner we took fresh beers and went to Huey's hot tub that had a huge big screen TV directly in front of it.

I said, "Huey do you watch much TV out here?"

Huey said, "Every night. I finish dinner and sit in the tub out here. It relaxes me enough that in a couple of hours I can get to sleep."

Michelle said, "Huey, where do you want us to sleep?"

Huey said, "The other end of the house has a bedroom with a view and a bathroom. Just make yourself at home. I get up early to go to the boatyard so you two sleep late and enjoy. Nash there's keys to my other car in the ignition. Take it and try not to dent the thing. It doesn't get driven too much so it might be slow to start. Oh and my house keeper will be here at eight. She'll be happy to cook breakfast for you if you want."

I said, "Thanks Huey your hospitality is great as always."

Michelle said, "Yes thank you Huey. Thank you very much."

We sat back in the tub and watched the film that was on. In another hour Michelle was falling asleep in my arms and I woke her up and the two of us went to bed.

We woke up the next morning and the sun was shining in our window. We hugged and were slow to get up from the bed and before we did it started to rain. A good summer downpour was on us and we lay together and watched it rain with the city of Guayamo below us as a background for the deluge. The rain stopped in another hour and it did so as quickly as it started. We got out of bed and after showering went to the kitchen. Huey's housekeeper was there and offered breakfast to us but we cooked our own guessing she had plenty of work to do picking up after Huey. We left her the dishes in the sink with those from the night before and went to the garage to get Huey's second car. We hadn't seen the car the night before but it was sweet in the daylight. Huey's second car was a perfectly restored 1957 Ford convertible which was pure white.

It was truly beautiful and when she saw it Michelle said, "Wow! We get to drive this?"

I said, "Apparently so. It's the only car here and the keys are in it let's take it for a spin."

We climbed inside and I reached for the key. It turned over fine and it started the third time I tried the switch. The big V-8 roared to life and I looked at Michelle who was smiling.

I said as I backed the Ford out of the driveway, "Mrs. Hedberg where would you like to go first?"

She said, "Mr. Hedberg can we go find a hotel that has a nice beach and room service?"

I said, "Sure we can. It will be at least a week 'till the boat is fixed and we have some time to kill. Other than finding Rojas and talking to him all we have to do is watch our backs."

Michelle and I drove down the hill from Huey's house and turned right when we got to the coast road. I drove us along the coast to the town of Barahona where we could turn north to drive over the mountains to Aricebo where I knew there were nice beach resorts Michelle would like. The mountains were a great drive and we went into the clouds that were left from the morning squall that rained on us earlier at Huey's house. When we reached the coast I drove us around and Michelle looked at the hotels deciding which one she wanted to stay in. She liked the look of the beach in front of the Hilton so we parked the car and went inside to see if they had any room available. They were down to only suites and Michelle said that would do fine for us. I winced a little at the price but decided the extra space was worth the money so we signed the register and took the key. We didn't go to our room directly but gave our bags to the bell man and left the hotel. We drove back to the boat yard where we collected enough clothes to see us through our little vacation.

Huey was at the yard and when we saw him he said, "You two find a place yet?"

I said, "The Hilton in Aricebo. Call us there if you need us. We're registered under Hedberg."

Huey said, "I heard from Rojas this morning. He's waiting for you to call."

I said, "I will after lunch do you want to come with us?"

Huey said, "Sure are you buying?"

I said, "I am. Where should we go?"

Huey said, "I've got just the place. Let's go."

We took Huey's car and he drove us to a small island restaurant which most likely had been owned by the same family for years. I was open air and had a great breeze flowing through it.

We sat down and Huey said, "Get the special it's always fantastic."

Three were ordered and the fried Conch was delicious. Michelle had never eaten the delicacy and she thoroughly enjoyed what she was eating. Mine was the best I'd ever had and Huey smiled through all of his. We finished our lunch and went back to the yard where Michelle climbed the ladder and got more clothes for the two of us. I drove us back to Aricebo and we took the two new bags to our suite. We got to our room and it was excellent. I opened one of the bags to put our clothes away and found our guns and ammunition inside along with our clothing. I smiled when I saw our heat and Michelle smiled back. When we finished we dressed for the beach having nothing to occupy ourselves with except the sun and the sound of the surf.

I called Enrique before dinner that night while Michelle was in the shower and it was good to hear from another old friend. I invited him to dinner the following night and we agreed to meet at one of the hotel's restaurants.

I asked Michelle what she wanted to do for dinner that night and she said, "I want to stay in tonight if you don't mind. I want to order a romantic candle light dinner and have it here with you. We can eat and look out of the windows and afterwards I'll make love to you until dawn."

I said, "That will be fine with me," and we turned on the TV and watched the news. It finished and Michelle picked up the phone and ordered our dinner. It was served at nine and we ate watching the beach and the action taking place below us. Michelle was good to her word and when the remains of our dinner were gone we settled in on the couch where we drank the rest of the wine and got intimate with each other.

The beach was our only chore the next day and we spent the day relaxing and having drinks that came with umbrellas in them. We had lunch at the outdoor restaurant by the beach and spent the afternoon playing on the wind surfers we rented. It was a wonderful afternoon and we napped through the evening news getting up to shower and dress for dinner with Enrique. We waited for my old friend to show at the bar that was connected to the restaurant. Enrique showed up with his girlfriend Julia at five of nine and they sat in the empty stools next to us at the bar while we waited for our table to be ready.

When they arrived Enrique walked up to me and said, "Que dice' amigo. Esta bien?"

I turned and got up from my stool and said, "Hey, Enrique, long time no see. How the hell are you?"

Enrique said, "Amigo this is my girlfriend Julia. Don't bother with introductions she already knows who you both are."

Julia smiled and shook our hands. She was from the states and very beautiful. Her hair was very blond and I expected this as Enrique had a passion for beautiful blond women. I hugged Enrique and the couple sat next to us and I motioned for the bartender to bring us a round of fresh drinks.

We were seated at our table shortly after our drinks were served to us and after sitting down Enrique said, "Nash what are you doing causing trouble in the Caribbean at your age? I thought you were retired."

I motioned to Michelle and said, "Buddy it's all Mrs. Hedberg's fault. I've been unretired since two days after I met her."

Enrique said, "Unretired is a small word for it. We've been hearing stories about you here for a month. Why is this puta after you in the first place?"

Michelle said, "The puta is my ex. I left him and his bullshit and he can't stand it. He either wants me back or in pieces. The other night wasn't exactly an invitation to come home."

Julia said, "We heard about it yesterday. Michelle you're getting to be a legend here in the islands."

Michelle said, "For fighting off the guys the other night?"

Julia said, "No for taming Nash here. That's really what people are talking about. When Enrique found out Nash was traveling with a woman he immediately said you must be someone really special."

I said, "She is really special and she's a bad ass with weapons."

Enrique said, "And not at all hard to look at. Michelle you are very beautiful."

Julia said, "Beautiful is an understatement. Girl you are the shit. I'm very happy to meet you. Will you come to lunch and go shopping with me tomorrow? Garcia said you were hanging around the boys way too much."

Michelle said, "I'd love to see you tomorrow for lunch and fun. Any friend of Garcia's is definitely a friend of mine."

Our appetizers were gone by this time and our entrées were put in front of us.

We began to eat and Enrique said, "Nash seeing that you're not retired anymore how would you like to help me with a run?"

I said, "Maybe, what are we doing?"

Enrique said, "Nothing bad, Julia will be coming with us. It's actually a good deed to balance all of the evil I do. I have a doctor brother who is taking care of the poor bastards in Haiti. There are lots of them and their dictator is an asshole. We'll be running medical supplies to him for his clinic there."

Michelle said, "Absolutely We'll help you. I have to atone for the evil I laid out the other night and this will do fine."

I said, "There you go Enrique. Mrs. Hedberg has spoken."

Enrique said, "That she has and I agree with her. The rest of what we're going to do is help some friends get off of that island and bring them to this island. Will that be OK?"

I said, "OK, we're in. When do we leave and what kind of boat is it?"

Julia said, "It's an eighty foot schooner we're borrowing from a friend. We'll pick it up from Huey's boatyard two days from now if that's all right."

I said, "Eighty feet? That's pretty big. Is it modern and does it have all of the new navigation stuff?"

Enrique said, "It does indeed. Huey restored the boat for the owner two years ago so I'm sure it's good. Call Huey and check. You know me, I know shit about boats."

I said, "So you really need us to sail you there and back."

Julia said, "That's it exactly. Please come with us. I trust you two and Enrique will most likely just run us aground in Cuba if I let him drive."

Michelle said, "Julia we'll do it. I don't want you in Cuba at all. Now what will we be up against going and coming?"

Enrique said, "The Haitians don't have much of a navy which is easy to imagine. There might be a patrol or two watching the beaches but we'll be unloading out in deep water. The most dangerous thing will be landing our passengers when we get back here. The Puerto Rican government doesn't think much about Haitians coming ashore but that's just inter-island rivalry. There's a dark night coming up soon so we should be able to land them in old San Juan. It's crowded but it's not watched much because it's so obvious."

Michelle said, "What if we get caught bringing them in."

Julia said, "Not much. We'd be talked to sternly and told not to do things like that but they would be sent back to their government and that's not good."

Michelle said, "What would happen to them?"

Enrique said, "More persecution but they're used to that. Their government can't keep them in jail because they don't have the food to feed them. The poor Haitians are in a hell of a jam and most of them want out."

Desert was served to us and brandy to go with it. When the waiter left I asked, "Enrique when do you want to leave and how long will we be gone?"

Enrique said, "A week to ten or eleven days. I'll buy the food and we'll eat well every night. You and I can sail the boat and watch the girls sunbathe. Today is Tuesday so let's leave Friday morning. I'll have my crew do the loading so you two won't have to work."

Michelle asked, "What kind of weapons should we bring?"

Enrique said, "Well listen to the new girl. Nash what have you done to her? Michelle just bring small arms and ammunition. Julia and I will bring our own too."

We finished our dinner and Enrique and Julia went back to their home and Michelle and I went to the beach to walk on the sand together.

We walked holding hands for a long time and then she said, "I think I'm going to like this trip with Enrique and Julia."

I said, "Why's that?"

She said, "I really do want to do good for someone. I keep thinking about blowing that boat up the other night."

I said, "I don't mind doing good will missions like this one. I've got lots of bad karma to pay for myself. All of those guns and drugs years ago can't have been good for all concerned. As a matter of fact that's one of the reasons I retired."

Michelle said, "So you do have a conscious about what you were doing for so many years?"

I said, "Of course I do, all of us do. Especially Hector. He's always afraid his karma will drift to his family. He gives a lot of money to the charities around the islands to try and balance it all out."

Michelle said, "Good, then I don't feel funny about doing this anymore. It's good. Let's go back to our room and get some rest. I have a difficult day of eating lunch and shopping tomorrow."

We went back to the hotel and Michelle began kissing me playfully in the elevator. I kissed back and we had quite a night playing in our suite.

Julia picked up Michelle at noon the next day and I went to the boatyard to see how the work was going on the Mo Cuishle. Huey had the repairs well on the way and I was happy my boat was getting fixed. Michelle came home that evening before dinner smiling and carrying a lot of packages. The girls had a great afternoon and they were bonding with each other nicely. Michelle and I drove to another part of the island and had a great meal in downtown San Juan. We played at the beach for the next two days and then checked out of our hotel to meet Enrique at Huey's boat yard. At the front desk were settled up on our room and the incidentals we incurred during our stay. Michelle surprised me by pulling out a wad of cash and paying for our suite. I was pleased and remembered she came with quite a bit of money. The drive to the boat yard was fun and Huey walked up to us as we parked the Ford in the yard.

He said, "No dents?"

I said, "No dents amigo, thanks for the loan. Is Enrique here yet?"

Huey said, "They're already on the boat. It's all fueled up and ready to go. I put it in top shape for the owner and it shouldn't give you any trouble."

Michelle said, "Thank you Huey. Thank you for everything. How's the work going on the Mo Cuishle?"

Huey said, "Well enough. We're making progress every day and you should be able to sail when you two get back here. I think your doing this run with Enrique is a good thing. His brother is really helping over there and those poor bastards really need all of the help they can get."

I said, "I think so too."

Huey said, "You two had better get to the boat and get on the wind. Do you want some help with your bags?"

Huey picked up one of our suitcases and I took the other two. Michelle stopped at our boat for the M-16s and extra ammo and said she'd meet us on the schooner. Her trip didn't delay us long and we were underway in another half hour. I motored us out of the harbor and to the end of the channel. Enrique and Julia stood to the helm while Michelle and I set the huge sails. The wind was good and the schooner was pretty fast for what it was. When I had her sailing well I set the course and turned on the auto pilot. The boat stayed on the wind nicely and we began to relax on the cockpit cushions with Enrique. Julia came up from below and brought a tray of bloodymarys to us. When we all had our drinks she sat with us in the cockpit.

Enrique asked, "Nash how long a trip do we have?"

I said, "What's our destination?"

Enrique said, "Off of the coast of Tiburon on the end of the western peninsula."

I picked up the chart and looked. The trip would be about 400 miles and I said, "It's about 400 miles there so I figure four days with good wind and weather. Is that fast enough?"

Enrique said, "That's fast enough. Four days in the sun is good for me."

Julia said, "Well I don't want to listen these boys talk for four days. Michelle lets go put our things away. When we're done we can get into some sun. Enrique plan something nice for lunch. If it's good Michelle and I will make dinner for you two maniacs.

The girls disappeared below and Enrique said, "What should we cook for lunch?"

I said, "What do you have on board?"

Enrique said, "Pretty much everything. I bought heavily because Julia said she wouldn't go unless the food would be great."

I said, "Do you have salad fixings and crabmeat?"

Enrique said, "Sure."

I said, "Well we can have crab salad for lunch then. I have a good recipe for the dressing. The girls will like it and we'll get a nice dinner tonight."

Enrique said, "Nash where did you learn to cook?"

I said, "I taught myself. It's part of my retirement. I learned mostly out of necessity. I stay on islands that don't have many restaurants on them and I got tired of peanut butter so I read a book and learned how to cook."

Enrique said, "Will wonders never cease. You really are becoming more civilized. Are you going to keep the girl?"

I said, "I'd like to but I think it's up to her. I'm the one who's old enough to be her father."

Enrique said, "Look here they come now."

The girls were coming up through the forward companionway bringing cushions from below and wearing nothing but the bottoms of their bikinis. Enrique and I smiled at each other and then put our eyes back on two of the most beautiful women one could imagine.

We watched as the girls took their obviously fresh drinks and reclined in the sun on the foredeck. We stayed in the cockpit and talked about old friends and times until it was time for lunch. I took Enrique below and began to make the crab salad while he went about setting the table in the shade of the dodger in the cockpit. I had lunch ready before one and the girls were impressed it was so nice. They spent the afternoon until cocktail hour lying in the sun on the foredeck working on their tans and Michelle's darker skin was very sexy. It was the girls turn to cook that night and Enrique and I sat back in the cockpit until it was served. Julia and Michelle had fried a chicken and made fresh potato salad and it was excellent. We stuffed ourselves sitting around the table in the cockpit until Enrique cleared the dishes and took them to the galley to wash. We divided the watch into teams and Michelle and I took the first watch that night. We would be up until one and would wake Enrique and Julia then for their watch at two o'clock. Our friends went to bed early and we could hear them making love when we went into the main salon an hour later.

Michelle smiled at the noise they were making and when we were in the cockpit sipping our cold drinks she said, "I really like them. Julia is so great she's like finding a new sister."

I said, "Do you like her better than Garcia?"

She said, "I like her in a different way. We both have the hots for Garcia but we're not lesbians. Julia is just like me I think. We like the same things and have the same taste in clothes and music."

I said, "I'm glad you have another woman to relate to for awhile."

Michelle said, "I am too. That was something I missed when the puta was holding me. I wasn't allowed to have girlfriends at all. The only times I could talk to other women were the odd moments when I would be left alone at parties."

I said, "Are you going to miss having another woman around while we're seeing the world?"

Michelle said, "I don't think so. I really love being with you and as long as we can visit the people I like I think everything will be fine."

We sailed on into the night and woke our relief at one for their watch. After they had been instructed about our course we left the boat to our friends and went to our stateroom where we made love for quite awhile.

The next few days went perfectly with the exception of some rain we encountered along the way. It was just rain and with no strong winds so we just stayed on deck and enjoyed the fresh water that washed the salt from our bodies and made us feel clean.

We were fifty miles from our rendezvous point and Enrique got on the radio and confirmed we would be met at a specific longitude and latitude off of the Tiburon peninsula at midnight. The transfer of the medical supplies went perfectly and just when it was done another boat came slowly up to us with our passengers. There were three couples that had two children between them and we took them on board and sent them below. They were all professional people and they were very happy to be getting away from the island. Two of the men were lawyers and the other couple were both architects that wanted out. On our return they told stories of the hard times on the island and how all of the necessary supplies for decent living were stolen by those in political power. Their stories made us feel very good about helping them escape.

Michelle and I were at the helm a couple of hours after the transfer when a search light shined on us from a half mile away. What was left of the Haitian navy were trying to board us and kept trying to hail us on the radio. As they got closer we heard their demand coming from a loud speaker telling us to heave to and let them board. Enrique solved this problem by coming up on deck with a rifle and with one shot he put their light out of business. Our shooting at them was enough of a deterrent to make them fall away from our course and we kept our course to the south distancing ourselves from our antagonists. I guessed that with the poor condition of their government and their island they may not have had guns. They at least had no stomach for a fight and we got away without any more conflict. As it got light outside the girls went below to cook breakfast for all who were on board. As our guests woke up and came into the salon they were fed and pampered as much as we could. Two of the six became seasick on that morning and we did what we could for them. Sea air is best antidote and they were instructed to sit on the foredeck and watch the horizon to settle their inner ears that were causing their discomfort. They were OK in another day and seemed to enjoy the trip when they stopped throwing up. The days passed and we motored into the harbor in Old San Juan at two in the morning on our eighth day out. The scenario was as Enrique expected and there was no one around when our passengers were dropped off at the dock. We let them go and stayed tied up until the next morning when we left the harbor and sailed the boat around the island back to Huey's boatyard in Guyamo. We had a wonderful time on our little journey and Enrique invited us to dinner the following night at a wonderful restaurant. Huey was invited too as he supplied the boat and we all had a great time at dinner.

During the meal Enrique said, "Nash I heard from a friend that X is in South America for awhile."

I said, "Does anyone know when he'll be back?"

He said, "That's debatable. My friend said he's on a mission to help out one of his connections in Antigua."

I said, "Who would that be?"

He said, "Ziggy Dubois. I think you remember him. He's from New Orleans. He came down here years ago to get away from some time he owed the man there. We do business from time to time like all of us do. I think you and Michelle should sail to Antigua and find him. He might be X's next stop in the islands. If he is and you two are there your problem will be solved."

I said, "Antigua is always nice. Going there is a good idea and I'm sure Michelle will like it."

We finished our meal with our friends and went to Enrique's house to spend the night. It was late when we got there and Enrique and I were tired and went to bed. Michelle and Julia stayed up with a bottle of good wine and talked until the late hours. I was joined in bed by Michelle just before dawn and she held me tightly as she went to sleep.

We were up at ten the next morning and were given a ride to the boatyard. Huey had said the night before that our boat was ready and we spent the rest of the day moving our lives back into the boat. I called the grocers that afternoon and arranged for a delivery of supplies the next morning. Michelle and I spent the night on the boat and woke up at nine when the grocer arrived. I paid for the groceries and tipped the delivery man before he left. Michelle was putting all of our supplies away and I went about checking the diesel and the generator for vital fluids.

Just as I was finishing Huey walked up to the boat and said, "Nash are you ready to leave?"

I said, "Just about Huey. We just need fuel and fresh water."

Huey said, "Then let's go to the fuel dock."

Huey got on board and I started the diesel and Michelle untied the lines. We motored the short distance there and Huey helped us fill up our tanks. Before we left he said, "It was a pleasure to have you two here. You two come back when you can stay awhile. Damn I'm jealous of you two. Nash seeing you leaving on your boat is just like the old days. I wish I was going with you."

Michelle said, "I wish you were too Huey but we'll be back soon. Thanks for everything and especially the use of you car. That was really fun."

I said, "It's too much like the old days. I'm realizing why I retired in the first place."

Huey said, "Ahh this beauty will make you young again in no time. You two enjoy yourselves and be safe out there. Remember it's treacherous out on the ocean."

We all hugged on the dock and said our final goodbyes. It was noon when we motored out of the harbor and set our course for Antigua.

CHAPTER SEVEN

I sailed the boat and Michelle put all of the things we'd taken from the boat back in their proper places.

When she was done she came to the cockpit and sitting on the cushions said, "It's really good to be back on board again. We're going to Antigua is that right?"

I said, "That's right we're going to find Ziggy Dubois. X is supposed to be coming to him after he comes back from South America."

Michelle said, "What's he doing there?"

I said, "It could be a number of things. He's most likely visiting one of the cartel bosses there to keep the supply running to the states."

Michelle said, "You know I never dreamed the people in that business could be so nice. I always expected them to be sleazy and rough."

I said, "They can be rough when they want to but the sleazy part comes in the states where the hoods and punks get a hold of the stuff."

Michelle said, "That must be why my ex had such sleazy people around him all of the time."

I said, "Well that's the difference between the big time and the small fry. Most of the people who you've met do all kinds of things. We used to move anything that was profitable."

Michelle said, "Did you ever move heroin?"

I said, "No we didn't. That stuff really ruins people's lives in a bad way. Besides most of it comes from the Mediterranean because it's processed in France. Also the authorities really take a dim view of heroin. If you got caught with coca, pot or guns the story in court would be very different."

Michelle said, "I can understand that completely and I feel the same way." I changed the subject asking, "Tell me are you still in love with me?"

Michelle said, "Yes, even more so. Your friends have so much respect for you it's wonderful. I like that they automatically respect me because I'm with you. It's very nice when they make me feel so at home."

I said, "They're all really happy that I've got someone to travel with finally."

Michelle said, "Why is that? I would think that you always had your choice of women."

I said, "I did have my choice but most of the women I was attracted to weren't really the type to have adventures. They were the type of women that wanted me to have a home and ties to land. You've seen the way I live. I like changes in scenery and sailing my boat."

Michelle said, "So you didn't have girlfriends?"

I said, "I had girlfriends but only when I was in port. You know about sailors, a girl in every port."

Michelle said, "So they're really not kidding when they talk about me taming you?"

I said, "No they're not kidding at all. They mean what they say."

Antigua was about three hundred and fifty miles from where we were and was located on the Atlantic side of the Lesser Antilles chain of islands. Our course would take us to the ocean side of the islands and we would go through the islands south of St. Croix and north of St. Kitts to make our land fall in Antigua. The trip would take us about ten days depending on the wind and the tropical storms that could blow through the area. These storms could be of hurricane strength and the weather satellites would keep us apprized of their location. On our fourth day out we had a good tropical storm that grew from a low pressure system when we were south of St Croix. It wasn't a hurricane yet and its winds were blowing forty to fifty knots. The seas that accompanied it were running twenty to thirty feet and we sailed into the middle of it. I had done this before and I knew it would be nasty. We sailed under reefed sails for two days and Michelle was great at helping with the boat. I rigged Jack lines running fore and aft and we wore harnesses that when clipped to the Jacks allowed us to move around on the boat and not be washed overboard by some of the big waves that would come over the deck. We both wore strobe beacons on our flotation devices that would flash when they hit the water and a radio direction finder good for many hours of broadcast. Michelle and I split the work and she was surprised by the number of things that constantly needed to be done. We were both worn out when the storm was over and happy to get the sleep that we missed during the squall. We lost time because of the storm and arrived in Antigua on the ninth day. We were still exhausted when we motored into the harbor and went to sleep after we'd cleared customs and gotten our buoy assignment. There were no slips in English harbor as every one moored off of the beach to a buoy. We would have to use the dink to get back and forth to the landing. It was extremely beautiful there and Michelle loved it. At noon on our first day we put the dink into the water and I got the little outboard from the storeroom. We dressed for the island and taking our guns motored to the landing where we tied the dink and went ashore. I went straight to the phone and called Ziggy. He was in and had heard through our friends we were coming. He sent a car for us and we were taken to his residence a few miles from the harbor. He had a great view of the harbor and we could see our boat from his living room. We told him which one was ours and he said he would have one of his men watch it for us.

When we walked into his living room he said, "Nash bra. Good to see you. It has been years man. How's your retirement going?"

I said, "Zig, right now I'm not retired. You look well and prosperous is everything all right?"

He said, "I'm fine and the coca has made everyone rich in the islands. We used to be poor pot dealers but now we're rich coke demons. This must be the Michelle I've heard about. Damn you're beautiful. Nash you've always been lucky with the girls."

I said, "Michelle this is Ziggy. We're both from the gulf coast and got into the business the same way. Except that Ziggy is much younger that I am."

Michelle said, "Ziggy it's a pleasure to meet you."

Ziggy said, "It's a pleasure to meet you. You're almost into celebrity status here in the islands. Is Nash showing you the sights or has he made you his boat slave?"

Michelle said, "I'm working up to boat slave. I started out as just a sex slave but I'm trying to get a leg up."

Ziggy said, "Nash how did you find her?"

Michelle said, "He made the mistake of taking me sailing. Before he knew it I was living on his boat and getting him into far too much trouble."

Ziggy said, "Nash is that the truth?"

I said, "It is but I never knew she would be such a liability."

Ziggy said, "I've heard she is. Listen there have been strangers on the island that don't look good. They might be here for you two so keep a weather eye over your shoulders. I'll try to find out more about who's on my island. Do you two need transportation?"

I said, "Sure we could use some wheels. What have you got?"

Ziggy said, "I've got a pair of scooters that will get you around will that be all right?"

I looked at Michelle, who said, "Motor scooters? Great I love motor scooters. Thank you so much."

Ziggy said, "Not at all it's my pleasure. What are you doing for dinner? Would you like to go out with me and my girlfriend tonight?"

Michelle said, "That sounds like fun. We could use some restaurant food. We haven't felt right since working through that tropical storm."

Ziggy said, "Did Nash sail you through that nasty weather? That's typical of him. He did the same thing to me once on a run to Panama. He scared me to death and I threw up the whole time."

I said, "Yes and I had to sail the boat by myself for two days while Zig puked his guts out over the starboard rail. He must have lost fifteen pounds because he didn't eat for almost three days."

Ziggy said, "Michelle I lost so much weight I had to tie up my shorts with a length of rope and it took me a week to feel right again."

I said, "What about X?"

Ziggy said, "He's supposed to be here any time or week. He said he was going to check on me when he got back from his trip. He could show up tomorrow for all I know."

I said, "We just might wait for him here then."

Michelle said, "Sure it's beautiful here I don't mind at all."

Ziggy said, "Let's get you two on some scooters then. I've got business this afternoon that I can't defer. Meet me at nine tonight at the Jolly Roger restaurant. Its a few miles up the road from where you're moored in English Harbor. It'll be a nice ride."

Zig took us out to the garage where he kept the scooters and after giving us a little instruction we shook his hand and were off down the gravel road and back to the landing where the dink was tied up. We left our scooters in the parking lot and took the dink back to our mooring. We got out of the dink and I tied it to the port stern cleat and we went below to nap through the afternoon.

Our nap did the trick and we felt wonderful when we woke up after the sun had set. We showered and dressed for dinner with Ziggy later that evening. The two of us took the dink to the landing and rode to the restaurant in the perfect weather. Parking our scooters in front of the restaurant we climbed off and went inside. Ziggy was already there with his girl sitting next to each other at the bar.

We walked up and Ziggy said, "Nash and Michelle this is my girlfriend Beato she's a native of this island and other than a few trips I've taken her on she's been here all of her life.

We shook hands with her and Michelle sat by her and said, "Beato you have a beautiful island. You're so lucky to have grown up here."

Beato said, "I was lucky but you know how it is when you're growing up. You hate the place you are. I like it now though."

I said, "That's true. Islands can be awfully small."

She said, "Right you are. The worst thing was everyone knew you and your parents. I couldn't do anything without my parents finding out."

We all laughed and went to our table which was ready for us. We sat and ordered our food and the conversation was light and wonderful. I loved watching Michelle's personality come out and she was wonderfully gregarious. She had a great knack for making people feel at ease with her. We chatted through dinner and she and Beato made plans to go shopping the next day. When dinner was over we stayed at our table and danced to the island band that set up for the after dinner crowd. The girls danced Ziggy and me into the parkay floor and we finally begged off to sit and drink. Beato and Michelle stayed on the dance floor dancing together while Ziggy and I watched them. Last call was finally made and we gathered our things to leave the restaurant. Michelle and Beato were pretty drunk and we all hugged many times in the parking lot before leaving.

The wind in our hair felt great as we cruised slowly along the road back to the boat. We were driving through one of the small towns along the way when suddenly a station wagon pulled out in front of us. We tried to stop but Michelle hit the station wagon where the front wheels were and flew over the hood landing on the road beyond. I hit my brakes and slid sideways into the vehicle smashing my hip into the metal. I was trying to get free and get to Michelle to see if she was all right when the car behind me pulled up close and six men got out. They grabbed me and started to work me over beating me everywhere on my body.

I fought back as well as I could and I could hear Michelle screaming, "Get off of me you bastards, leave me alone!"

I could see she was being taken by the men and as the men on my side of the station wagon pounded on me I heard two gunshots that sounded like Michelle's .32 going off. That was all I saw that night as I woke up with strangers reviving me on the side of the road. The station wagon was still there and there were two bodies lying in the road where Michelle had been attacked. I touched my face and it was sticky from blood. The ones who revived me took me to town and the emergency clinic where I was patched up complete with three dozen stitches in my head. I had several broken ribs that hurt like hell when I breathed and my right hip was seriously bruised from where I contacted the car. I was a mess and could barely walk. I made my way to a phone and dialed Ziggy's number.

He answered and I said, "Zig, they've got Michelle."

He said, "Where are you?"

I told him the name of the hospital and he said, "I'll be right there. Stay put."

Twenty minutes later Ziggy walked through the doors of the emergency room and I was glad to see him. I got up and finding the nearest pair of crutches I left the hospital without saying a word and got into Ziggy's car. We drove to his house with Beato holding me in the back seat. My friends took me inside and I went to the couch in the living room and collapsed onto it. Beato went to the kitchen and came back with a bottle of black rum and a cold towel for my head. I took both and drank heavily from the rum. Ziggy was on the phone and stayed there for almost half an hour while I listened from the couch. It was obvious he was closing the island and directing all that he knew to the airport and other ports of embarkation around the Island.

He finished all of the calls and came to the couch where he said, "How many of them were there."

I said, "Eight I think but Michelle got two of them with her .32. I didn't see their vehicles but they must have taken her in a separate car or van. The guys looked Hispanic and black and they hit like line backers."

He said, "You're pretty messed up. Want some pain pills?"

I said, "No thanks but maybe later. I'd love to nod out but I have to stay on my toes for this one."

Enrique nodded and said, "I've got everyone on the island watching all of the exits. They still might get her out still but I think they'll wait for awhile."

I said, "What about us?"

"Enrique said, "I don't think we have to worry but I have two men here guarding us. If they'd wanted you dead you'd already be there. They didn't kill you because of who they know you are connected with. I don't think they know Michelle is just as connected as you are now."

I said, "Let me use the phone."

Enrique brought me the wireless handset and I took another pull off of the rum. I dialed Garcia's number and she answered sleepily. I said, "Garcia they've got her."

She said, "Who is this? Is that you vato?"

I said, "It's me, Nash. Michelle and I got jumped tonight and she's been taken prisoner."

Garcia said, "Where are you?"

I said, "Antigua with Ziggy. I'm at his house."

She said, "Blanco you don't sound so good."

I said, "I'm not good. I ran into a car on the scooter I was riding and the men that took her beat the shit out of me."

Garcia screamed, "Bastas! Chingasos! Nash I'm on my way. Stay there."

She went off in a screaming of barely intelligible Spanish that I could hear before

I hung up the phone. My next call was to Enrique who said he was leaving when the phone died. I called Hector who was furious when he heard the news and said he would be there as well. Ziggy got back on the phone as a ton of radio equipment was brought into his living room and was set up. I thought, "Good we'll need our own communications for this. No sense in letting the phone company in on it."

Beato was right there with me and when I finished my calls she forced me to lie down on the couch where I woke up four hours later stiff and sore with a splitting headache. Beato gave me some pills for the headache and I ate some eggs and tried to walk. I could stand but was too stiff to walk. I picked up the bottle of rum and after a few shots I could move my legs enough to go to the bathroom with the help of the crutches I'd appropriated.

I finished relieving myself and went back to the living room just as Garcia was coming in the front door.

When she saw me she said, "Jesus Christo vato you're a mess, who did this to you? They're dead men already. They just don't know it. They shouldn't have fucked with my Michelle either. That will make it a slow death. I'll have them eaten by ants those fucks. How dare they fuck with my family?"

Lene' was coming in with their suitcases by this time. She dropped the bags when she saw me and I watched as tears came to her eyes. Garcia was quizzing Ziggy about what he'd arranged for closing the island and when they finished talking Garcia got on the phone while Lene' and Beato laid me back on the couch to try and keep me from moving.

When Garcia was done on the telephone I said, "Garcia how did you get here so quickly?"

She said, "Vato you haven't been in my jet? When you get better we'll go somewhere. Just you and I like the old days."

I said, "Where did you learn how to fly?"

She said, "Lene' taught me a year ago. The bitch is a flight instructor. Did you think she was just another piece of ass?"

I laughed and said, "I should have known. Garcia you never cease to amaze me. What's going on now?"

She said, "Ziggy got the island closed and I have fifty men and ten angry lesbians coming to the island pronto. Hector called me in the air and he'll be in tonight. His men are pretty much shutting down the Caribbean and the Gulf rim. There's going to be no place for them to go. Hector has the L.A. connection working and they're looking for Wise. That puta doesn't even know what he's started. I'm going to have his eyes eaten by birds when I catch him. One at a time so he can watch the first one go in a mirror. Did you call Enrique?"

I said, "Yes he's on the way."

She said, "What's his sat phone number I need to talk to him. What about Desmond?"

I said, "I didn't call Des. He's always too stoned to do anything but business and he'd never leave his bitches."

Garcia laughed and said, "Is he still with the two white girls? I always liked the tall blond."

Garcia went back to the phone and I watched her directing the closure of a whole Island. I had to admit that her standing there on the phone with her black hair and gorgeous body wearing a T shirt and weapons belt was a beautiful sight and I wished Michelle was around to see it. I fell asleep on the couch and didn't wake up until Enrique walked into the room.

He came to where I was lying and said, "Nash, everything is going to be all right. All of the Caribbean is with us on this one. You know how they hate those cowboys from LA. We'll find her and bring her back here to you. Can you walk?"

I said, "Not bloody well but I will in a few days. I'm just stiff and sore and my head hurts from the stitches. They gave me a pretty good beating last night. I'll get over it soon enough though. I have to get my girl back."

Enrique said, "Don't worry about that now. We're here and everything is under control. I feel for the poor bastards that took her. There's a line of your friends that want a piece of them. Especially Garcia. I've never seen her so angry."

I said, "She's pissed all right. Just look at her eyes. I haven't seen her like this since we had to fight our way out of Colombia that time."

Enrique said, "I remember that. If they'd stopped you the two of you would probably still be in jail. How many people did you two kill getting to the boat?"

I said, "I can't remember how many but the barrel of my rifle was so hot it would take your skin off if you touched it. I burnt myself twice when I was running with it."

I lay my head back down and went out while the team was busy finding out all they could about what had taken place. Garcia had her people set up an interrogation room in the garage and there were already people being brought in for questioning. I thought, "This woman is as bad as Castro. She should have her own country to rule."

It was late that night when Hector came in the door wearing full battle gear that barely fit him anymore.

He came up to me and said, "Amigo, how are you feeling?"

I said, "Hector I feel like shit. How are you?"

He said, "I'm pissed off that's how I feel. I put the price of a hundred thousand up for Michelle's return and that might get some results. I also put the price of a hundred thousand dead or alive on Wise that fuck. He'll have to hunker down somewhere. We'll get Michelle back and when we get Wise I'll give him to you personally. What will you do with him?"

I said, "Shit I'll just give him to Garcia's gang of angry lesbians and tell them what he did to Michelle for five years. What could be worse?"

Garcia laughed his big laugh and said, "Damn Nash you are mean! Tell me; are you in love with her?"

I said, "Yes I'm in love with her."

Hector said, "Then we'll get her back to you old friend. I'll have the gulf drained to find her for you. You are not going to let this one get away. Now go back to sleep and let those that love you work."

I was given some pills by Lene' and was out for the duration of the night.

I woke up the next morning and Beato was sitting with me on the couch I looked at her and she said, "Nash how are you feeling this morning?"

I said, "I don't know let me assess myself," I took inventory on my body and then said, "I'm better than yesterday. My head doesn't feel so bad today."

I said, "I'm hungry though can I have something to eat?"

Beato said, "It's on the way. Lene' is making it for you. Are bacon and eggs OK?"

I said, "Yes that's good. Better bring me a beer to wash it down. I need to loosen up my legs. I have to walk."

Lene' brought me a beer and I drank while she fed me eggs. It was better when my stomach was full and I'd had two beers in me.

Lene' took away my plate and when she came back she said, "OK Nash, Bath time."

I began to complain but was instantly told to shut up. The girls picked me up onto my feet and after they put the crutches under my arms made me walk towards Ziggy's hot tub. I was able to move better and it was slow but better than the day before.

When I got to the tub they said, "Nash sit down. We're taking your clothes."

I started to complain but the two started getting my clothes off of me. I was being stripped by two beautiful women and even as hurt as I was it was pretty erotic. I had to enjoy the attention and they had me stand naked on my crutches while they helped me to the tub. They let me down into it and the hot water felt great. I was soaped clean and the longer I soaked the better I felt. Lene' went to change the bandage and dressing that was covering my stitched up head. Just as she had the old dressing off Garcia came by the tub.

She stood on the side of it and said, "Damn Nash what did they hit you with? It looks bad. Does it still hurt?"

I said, "Yes it hurts. What are you doing here? Go find my girl."

She said, "Shut up vato. We're finding her. I just came out here to see you naked. I always did like the way you look with your clothes off. I just didn't think your head would be so gross. Vato you should take better care of yourself."

I said, "Thanks a lot. I love you too. Now go find Michelle."

She said, "Ungrateful, I give you two of the hottest bitches on the planet to bathe you and all I get is do some more."

Garcia laughed and walked away back to where the captured were being brought in for questioning.

When she was gone Lene' said, "Nash you are something. I think you are the only man she truly loves. You should have seen her after your phone call yesterday. She went completely nuts and started shooting her .45 in the house. I've never seen her like that before."

I said, "Well we go back a long way and we swam the same ocean together more than once."

Lene' said, "Nash, I want you to know you can swim the ocean with me any time you want. All you have to do is call."

I said, "Lene' are you making a pass at me?"

She said, "Un huh, that's what I just did. I think you're wonderful and if you want Michelle to join in I'd like that too."

I said, "Lene' that's very flattering but do you really want Garcia to cut my balls off when she finds out?"

Lene laughed and said, "OK time to get out of the tub. Nash you're beginning to prune."

I said, "I'll need some clean clothes."

Lene' said, "We've already been to the boat and yours are here. Now sit down so I can dress you"

Lene' helped me into my clothes and I was taken back to the couch to lie down and rest. I did feel much better and the clean clothes were good.

Garcia came into the room and coming to where I was resting she said, "Vato, its bad news. She's off of the island. They took her straight to a helicopter and she's gone."

I said, "Shit where did they go?"

She said, "We're trying to find that out right now. It took a hot knife to find out she is off of the island. Hector has his men finding out where they might have gone by figuring out the range of the helicopter. They probably took her to a place where they can get her on a boat. A helicopter would be limited to about two hundred miles but would have to refuel to get back. That leaves airports and there's not too many of them. Most likely St. Kitts or Guadeloupe. Hector is looking into fuel sales on the smaller islands in the area and Enrique is working on the satellites. I think one of these locals will talk to us and spill the beans. The one who told us she was off the island is plenty scared but we might let him live if he gets his mouth working quick enough."

I said, "Who's calling the helicopter services. Someone had to rent them the air time unless they got that chopper far out of town and that's unlikely."

Garcia said, "Good idea Nash. Pretty good thinking for a retired guy. I'm hoping they don't try to hole up until the heat dies down. They'll be easier to spot if they keep moving."

I said, "Remember Michelle will be trying to get a message to us. She can be pretty resourceful."

Garcia said, "How are you feeling?"

I said, "I'm better since the hot tub but my head still hurts like hell."

She said, "You'd know why if you saw it. I'll send out for a Polaroid and take some gross pictures of your wound for you. Then you'll know why it hurts. Most people would probably be dead from getting hit that hard."

I said, "Garcia are you trying to tell me I have a hard head?"

She said, "You said it vato, not me." And laughed as she walked away.

I lay there on the couch wishing I could do more to help and after Lene' gave me some more pills I slept until that evening. I woke up with Garcia, Enrique and Hector sitting by me talking about the information they'd gathered so far.

I just listened and asked, "Where did they get the chopper?"

Hector said, "They hired it on St. Kitts. Carlos is on his way there with dos hombres to talk to the owner. We'll find out in the morning or before where they went. Are you hungry amigo? What do you want to eat?"

I said, "I need fuel, how about a steak."

Garcia said, "I'm hungry too let's start the bar-b-que."

I heard things being moved around and the next thing I knew they said, "Nash we're out here on the patio come and join us."

I knew what they were up to and struggled to my feet with my crutches. I got my balance and made my way to the patio where Lene' was firing the coals up to cook. They had a bottle of tequila that they were passing and when it came to me I took a big slug before I lay down in the couch that was there for me.

I said, "Thanks for the help getting out here. Are you three trying to see how tough I am?"

Garcia said, "No vato. You walking on crutches is just entertaining for us. You should see yourself. You should be on TV."

They all laughed and I had to laugh with them. They were helping me get well by making me move around by myself. It was difficult but I knew the sooner I was moving the sooner I would get well.

I said, "There's someone else we can call."

Hector said, "Who's that amigo?"

I said, "I have a friend who owes me a favor who is a coast guard commander."

Garcia said, "Which coast guard?"

I said, "The U.S. Will someone get me my phone book?"

My book was brought to me and I looked up the number of Commander Tommy James. I didn't get him but talked to his wife who said she would call him on the ship and have him call me.

I put down the phone and Enrique said, "What are you thinking amigo?"

I said, "If they got her to a boat they'll be transporting her somewhere. I think they're stupid enough to run the boat at high speed."

Hector said, "Right they'll look like rookie smugglers in a hurry."

I said, "They'll be the only ones running fast out there. I think James will be able to cut in the navy as well. They have better satellite service than we do."

Garcia said, "Vato what are you doing hanging out with the enemy?"

I said, "I picked James and his wife up off of their boat two years ago when they got it stuck to a reef. I was asked to keep the secret as coast guard commanders aren't supposed to run their boats aground."

Hector said, "It's worth a try then. They can help find Michelle with some of that fancy technology they use on us."

I said, "Exactly so. If we can track the fast moving boats we might find out where they are going."

By this time our steaks were done and I sat up to eat. I had trouble cutting mine and Lene' came and sat next to me and helped me make my steak into smaller pieces. When we were done eating I got up and headed to the bathroom. It was a serious challenge to get there and when I was done I came into the living room and said, "I have to get into the hot tub. Who's coming with me?"

Everyone got up and followed me to the tub on the patio. Garcia helped me undress and they let me down into the tub. She gave my ass a nice squeeze as I was being lowered and I smiled when I felt her hand. The tequila was brought and we sat in the tub drinking with the telephone near us. It rang in half an hour and it was Commander James on the other end. I explained the situation to him and he said he would help us. I was pleased to hear this and thanked him when the conversation was done and hung up the phone. Lene' got out of the tub and went to get fresh bandages for my head. She changed the dressing while my friends ragged me about how gross I looked and told me how much of my hair had been cut off at the hospital. When my bandage was finished Lene' sat in the tub next to me with Garcia on the other side and they both massaged me while the conversation went on.

Garcia said, "If I'm right they'll try to get her to the west coast where the puta is."

Enrique said, "Then they'll have to get her to a major airport to get a flight there."

Hector said, "Or at least a landing strip in the islands that can handle a plane big enough to fly to Central America or Mexico."

Ziggy said, "What about the Dominican or Haiti. People are desperate there."

I said, "I'd personally try Trinidad or Caracas. If they were to go there they would be able to hop up the west coast to California."

Garcia said, "Or they might try to go from Jamaica to Honduras or Guatemala."

Hector said, "It's a long shot but this cowboy might try to go north through Cuba thinking we won't look for her there. I'll call Manuel and see if he can get the Castro government to watch for her. They're hard to deal with but money really talks there since the Russians pulled out."

I said, "I know Desmond is always stoned out of his mind but he does run most of Jamaica and his government connected brother might help. If we get Jamaica closed it would make it hard for them."

Garcia said, "It shouldn't be too hard to get the Venezuelans to work with us. All we have to do is drop the word that they are running drugs. I stopped using Venezuela a long time ago because of their American connection to the oil."

Enrique said, "What about Panama? Since America got them on the anti-drug program they would look too."

I said, "Damn are we going to have to shut down the whole of Central America?"

Hector said, "Maybe so. It has one distinct merit though. Everything that gets shut down will piss the small timers off and when their supplies get low they'll be pissed at the person who caused it."

Garcia said, "Good idea let's work on the angle of making sure everyone knows the puta is responsible for nothing moving. That should make things very hard for him."

I said, "That's good thinking. Who thinks they'll go by plane or ground?"

Ziggy said, "I think by plane. They're in a hurry."

Garcia said, "They'll go by plane. I think our cowboy will try and get her back to his territory as fast as possible too."

Hector said, "I'm leaning towards ground transportation. It's harder to watch and the people involved are easier to bribe."

Enrique said, "I'll have to go along with ground that's the way the majority of illegal people move from country to country on the mainland."

Garcia said, "Enrique that's a good idea. What if this puta did the snatch but is planning on moving her along with the rest of the wetbacks. He would have to go through one of the coyotes that can deliver reliably."

I said, "Not to bring up old annoyances but have any of you three pissed off anyone lately that might be helping them?"

Hector said, "I don't think so. I haven't burned anyone in a long time because I haven't had to."

Garcia said, "Not that I can think of. The last one I pissed off wound up in hell."

Enrique said, "Same here Nash. Things have really stabilized since you retired. Everyone has been working together nicely for quite awhile. There hasn't been much excitement."

Hector said, "That's enough for tonight. I'm getting tired and we won't find out anything more until tomorrow morning so let's go to bed."

I said, "I'm tired too but I have one last question."

Garcia said, "What's that vato?"

I said, "Do you think we should move our headquarters somewhere else. Somewhere where we have better access to the mainland?"

Enrique said, "That might be a good idea and it would give Ziggy here a break."

Ziggy said, "Don't worry about me but I think a more accessible location might be good."

Garcia said, "Let's figure this out in the morning. I'm tired and drunk and the night shift will wake us up if anything is heard."

We got out of the hot tub and Garcia, Enrique and Ziggy went to their rooms to get some rest. It took me longer to get out of the tub and I had to have Lene' and Garcia help me. They got me out and I held myself up on my crutches while they dried me off. I put my shorts on and started back to the couch where I had been for the last two days.

When I got to the living room and started to settle onto the couch Garcia said, "No vato. You're sleeping with us tonight. There's nothing like two beautiful warm bodies next to you to make you feel better si?"

I said, "Garcia don't you two want some privacy?"

She said, "What for vato?"

I said, "Well you two might want to make love."

She said, "What if we do?"

I said, "Won't I be in the way?"

She said, "Vato we might play and you can help if you want to. If you don't want to help you can watch."

I said, "OK but remember it's your idea."

Garcia came close to me and said, "Nash you know I've been in love with you for years. It took this incident to make me realize just how much. Now come with us and get into my bed."

I followed to Garcia's room and they helped me into bed and climbed in one on each side of me. I was hugged for awhile and eventually Lene' and Garcia started kissing. They kissed me as well and they made love together with me helping from time to time.

I did manage to sleep that night and the next morning over breakfast it was decided we would move our head quarters to the Virgin Islands because of their access to major airports and rentable aircraft should we need to go some where in a hurry.

CHAPTER EIGHT

Garcia orchestrated the move and all of our equipment was removed from Ziggy's house and taken to air freight. My boat was to be sailed there by professionals and would meet me there in a week. The rest of us went to the airport after we'd packed our bags and went to the executive terminal there. Garcia had called ahead and her Gulf Stream private jet was waiting for us running and ready to take off. Our bags were stored and we boarded Garcia's jet. There were eight seats in the fuselage and we took seats as we wished. I sat across the table from Hector who needed two seats to be comfortable. Enrique and Ziggy took the other pair facing each other in the back of the plane and began to make calls regarding the ideas we had the previous evening in the hot tub. Garcia and Lene' went to the flight deck and when we were settled in the door was closed and Garcia began to taxi out to the runway while speaking to the tower on her head set.

She turned the jet onto the runway and called back to us saying, "Fasten your seatbelts or hang on tight. I'm putting the hammer down."

She pushed the throttles forward and the jet bolted down the runway. Three quarters of the way down it she pulled back on the yoke and the plane rotated up and climbed at a fantastic rate. She leveled off at about fifteen thousand feet and then she left the jet to Lene'. She came back to where we were sitting and then played stewardess making drinks for all of us.

She sat next to me and said, "So how do you boys like my jet? Isn't it the shit? I love flying it."

Hector said, "Very impressive. Is it hard to fly?"

Garcia said, "Not at all. Lene' could teach you in no time."

Hector said, "Do you think I can afford one?"

Garcia laughed and said, "Hector you'll never believe where I bought this one. I got it for next to nothing at an auction where they sell all of the stuff they confiscate from the drug dealers they catch."

Hector said, "No! You didn't?"

Garcia said, "I sure did. It went for one third as much as a used one in good shape would from a dealer."

I said, "Damn Garcia that's impressive."

She said, "Lene' taught me how to do it. Owning a jet is fun. It's so easy to zip off to somewhere and spend the weekend. Hector you should get one, your family would love it."

Hector said, "No doubt they would but it's hard enough to keep up with the way they spend in Florida. I don't think I want to open the rest of the world to them."

We landed forty minutes later in St. Thomas and when the plane was unloaded we rented cars and drove to the Ritz Carlton Hotel were we were given two huge suites back to back.

Garcia and I were in the elevator and I asked, "Damn Garcia who's going to pay for all of this?"

She said, "Don't worry about it vato. I've got it covered ten ways to Sunday."

I said, "How's that?"

She said, "The owner of this hotel owes me a favor. I saved his kid a year ago in Grenada. The kid got in trouble and I got him out of it. Simple as that."

I said, "What did he do?"

Garcia said, "The usual. Just another dumb college kid going to make a score in the Caribbean and bring it home. His mistake was he bought from a DEA agent the little shit."

I said, "How'd you hear about it?"

She said, "From my attorney. He knew the boy's father and one call led to another."

I said, "How did you get him away from the DEA?"

Garcia said, "What are you doing? Writing a book Nash? I let the DEA have a lowlife that had been bugging me for a long time. I rolled him over to the man and the kid was sent to me. I used him for a house boy for a month before I sent him back."

We got to our room by the time the story ended and we all went inside. It was palatial and beautifully decorated.

The bed rooms were divided up and when I looked at the one I wanted Garcia said, "Not on your life vato. You can keep your clothes in there but you sleep with me until you're well."

I said," I'm just thinking about Michelle and what she might say about the threesome we're having."

Garcia said, "Vato that's so sweet. It's completely unlike you. Tell me are you in love with my Michelle?"

I said, "I'm afraid so."

Garcia said, "Don't worry vato she's in love with you too. You let me handle this and don't think you're sleeping anywhere else. I promised Michelle I'd take care of your Blanco ass and that's what I'm going to do."

An hour later we were settled in and the calls were being made as they had been continually from the morning after Michelle was kidnapped. Information was being gathered and Michelle's trail hadn't showed itself yet. I was getting nervous about where she might be and was worried that the ex might have done away with her. We got a break that afternoon just at cocktail time when Garcia got a call from one of her contacts in Guadeloupe where the helicopter apparently had been flown. The information came from a local there who saw the helicopter land at a cove that was continually being used for smuggling in and out of that island. The chopper had landed in the cove and there had been a boat there to meet it. The passengers had gotten out and the boat which was described as a large trawler left with the passengers. The local was adamant that there was a female with dark red hair with them that was putting up a good fight from the chopper to the boat. He said the direction the boat went was to the south once the boat had cleared the entrance to the cove. That gave us a place to start from and the effort to find Michelle was concentrated in that area. That was forty eight hours ago and even at the slow speed the trawler moved at it could easily have put them two hundred miles away. The team went into action with calls to Martinique. St. Lucia and Dominica where there were good airports. St. Vincent and Grenada were not left out and calls were made there as well.

When the calls were made I said, "Hector where do you think they're going?"

He said, "I really don't know. I'm guessing they will be headed to an airport but you never know. They could go anywhere but it's my guess they will try to get on the mainland to give us more places to look."

Garcia said, "I don't think so. The mainland on the northern coast of Venezuela is mostly rainforest and it's difficult to go overland in that part of the country."

Lene' was making cocktails by this time and we waited to hear where the boat might land. When cocktails were done we went to the restaurant in shifts to eat and kill some time. I stayed in the suite and ordered room service with Hector who didn't want to go out. We ate together and ordered crab and lobster which we devoured instantly when it arrived. The others were back by ten and when they came in Hector, Enrique and Ziggy all went to bed. I stayed up with Garcia and Lene' drinking wine while we waited for the phone to ring. Lene' had the television going and we paid sporadic attention to it as the hours passed. We finally went to bed after I was given a bath and had my dressings changed by the girls. The hot water was good for my bruises and I could walk much better when I got out of the tub. Lene put me into their bed and I slept wonderfully that night.

I woke up the next morning between the two girls and I had to wake them up to get out of bed and go to the bathroom. Lene' was up by the time I'd finished and was in the kitchen making breakfast for all who came into the kitchen. Enrique was first on the phone and I could hear him talking to our contacts in various places.

Enrique came into the room and said, "Good news! They were in St. Lucia yesterday and tried to get on a plane at the airport. Apparently Michelle caused a stink and got them all grabbed by the cops. They bribed their way out of the airport and went away. As far as our friends know they're still on the island. After that no one knows. We do know they haven't tried to get a charter plane because the charter companies are all in our pocket."

Hector said, "Maybe we should go there right now?"

Garcia said, "No they've just changed plans I'm sure it's back in the boat for them."

I said, "I'm inclined to agree with Garcia. I think they will go for the boat ride."

Just then the phone rang and it was another of our contacts in St. Lucia. Enrique listened and spoke back in Spanish to the person on the other end.

He hung up the phone and said, "That was Jaime. He said they got back on the trawler and went west. This time we've got numbers and a good description of the boat."

He wrote the particulars on the note book that we were using to keep the information and I said, "I'm calling the coast guard."

I waited for awhile and talked to Commander James. I filled him in and he said he would call me back after he looked on the satellite photos that were taken in the last 24 hours. I sat back down and Garcia was coming back into the room with a sheaf of maps.

She spread them out on the floor in front of us and said, "They're going west into the big part of the Caribbean Sea. There's nothing to the south of them for a thousand miles except for Caracas and Curacao. The east coast of Central America is a long way off and so is Jamaica. Even if we know their exact longitude and latitude they'll be hard to find."

I said, "Not exactly hard to find but difficult to stop. I don't want to blow them out of the water with Michelle on board."

Hector said, "No we don't want to do that. Landing in front of them in a seaplane isn't good either. We may have to wait for them to land in a port where we can easily get to them without killing Michelle."

The telephone rang and I was handed the phone. It was the commander and I was told that he had a fix on the getaway boat and would keep us apprised of its direction and position."

I told the others what he'd told me and said, "It looks like we're going to have to wait until they choose a port."

Hector said, "What if they drop a plane out of the sky and take her off of the boat?"

Garcia said, "They could do that. But I think the coast guard would notice."

I said, "They told me the boat would be monitored 24/7. If they try to take her off by plane I'm sure we'll hear about it."

We went about our day and finally Garcia said, "Damn it Nash let's go get her. Call that coast guard filth and see when they can intercept and hold them on the ocean?"

I said, "OK but how are we going to get there?"

Garcia said, "You leave that to me vato. I'll make the arrangements when the time comes."

I got on the phone and spoke to my friend the commander. After he did some checking he said, "No problem Nash. We can intercept in thirty-six hours."

I said, "What kind of vessel?"

He said, "The big deal. A 180 foot cutter with a full compliment of men and weapons. What are your plans?"

I said, "I'm not sure yet but I'll have to call you back."

I hung up the phone and waited for Garcia to hang up from her conversation. When she did she said, "Its set, Crazy Larry is on his way here to get us. Who wants to go and when can the coast guard intercept?"

I said, "Thirty-six hours to their intercept. That should be the day after to-morrow at let's say six in the morning."

Garcia said, "Perfect Crazy Larry can get us there at six. What's the ocean do-ing out there?"

I picked up the phone and made a call. When I finished listening I said, "The seas are calm two to three feet."

Garcia said, "Call your coast guard friend and ask him to stop them at six in the morning the day after. Get the aircraft frequencies from him so we can get their exact position. I don't want to miss them."

I called my friend back and he was great about giving me the radio frequencies and said the boat would be stopped and held for us.

When the deal was done I said, "OK Garcia tell me the plan."

She said, "Crazy Larry is on his way here in his flying boat. It's a PBY Catalina like they used in World War Two. They have tremendous range and can set us down on the water next to the coast guard. He'll let us get Michelle and fly her back here. Now who wants to go?"

Hector said, "I'm definitely in."

Ziggy said, "Sorry Garcia I get air sick too easy."

Garcia said. "Blanco pussy. You'll miss all of the fun."

Enrique said, "I'm with you. I couldn't miss it Julia would kill me."

Garcia said, "Vato?"

I said, "You bet. Just bring me some clean bandages and my combat gear."

Garcia said, "Good, Crazy will be here tomorrow morning and it will take us ten hours to get to the meeting point. Just enough time to sort out the details and fly there for six am. Those poor bastards will never know what hit them. Wait until we drop out of the sky on them."

We spent that afternoon getting ready for our commando raid in the middle of the Caribbean. Our gear was checked and re-checked before it was all taken to the dock where Crazy Larry was to meet us. I was still having trouble moving but managed another hot tub that night after dinner with Garcia and Lene'.

Garcia was relaxing with Lene' sitting next to her and she said, "So vato are you nervous?"

I said, "A little but mostly because I'm not a hundred per-cent. If there's trouble I might not be able to help much."

Garcia said, "I hope there's trouble. I want some pay back. My Michelle better be OK for their sake too."

I said, "What are we going to do with the kidnappers?"

She said, "We'll give what's left of them to the coast guard or the sharks."

We went to bed after that and went right to sleep knowing the next day would be a long one. We breakfasted the next morning and went to meet our pilot and plane owner at the docks. He was two hours late and Garcia was visibly annoyed. When he finally showed up he taxied the plane in and we went about stowing our gear and turning our plane around. When it was set to go we took a break and went to dinner.

We flew away from the island at seven-thirty with Larry and Lene' at the controls of the Catalina. Our tentative destination was figured and the plane flew into the night. I was still very sore and moving slow doing my best to rest on the flight there. Garcia contacted the coast guard at five AM and they were shadowing the trawler from just over the horizon. They would move in and force the boat to heave to at six and we had coordinates that would get us close enough to have a visual of the position. It all went perfectly from the start. The trawler was stopped on the water and Larry brought us down and landed us on the surface taxiing us to a safe distance. The coast guard was already aboard the boat and had the crew out on deck handcuffed to the starboard rail. The only problem was that Michelle wasn't there. A launch took us to the boat and I struggled aboard anxious to find Michelle. When it was reported Michelle wasn't on board Garcia went nuts and began to search the boat herself cursing in Spanish the whole time. She and Lene' and Hector and Enrique combed the boat stem to stern finally finding Michelle drugged and stuffed into the chain locker in the foc'sel. They pulled my girl out and got her topside in a hurry. Michelle was out but still alive. I was frightened to death when I saw her and we gave her to the coast guard who rushed her aboard their vessel and their sick bay.

Garcia was right at her side as she went aboard and my friend the commander came up to me and said, "Nash is that your girl?"

I said, "Yes that's her all right."

He said, "I've already got word from command to bring these guys on the trawler in and the boat as well. Do you want a piece of them before they find the brig on the cutter?"

Hector said, "Commander, Nash isn't quite up to snuff today would you mind if I took his place?"

The commander said, "Not at all Hector. You've been gaining weight though."

Hector said, "Do we know each other?"

The commander said, "We do, remember the load of weapons you lost off of Trinidad about fifteen years ago? I was the lieutenant that boarded your boat that morning."

Hector smiled and said, "I do remember. That was not a good day for me but I see you've been promoted."

The commander smiled and said, "It seems that we've both been promoted. I think my men and I will investigate the stern of the boat while you explain to this crew about kidnapping."

With that the commander and crew left the bow and Hector started in on the captain who was already pissing in his pants and standing in yellow liquid. In no more than five minutes later the captain had told Hector all that he wanted to know and the others were readily volunteering information.

We were taken to the cutter when Hector was done and got to see Michelle in the sick bay. She was flat on her back and barely conscious.

I walked to where she was lying on her back and she said, "Nash do you still love me?"

I said, "I do but sometimes you're a lot of trouble."

She said, "I am a lot of trouble but look at you. You're a mess. I let you out of my sight for five minutes and you get all banged up. What am I going to do with you?"

I leaned over and kissed Michelle's beautiful lips and they felt wonderful. I hugged her and looked over my shoulder where Garcia was speaking to the doctor.

She came to me and said, "Nash the doc says she's going to be OK but needs a hospital soon. He said it would be best if we flew her to the Virgin Islands with us. Get ready to leave. We're out of here as soon as Michelle can be loaded into the Catalina."

I stayed by Michelle's side while the preparations were made to get airborne again. We were on the way down the ladder with Michelle and Garcia started after us.

She was on the ladder and the commander said, "Nice to see you again Garcia."

Garcia said, "It's nice to see you not chasing me for once. How's your family?"

The commander said, "They're fine, how's yours?"

Garcia said, "This is them here with me. As you can see they're very good."

The Commander said, "Nice to see that you do humanitarian work too."

Garcia said, "Of course I do but don't let that story get out. I have a reputation to hold up."

The commander smiled and said, "Of course you do. I'll see you around the Gulf soon enough Garcia."

I listened to the conversation as I was putting Michelle into the launch with the sailors that were assigned to help me.

When our gang was inside and Lene' and Larry were getting the Catalina off of the water I said, "Garcia, the commander is an old friend?"

Garcia said, "He's chased me a few times. We know each other."

I said, "It sounds like you know each other pretty well."

Garcia said, "OK, OK! He was cute years ago and I had to use my ass to get out of trouble once. Do you want a play by play?"

Hector said, "It's OK Garcia. I had to dump my contraband just before he caught me fifteen years ago when he was a lieutenant."

Garcia said, "Really? You knew him too?'

Hector said, "Unfortunately yes. He cost me a lot of money but I think he enjoys us for the chase and the game."

I said, "Well he was certainly nice to us today."

Garcia said, "That was today but you can bet he'll be right behind me next month."

Michelle was feeling well enough by this time to enjoy the repartee' that was taking place. I held her head in my lap all of the way back to the Virgin Islands and she slept most of the way there. While all of us rested I thought about finding Mr. X and finishing this business. Wise was certainly not going to stop his sick quest for Michelle and we were not going to stop keeping her safe. I vowed to be more careful in the future.

Crazy Larry landed us back in the Virgin Islands several hours later and we took Michelle to the local hospital and had her looked over. The doctors pronounced her in decent shape and kept her there overnight for observation. I stayed with her and Garcia did as well. The next morning came and Michelle was much better as the drugs her abductors had been pumping into her were leaving her system.

I was sitting next to her when she turned her lovely face to me and said, "Where am I?"

I said, "The Virgin Islands. I told you we'd visit here."

She said, "How did you find me?"

Garcia said, "No big deal. We just had to mobilize all of the Caribbean. There's nothing like calling in a few thousand favors."

I said, "That is the truth. We had people looking for you on every island. How do you feel?"

Michelle said, "Stiff, bruised and sore. I fought with those bastards every time I woke up. They finally got tired of me fighting them and pumped me full of something nasty."

I said, "Well that crew won't bother you again. They went with the coast guard and Hector found out where they were from and who put them up to your capture. Those that were a part of this will be running if they know what's good for them."

Michelle said, "You look like shit. What happened to you?"

I said, "Thanks a lot. I got this way from hitting the car you ran into and being beaten by the other half of the team that kidnapped you."

She said, "I remember getting out my pistol and shooting two of them."

I said, "I heard you fighting them. Both of the men you shot were lying in the road when some people found me and took me to the hospital."

Michelle said, "I killed them?"

Garcia said, "Deader than a Thanksgiving turkey."

Michelle said, "Am I in trouble?"

I said, "Not at all. You fought like a demon. Good girl."

She said, "Where did Hector, Garcia and Enrique come from?"

I said, "They got here the next day to help me find you. I was pretty much incapacitated for several days."

Garcia said, "Nash was a mess girl. He spent the first two days on the couch flat on his back. We had to fill him full of tequila and hot tub him several times a day until he could walk on his crutches."

Michelle said, "My god. You were that hurt?"

I said, "Yes, besides my stitched up head I slammed my hip against that car. It's still pretty badly bruised and I'm sure I have several broken ribs from those guys stomping me."

Michelle said, "Where's the boat?"

I said, "She's tied up here waiting for us to get well and sail away."

Garcia said, "Except that Lene' and I are going with you. Nash has already proven he can't take care of himself let alone you. We're going along to make sure that both of you are safe."

Michelle said, "Is that true David?"

I said, "Garcia says she's going with us and I'm not well enough to fight with her so I guess she is."

Michelle said, "Thank you Garcia. The whole time I was held captive I worried about David. I thought he might have been killed."

Garcia said, "He might have been if it wasn't for that hard Blanco head of his."

I said, "Do you feel like getting out of here?"

Michelle said, "Please get me out of here it smells like rubbing alcohol and medicine."

Garcia got up and kissed Michelle and went to finish the paperwork for her release. I stayed with Michelle until Lene' walked into the room with clean clothes for her to wear on the way to the hotel where we would meet up with the rest of our gang who were doing the follow up on the kidnapping.

I helped Michelle dress and was surprised to find she had bruises all over her body from fighting with her captors. When I had her dressed I took her downstairs in a wheelchair to the parking lot. Garcia was waiting there for us and helped me load Michelle into the car. We drove the short distance to the Ritz Carlton hotel and went to our suite. Hector and Enrique were there on the phones arranging god knows what for the perpetrators of Michelle's kidnapping. I wanted the worst for them but at the same time thought about what they would receive for their dark efforts.

Garcia put Michelle on the couch where she could be with us and Lene' fixed drinks for us all. We celebrated Michelle being back and I could tell she was happy to be with us.

She finished half a drink and said, "I don't want to be a bother but I'm desperately hungry can we get some room service?"

Garcia said, "Of course bambina what would you like?"

Michelle said, "One of everything. Those bastards only gave me crap and most of the time I threw it at them. When I was unconscious they gave me nothing. I feel like I've lost ten pounds."

Garcia said, "Chiquita you don't have ten pounds to lose. We'll get you some food. How about some lobster?"

Michelle said, "I don't care if it's peanut butter and jelly. I'm hungry."

I said, "Room service coming up right away madam. You can eat until you pop if you want."

Michelle said, "Thank you. Thank you all for finding me. I was so scared when those guys had me. It was horrible."

I said, "What happened in the airport?"

Michelle said, "Those bastards were trying to get me onto a plane while I was drugged. I started to wake up and realized where I was. I started screaming and the cops came and hassled them. I passed back out and don't know what happened after that."

I said, "You caused enough trouble there that we heard about it. When the airport was no longer an option they took you back to the boat and tried a getaway on the ocean."

Michelle said, "Why are we here in this hotel?"

Garcia said, "We're here because we needed a central place to conduct our search for you. Hector and Enrique are calling off the search as we speak. We weren't kidding when we said half of the Caribbean was looking for you."

Lene' said, "And we want you to be somewhere nice while you recover'.

Michelle said, "How long can we stay here?"

Garcia said, "As long as you want Chiquita. We'll put you in the sun tomorrow. You and Blanco need to heal up."

Michelle said, "David are you going to be all right?"

I said, "I think so. I should have Garcia take my stitches out in a few more days if she thinks I've healed enough."

Garcia said, "You should have seen him the morning after you were taken. He was a complete mess. His head was fully bandaged up and I saw it when Lene' had him in the hot tub bathing him and changing the bandages. It was really gross."

I said, "It was a pretty bad headache for a few days. Those guys weren't playing with me on the road."

Michelle said, "I remember flying over the hood of the car and landing on my back in the road. I was just getting up when they grabbed me. I pulled free and reached into my purse for my pistol. I remember shooting at two of them and then the lights went out."

I said, "That sounds about right. I don't remember much after the two shots."

The food was delivered from room service by this time and we all stopped talking to eat. Michelle ate like she was desperately hungry and it was amusing to see her eat so much. We spent the afternoon in the living room and when it became dark we ordered more food and Michelle packed it away as she had before. After dinner we all got into the hot tub and Michelle said it made her feel much better.

We stayed in for a couple of hours and Michelle asked to be put to bed. We took her to the room and slid her under the sheets which were nice and cool from the air conditioning. I slid in beside her and I turned off the light. She reached for me and I held her very tight. She started to cry softly and then her tears flowed like a waterfall. She made little noise but cried for a very long time while I held her. She finally stopped crying and I let her fall asleep as I lay behind her and held her tight through the whole night.

CHAPTER NINE

Everyone slept late the next morning and Garcia woke us well after the sun was up. Lene' was arranging the table for the food room service had brought to the room. We sat down to a very nice breakfast complete with a hotel waiter standing by and serving us.

During the meal Hector said, "I love being here with everyone but I have to go home. My wife is beginning to think I've divorced her."

Enrique said, "Same here. I was on the phone with Julia last night and she was getting annoyed I wasn't there."

Garcia said, "All of the work is done and you can't stay for the fun. What's happened to you two? Stay with us and spend a few days at the beach."

Michelle said, "Yes, please stay for at least another day. You've all been together looking for me and I feel left out because I wasn't there."

Hector said, "OK you've got me for one more day. What about you Enrique?"

Enrique said, "I agree. We did have some pretty good times together while you were captive. I can stay another day too."

Garcia said, "Great let's spend the day drinking on the beach and lying in the sun like we used to do between runs."

We all toasted with the Mimosas we were drinking and after our breakfast was eaten and pushed out into the corridor leading to our suite we went to our rooms to prepare for the beach.

Michelle and I dressed for the beach and we hobbled to the elevator that would take us to the main floor and the white sand. We got towels from the beach shack and found Garcia and Lene' already lying on the sand next to Hector and Enrique who looked like they hadn't been to the beach in years. Garcia already had a waiter watching for us and as soon as we were settled drinks were brought to us.

As we walked up Garcia said, "Michelle my god you're covered with bruises!"

Michelle said, "That's from fighting with those bastards that were holding me. I got some licks in though. One of them is missing a couple of teeth."

I put my towel down and after taking a drink I headed to the water to get some salt on my head wound. It stung a bit at first and felt better a few minutes later. Michelle joined me so the salt water could take care of her bruises and we stayed in the water for a long time. When we got out Michelle announced she was hungry again and put in an order with the waiter for some food which she devoured the minute it was delivered.

While we were lying on the sand Garcia said, "Nash what's up? When you two are well enough to travel where will we go first?"

I said, "We've still got to find Mr. X and get Wise's supply shut off. Are you two really going to come with us?"

Garcia said, "I wouldn't miss it. Someone has to look out for you two and I think it will be fun. I can take the time off. Jose' will take care of everything and my house staff loves it when I leave. It's like a vacation for them. Do you two want to stick with the boat or would you like to get in some jet time?"

Michelle said, "I'd love to go some where in your jet. Where could we go?"

Lene' said, "Anywhere you want. Have you been to Paris or Rome?"

Michelle said, "No I haven't could we really go there?"

Garcia said, "Sure why not. Lene' loves it there and you need some new clothes Chiquita. You too Nash. You looked good in that sports coat and should have some more if you want to compliment this beauty here."

I said, "I have no problems with any of this. I haven't been to Paris in years and the four of us traveling together will be fun."

Hector said, "Which one of you is going to pay for this trip?"

Garcia said, "I can always do some business over there. I've been moving things around in the Arab countries for a couple of years. Most of those guys live in France so it will be like a business trip."

The conversation faded as we passed out in the sun. We would occasionally get up to go in the water and cool off or order fresh drinks and we stayed on the beach until the sun was headed over the horizon. As the on shore breeze began to blow we picked up our towels and headed back to the suite.

Once inside Garcia said, "Are you two feeling well enough to go out to a fancy restaurant?"

Michelle said, "I feel good enough. What about Mr. Hedberg?"

I said, "I'm OK. Does everyone else want to go?"

The others were agreed and we retired to our rooms to shower and change our clothes. We left the hotel and walked two blocks to a fine restaurant that was two blocks away. I noticed Garcia and Lene' were packing and there were bulges under the coats of Hector and Enrique. We were seated at our table and the Maitre'd came up to our table and began to say hello to Garcia.

He said, "Hello Garcia, hello Hector and hello Mr. Nash. Nash it's been a long time since you've been here. Do you remember me?"

I said, "Hello Phillip how have you been?"

He said, "Wonderful thanks. It's great to have you back in my restaurant again. I don't know if you know it or not but Garcia helped me buy this place a few years ago. I'm the owner now and I'd like to buy your table some champagne."

Garcia said, "Thank you Phillip that would be very nice of you."

Phillip left and a waiter brought two cold bottles of the bubbly for us a few minutes later.

The champagne was poured and Garcia stood and raising her glass said, "To the Hedbergs and especially to Mrs. Hedberg who we all love very much. It makes me very happy you're back with us."

Michelle was next and stood raising her glass and said, "To all of my friends. Thank you very much for finding me. I'm very flattered you all came to get me. It makes me feel very special. Thank you all so very much."

Michelle sat back down and we perused our menus and began to order our dinners. The food was excellent and the conversation was light and friendly during dinner. Stories were told and told again of past times we had all shared. We danced after dinner until we were tired and walked back to the suites we had in the hotel. Michelle and I went to our room and stood together undressing each other.

Michelle said, "David, do you feel up to making love to me tonight?"

I said, "Yes I feel very much up to making love to you. Just be careful of my hip. It's still very sore."

We got into bed and made love slowly and softly until we collapsed from our release. I took Michelle into my arms where she stayed until morning.

We woke up the next day and I was feeling much better, as was Michelle. We helped Hector and Enrique put their things together and after breakfast we put them into the hotel limousine for their ride to the airport. We were sad to see them go and Michelle hugged and kissed them goodbye until there were tears in her eyes.

The four of us waved them off and when they were out of sight Garcia said, "Who wants to go to the beach?"

We all answered in the affirmative and headed upstairs to change for the salt water that was helping us heal. We spent the morning on the sand and in the water until it was time for lunch at the outdoor restaurant.

When our food was served Garcia said, "Are you two feeling well enough to sail tomorrow? I'm getting bored here on the beach and Lene' wants to get moving. Where do you think we should go?"

I said, "I think we can sail and I think we should island hop towards Trinidad. We still need to find X and he might be near there if he's been in South America."

Michelle said, "I feel well enough to sail and to tell the truth being on land makes me nervous. I want to be on the water where I can see these bastards coming at me."

Garcia said, "Good we'll leave tomorrow after we provision the boat."

Michelle said, "Why don't we provision the boat today and leave early in the morning after we get fuel and water?"

Garcia said, "Chiquita you really are nervous about being here. I can't say as I blame you after what you went through. Let's go get dressed and get the boat provisioned then."

Michelle said, "Thank you Garcia. I'll feel a lot better when I can't see land anymore and the radar will bark at me if anything comes close to us."

We changed our clothes and checked out of the hotel bringing our belongings with us to the boat. We spent most of the afternoon arranging the boat so it would be comfortable for the four of us and Michelle gave up her stateroom to Lene' and Garcia. The girls put their clothes away and I was on deck when the grocer arrived with our stores.

Michelle and Lene' and I began to put them away when Garcia said, "Would you three mind if I leave for awhile? I have an errand to run."

None of us disagreed and Garcia walked to the beginning of the harbor and hailed an island taxi. We went back to putting the stores away and when we were done Michelle went about putting my stateroom in order while Lene' and I did maintenance on the generator and the diesel.

It was all done in a few hours and we were showering on the dock when Garcia walked up and said, "Done already? Good, I'm glad I missed all of the work."

Michelle said, "How about a shower then," and turned the dock hose on Garcia who dropped her package after the stream of water hit her and picking Michelle up threw her off of the dock into the crystal clear water. Lene' and I laughed and Michelle shrieked as she flew through the air before she hit the drink. Garcia laughed and stripped off her top and jeans picking up the hose to continue the shower Michelle had started for her.

Michelle was back on the dock in another minute and as she walked up Garcia said, "Chiquita, I'm glad you're feeling better. Come here."

Michelle was given the biggest of hugs when she got close enough and it was nice to see my girl was feeling herself again. We finished our shower and dried off in the cockpit of the boat.

We went below and Garcia handed the package to Michelle and said, "A present for you Mrs. Hedberg."

Michelle said, "What is it?"

Garcia said, "Open it and see."

Michelle ripped at the wrapping paper and got to the box that was underneath. She opened the box and inside was a stainless steel, ivory handled .45 caliber semi-automatic pistol with a new holster, gun belt and storage for several magazines.

Michelle looked at Garcia and said, "Thank you Garcia. I need this and I don't know what happened to the .32 Hector gave me. This will do nicely."

Garcia said, "No worries, that pea shooter Hector gave you was nice but you need something with more stopping power. I hope this will help you feel safe."

Lene' said, "Excellent, I'm going diving for dinner who wants to come with me?"

I said, "I will. Will somebody work on the rest of dinner for us while we're gone?"

Michelle and Garcia said they would be glad to and Lene' and I gathered the masks and spear guns and headed for the nearby lagoon. We walked into the water and floated on the surface together looking for something good to eat near the bottom. Lene' pointed soon enough and there were a pair of decent sized Flounder together. We dove down and shot at the same time sticking both of the fish to the bottom of the lagoon. We pulled our spears in and swam on the surface to the beach.

We sat there for a minute and Lene' said, "Nash are you sure Garcia and I going with you two is OK?"

I said, "Positively, we can use two more people. That night when Michelle nailed that attack craft we were plain lucky. Michelle really doesn't know how close we came to being dead. We were out gunned and it was lucky for Michelle to score with the RPG."

Lene' said, "There was more than luck involved in it. You two make a good team. You could use another four hands though."

I said, "What about privacy? Michelle doesn't know about our little three-some."

Lene' said, "That was hardly a threesome. You were so hurt you didn't do much but pet and watch. I have no problems with you or Michelle being around when we make love. If you haven't noticed Garcia and I are in love with your girl as much as we're in love with you. Besides I think it will be good for Michelle to be around two women for awhile. She can talk to us about her kidnapping in ways she can't talk to you."

I said, "How's that?"

Lene' said, "Nash sometimes you're a typical male. Can't you see Michelle is trying to be a tough girl for you? She loves you very much and doesn't want to appear to be weak in front of you. She can do that with Garcia and me without feeling like she's letting you down."

I said, "Right you are Lene'. Being a typical male I didn't think about that. I'm glad you reminded me."

Lene' said, "Nash will you do one thing for me?"

I said, "Sure what would you like?"

Lene' said, "How about one of those typically male kisses of yours. I really liked being kissed by you the other night and I think you kiss wonderfully."

I smiled at Lene' and we leaned together until our lips met. We kissed long and softly with our tongues and when we stopped and came up for air Lene' smiled at me and said,

"Thank you Nash that was wonderful."

We collected the fish and walked on the hard sand to the dock where we went to the boat and cleaned the catch. It was cocktail time and Garcia had made Sangria for all of us.

We put the fish in the 'fridge until it was time to cook and once we settled into the cockpit Michelle said, "Mr. Hedberg where are you taking me next. Is this going to be another trip into hell or are we going somewhere nice?"

Garcia laughed out loud and put her arm around Michelle's shoulders and Michelle snuggled a bit closer to her. I said, "How about St. Croix. It's beautiful there and now that we don't have to be on our toes so much we can look for Mr. X at a more leisurely pace. Will that be OK?"

Michelle said, "St. Croix will be just fine thank you. I've always wanted to go there. Now that Garcia and Lene' are with us I feel two-hundred per-cent safe and you have three beautiful women to take care of you."

I said, "I know I do. I was just thinking about how I used to wish for a nice girl to sail with me. Now I have three fantastic women with me and I'm scared to death the three of you will gang up on me and make me your boat slave."

Garcia said, "No such luck vato. You're giving yourself far too much credit. You're only a sex slave and you're going to have to work your way up to boat slave the hard way."

Michelle said, "Yes, you're nothing but a sex slave and don't you forget it. Now that you're trying for boat slave get your ass below and bring up the rest of the Sangria. My glass is almost empty."

I got up from where I was sitting and went below getting the sangria and putting it on a tray. I put a large white napkin over my forearm and coming back into the cockpit went into my best boat boy routine pouring Sangria for all of the women.

Garcia said, "Enough, enough. Jesus Nash, you're still the only man in the world who can make me feel guilty. Now stop that routine and sit down here with us and enjoy the sunset."

I put the tray down and filled my own glass. As I sat down I said, "Yassum Miz Garcia I be gwan set down rite now."

This cracked Garcia, Michelle and Lene' up completely and Garcia said, "Damn it Nash stop that. You make me laugh too much. I'm supposed to be a hard ass lesbian and how can I do that when you keep making me laugh?"

Michelle said, "Mr. Hedberg, don't you ever stop making me laugh and I think Garcia is very beautiful and sexy when she smiles and I can see her teeth."

Garcia said, "Thank you Michelle. I've been being a hard ass for so long I forget what it's like to let my soft side come out. I do it so rarely it makes me uncomfortable."

I said, "I remember fifteen years ago when we got drunk together and your soft side got loose. We stayed in bed for two whole days."

Garcia said, "That was when we were in Cozumel right after Christmas. That was pretty nice vato. You almost had me thinking about marrying you."

Michelle said, "It's a good thing you missed your chance Garcia. He's mine now but you can borrow him when you want."

I said, "Michelle are you going to be in the habit of lending me to your friends?"

Michelle said, "Shut up sex slave. You'll do what I tell you. When I want you to dance you'll dance."

I said, "Garcia I think it was a bad thing to bring her to your island."

Michelle leaned over and kissed Garcia on the cheek and said,

"I think it was a very good day. Don't you Garcia?"

Garcia said, "A very good day Chiquita. Now if we can only get him to cook tonight'.

I said, "Sex slaves don't cook make your own dinner."

Michelle said, "Then it's up to us ladies."

The girls went into action and the flounder were grilled on the aft rail of the boat while I helped Lene' with the salad and the vegetables. It was all done at the same time and we ate as the last rays of the sunset faded into deep blue. We cleaned up after ourselves and had our after dinner drinks in the cockpit. Michelle was the first to get up and pull me by the hand towards our stateroom and our bed. We undressed each other and slid under the sheets.

When we were there Michelle put her arms around me and said, "Mr. Hedberg would you mind terribly if I made love to Garcia?"

I said, "No I wouldn't mind. Just make sure it's not permanent and it's OK with Lene'."

Michelle said, "You're sure?"

I said, "I'm sure, just get some ground rules straight with her and don't make things awkward for Lene' who would most likely want to join in."

Michelle said, "Would you want to make love to Lene'?"

I said, "I wouldn't mind. What if I make love to you right now and we'll see what happens with you girls later?"

Michelle said, "Yes make love to me now and we'll see what happens later."

CHAPTER TEN

We left the fuel dock the next morning shortly after dawn and I set the course for us to sail around the Virgin Islands until we could head almost due south to St. Croix. We had been out for about three hours and ran into some summer rain and a little wind. The rain was delightful and we enjoyed it from under the dodger. We all took turns soaping up in the rain on the stern and letting the fresh water rinse us clean. The rain stopped two hours later and it was hot and humid again within a half hour. The girls disappeared below and I saw them a few minutes later wearing next to nothing with cushions to lie on while they sunned themselves on the foredeck. I kept to sailing the boat leaving them to talk amongst themselves. Just before lunch Lene' got up and disappeared below leaving Michelle and Garcia together up forward. I went below a little later and Lene' was making lunch for us in the galley.

When I saw her I said, "How's Michelle?"

Lene' said, "She's fine and spilling her guts to us. The poor thing. She really went through hell on that boat."

I said, "Is she OK physically. I mean was she raped?"

Lene' said, "Almost, they tried but she fought them so hard they apparently decided it wasn't worth it. Good for her."

I said, "That's good news. What's for lunch?"

Lene' said, "Chicken sandwiches and potato salad."

I said, "That sounds good."

Lene' said, "When will we get to St. Croix?"

I said, "Probably tomorrow afternoon. The wind is light so we're not making much headway. It's good for sunbathing though."

Lene' said, "Did Michelle talk to you about making love to Garcia?"

I said, "She said she wanted to and asked my permission. I told her it was OK but she should make sure you were OK with it."

Lene' said, "It's OK with me but will I get to make love to you?"

I said, "If it's OK with Michelle then It's OK with me. In fact I've thought about it and I'd like very much to make love to you. You're very attractive to me."

Lene' said, "Wonderful I've been hoping this would happen. I've wanted you since I first saw you. This is going to work out beautifully."

Lene' kissed me playfully on the cheek and I went back to the cockpit to sail our course. I watched as Garcia and Michelle sunned themselves on the foredeck and thoughts of making love to Lene' ran through my head. Lunch was an hour later and it was very good. Lene' offered to take the helm for awhile and I went to my stateroom for a decent nap that took up most of the afternoon.

The girls woke me for dinner and I found out Michelle had cooked and it was excellent. I cleaned the galley with Garcia and took the first watch when it got dark. The girls stayed in the main salon watching a movie on TV and I stood to the helm. In another hour I began to see lightning flashing on the horizon and I checked the weather. There was a squall bearing down on us and there were things that needed to be done. I called the girls up and with Michelle at the helm we shortened sail and battened down the hatches. It was a good thing too because it was a nasty little squall. It hit hard and our visibility went to zero in just minutes. I stayed with our course watching the radar and the GPS. There was nothing near us but we were in for a rough ride for the next three hours before the squall began to slacken and the rain that had been coming down in sheets lightened up. In another hour it was done and we let the sails out again picking up speed and making better headway. I sailed the boat into the night while the three girls slept together in the main stateroom. I got tired at four and went and woke Michelle up. She sleepily woke up and began to get dressed to come on deck and take my place at the helm. I kissed her good night as I handed her a cup of hot coffee and went to my bunk to rest.

Michelle sailed us through the rest of the night and I woke the next morning well after dawn which was new to me. I thought about all of the help I had on board and decided it was nice to be able to rest more.

I dressed and went to the cockpit where the coffee pot was and poured myself a cup and sat down next to Garcia who said, "Welcome sleeping sex slave. It's nice of you to join us."

Michelle got up and handed me a roll kissing me on the cheek as she gave it to me and said, "My love did you have a nice sleep?"

I said, "I did, thank you very much for letting me sleep late. It's nice to have so much help sailing the boat."

Garcia said, "I'm having a great time. It's been years since I've sailed like this vato. I'd forgotten it was so relaxing."

Lene' said, "I'll say, I slept like I was dead last night and I felt wonderful when I woke up this morning. I feel better than I have in years."

I said, "Where are we?"

Lene' said, "We're about fifty miles from St. Croix. Where do we want to slip the boat?"

I said, "Chenay Bay is always nice. There are some good hotels and restaurants there and the beaches are very good."

Garcia said, "That's good enough for me. Do we want to get a hotel room?"

Michelle said, "Sure I've got plenty of the puta's money left."

Garcia said, "Keep your money Chiquita. I've been making millions for years and it's time I spent some of it. I'm on vacation and I like to have my comforts."

I said, "Great I'm beginning to like traveling with a little luxury. I've been keeping to my boat for a long time."

Garcia said, "Nash it's about time you spent some of that money you have coming in. You're just frugal. What were you paying to slip your boat on that dumpy little island where you met Michelle? I'll bet it wasn't more than two hundred a month."

I said, "Actually it was a hundred a month with electricity."

Garcia said, "Nash we'll have to teach you about spending. You're entirely too eccentric."

I laughed and got up to refill my coffee and get another roll from the table. I sat back down and asked, "Lene' do you have the course to Chenay Bay?"

She said, "Of course I do. Navigating a boat is no different than an airplane. We just don't have reefs and rocks in the air."

By three we were tying up in the bay and there were dozens of beautiful sailboats in the harbor. Many of which were very large and seriously expensive.

We were putting the Mo Cuishle the way it was best for port living and I said, "I remember now. This island is famous as a spot for cruisers to stop and spend time here. That's why there are so many boats here."

Michelle said, "Well we're in good company then. I wonder if there are parties that go on here at night."

Garcia said, "You bet there will be. One thing about people who own big yachts, they love to show them off."

Lene' said, "That's the truth. Very few people who have that kind of money keep the glitz to themselves."

Michelle said, "I wonder if we'll be invited to any of them?"

Garcia said, "Sure we will. Michelle you've been sheltered with that puta for too long. All we have to do is dress sexy and hang around on our boat where we can be seen. They'll be around like flies."

Lene' said, "That means only one thing."

I said, "What's that Lene'?"

She said, "Shopping of course. I want a new outfit to play in. How about you Michelle?"

Michelle said, "Yes, yes, yes. I definitely want to go shopping. I want something sexy to wear tonight."

Garcia said, "Shit, I hate shopping unless it's for new weapons."

Michelle said, "Come on Garcia come with us. Lene' and I will dress you up. It'll be fun."

Garcia said, "Do I have to? Michelle you aren't going to try and turn me into a girl are you?"

Michelle said, "I certainly am. You'll be positively gorgeous. Please come with us."

Lene' said, "Garcia you must come with us. You're on vacation and this is part of it."

144

Garcia said, "Well OK but it's only because I'm on vacation."

Lene said, "What about Nash?

Garcia said, "Are you coming with us Blanco?"

I said, "I think I'll pass on this one thank you."

Michelle said, "What if we buy you a new outfit to wear? You can't wear that old linen coat you have in your closet. We want you to look hot with us."

I said, "I'll wear a new outfit if you get me one but I know better than to go shopping with three women. That's a disaster in the making. Why don't you three go and I'll get us a suite in that nice hotel over there. That way you'll have a place where you three won't have to fight over the mirror when you dress up. You guys put all of the face paint and girl stuff you'll need in a bag and I'll bring it to the hotel. We can eat in their restaurant and then we can dress to impress afterwards. Don't forget to pack your weapons on this shopping trip. I don't want Michelle getting snatched from the lingerie department."

The girls instantly put their wheels into motion and rushed around packing the bag I was to take to the hotel. When it was done they all kissed me goodbye and left the harbor. I finished with the boat and sat in the cockpit with a cold beer enjoying the afternoon and being happy to be by myself.

I headed to the hotel after a few beers and got the room we wanted and made reservations for dinner at the restaurant for eight o'clock. I waited in the bar for the girls to return and they showed up at seven taking a pile of packages to the suite as they chattered about their purchases. They were down in a few minutes and we had a great dinner together. They didn't say much about what they had bought for the night but I knew I would see their outfits soon enough. When we finished dinner we went to the suite and I took a quick shower and shave coming into the living room in my boxers to be handed my outfit for the evening. The girls had done well and I really loved the eggshell white linen suit they bought me. I was given a very nice V-neck T shirt to wear under the coat and was instructed to wear my flip-flops with it on my feet. The girls said I looked fabulous when I was dressed and they shooed me out of the suite to the bar while they began to shower and dress.

CHAPTER ELEVEN

I sat in the bar for just over an hour and I was just about to call the suite to see what was taking the girls so long. I had just picked up the bar phone when they walked in. The three of them looked fabulous in their new clothes. From the way they confidently moved I could tell they were pleased with the results of dressing up. Michelle was wearing a gorgeous light cotton dress that beautifully showed off her figure and her long legs. Lene' was wearing a sexy linen pants suit that accentuated her ass and breasts and sandals that made her two inches taller. Garcia was the most impressive of them all. Michelle and Lene' had definitely turned her into a girl for the evening and she was as stunning as they were. They had dressed her in a sexy red cotton dress that was perfectly fitted. They had bought her lingerie that made her breasts look perfect and she was wearing stockings and small heels.

They all were perfect and when they walked up to where I was sitting I said, "Damn you all look great. All of the men are going to be totally after you and the other women are going to hate you."

Michelle said, "Doesn't Garcia look wonderful?"

I said, "Garcia you do look fantastic. I wish your father was here to see you."

Garcia said, "Nash I feel weird. I haven't dressed like this in a thousand years."

I said, "You look great and very sexy. Maybe you should dress like this more often."

Lene said, "She looks fantastic doesn't she? Wait until you see where she's packing."

I said, "Garcia, where's your heat?"

Garcia looked around the room and seeing we were pretty much alone she lifted up her dress. She was wearing garters and stockings complete with lace underwear. Her legs were completely sexy and I saw she had one of her smaller pistols tucked into her stocking on the inside of her thigh.

I said, "Garcia that's very sexy and look at you wearing lingerie. I don't think I've ever seen you even wear underwear before."

Lene' said, "Isn't she positively hot! I had to teach her how to fasten her garters if you can believe that. She said she'd never worn any before."

Michelle said, "Garcia you are positively a complete turn on. You're so sexy I can't believe it."

I said, "Who else is packing?"

Lene' said, "Mine is in my purse."

Michelle said, "Mine too. Where's yours?"

I said, "On the boat. I have to get my shoulder holster when we go there."

We left the bar and walked the short distance to the harbor. Michelle opened the boat when we boarded and I went below and turned on the cockpit and spreader lights. Lene' went to the galley while Garcia and Michelle folded the dodger away so we could be seen. Lene' came up with the drinks and we sat listening to some music watching well dressed people strolling to the yachts moored down from us. It didn't take very long before two well dressed men stopped and invited us to a party on one of the larger vessels. The invitation was accepted and we walked with them to their yacht. It was very big and lavishly beautiful. We went aboard and were introduced to people who were already socializing in the main salon. More people were arriving all of the time and the girls were getting plenty of attention.

Michelle and Lene' were instantly engaged in conversation by two men and I hung back with Garcia, who said, "Would you look at Michelle work the room? She really should have been a movie star. There's not an eye in the room that's not looking at her."

I said, "She's really fantastic isn't she? She's lit up like a Christmas tree from all of the attention. Lene' too she's getting her share as well. There are three men who are drooling over her while they're talking."

Garcia said, "You too Nash. Those women across the salon aren't looking at me. They're looking at those blue eyes that I love."

I said, "Garcia are you in love with me?"

Garcia said, "Yes damn it I'm in love with you. I've been in love with you since I was thirteen. I'm in love with three people and it's very confusing."

I said, "Michelle wants to make love to you. Do you know that?"

She said, "I know. I want to make love to her too. Will that be all right with you?"

I said, "Yes it will. I've already given her permission."

Garcia said, "OK are we going to trade girlfriends sometime."

I said, "I don't think there's any way out of it do you?"

She said, "I don't either. Vato do you want to make love to me anymore?"

I said, "Sure I do. I've always thought you were the shit, you know that."

Garcia said, "I used to know that but I thought you might not anymore."

I said, "Why's that?"

Garcia said, "Because we're older now. Am I still attractive to you?"

I said, "More than ever and you look hot as shit in that dress."

She said, "I think so too but it's been a long time since I've dressed up like a girl. Don't expect this often."

I said, "And why not?"

Garcia said, "Because this lingerie is completely uncomfortable and this bra is killing me."

I said, "But you do look fantastic. Look I'm going to get another drink. Why don't you go and find some men to torment. I want to watch them fall all over you trying to get into your pants."

I headed to the bar for another drink and Garcia went to where Lene' was talking to two men who I'm sure thought they were going to get lucky that night. I waited my turn by the bar and there was a very attractive woman who was waiting her turn standing next to me. We looked at each other and she smiled at me and said, "Hi I'm Patricia Owens."

I said, "Nice to meet you I'm David Nash."

She said, "Where are you from David?"

I said, "I used to be from the states but I live on my sailboat now."

She said, "How wonderful. I'm traveling with my husband. We own the next yacht over."

I said, "I'm slipped a few boats closer to shore from here. I have the Beneteau 473."

Patricia asked, "Are you with your wife?"

I said, "I'm not married. I'm with my girlfriend and two other friends. We're just cruising for the summer."

She said, "Was that your girlfriend you were talking to a few minutes ago?"

I said, "No she's just a friend, my girl is the one standing next to her in the short cotton dress."

She said, "Oh she's very beautiful. She looks like an actress or a model."

I said, "She is very beautiful but she's never done either of those things."

Patricia said, "Do you think she'd like to?"

I said, "I don't know. You could ask her though."

Michelle turned towards me and I motioned for her to come and join the conversation.

She walked up and I said, "Patricia Owens I'd like you to meet Michelle Murphy."

Michelle said, "Nice to meet you Patricia."

Patricia said, "Michelle you are a very stunning woman. Have you ever done any modeling?"

Michelle said, "No I haven't. I wanted to when I was younger but I got sidetracked."

Patricia said, "Well it's never too late. Models are getting older now and you don't have to be nineteen anymore. I own a modeling agency. Would you be interested in being in a swimsuit shoot we're doing here on the island?"

Michelle said, "I guess so. When would it be?"

Patricia said, "All of this week and the next. Let me give you my number on our boat. We're moored right next to this one. Call me tomorrow and we'll talk."

We had our fresh drinks by this time and Patricia handed me her number before she went back to the group she was with.

I said to Michelle, "Are you having fun Mrs. Hedberg?"

She said, "Yes I am and I'm very pleased to be here with the most handsome man in the room."

I said, "What do you think about the offer you were just made?"

Michelle said, "Do you think that was for real?"

I said, "Definitely. I tend to think that offers like hers that come on big expensive yachts are rarely bullshit. You should call her."

Michelle said, "What about the exposure? We're still hiding from my ex."

I said, "We'll watch you during the shoots. The publication won't be out for quite awhile and we'll be long gone by then. Besides what better way to annoy your ex than by being in a publication."

She said, "I've always wanted to put my looks to work for me and I need a way to make money. This cash I have with me won't last forever."

I said, "Michelle you know you don't have to have money with me. I'm happy to take care of our expenses."

She said, "I know that but I'd like to contribute if I can."

I said, "I like that, look at Garcia talking to those men. They're positively drooling over her."

Michelle said, "Look at her suck it up too. I think she's having a good time by her sexy body language. I'll bet those guys are offering her the world."

I said, "They can offer her the moon but they'll get nowhere with her. She's probably the richest person in the room."

Michelle said, "Is she really?"

I said, "Sure she is. Her father was plenty rich and Garcia has only made ten times his fortune. There's a lot of money in running guns."

Michelle said, "Where's Lene'?"

I looked around and saw Lene' sitting on one of the couches in the room talking with a couple of men in their thirties who were paying her extreme attention.

I said, "She's over there on the couch driving those two men out of their minds. Doesn't she look great?"

Michelle said, "Let's go talk to Garcia."

We walked to where Garcia was talking to the two men and joined her there. Michelle and I were kissed on the cheeks as soon as we walked up and Garcia said, "David and Michelle I'd like you to meet Tom and George Hanson from New York City'.

We shook hands with Garcia's two admirers and Tom said, "I understand you are cruising for the summer. How's the weather been?"

Michelle said, "Just perfect except for a couple of rain squalls. What brings you to the islands?"

George said, "We're here on business. We work for a company that takes over hotels that find themselves in financial trouble. What business are you in?"

I said, "I'm retired and Michelle is helping me sail our boat."

Tom looked at Garcia and asked, "Garcia what business are you in?"

Garcia said, "I run guns all over the world for a living."

Tom and George were taken aback for a minute and then started laughing. Tom said, "That's the best one I've heard tonight. Garcia you have a wonderful sense of humor. Running guns for a living. A beautiful woman like you would never do something like that. It's far too dangerous. Tell us what you really do."

Garcia said, "Actually I'm financially independent and my friend and I are just sailing with David and Michelle for the summer. We stopped here because we like the parties that go on here in the harbor."

George said, "Where's your friend?"

Garcia said, "My friend is the blond over on the couch speaking with the two men there'.

George said, "She's beautiful would you two be interested in going to dinner with us tomorrow night?"

Garcia said, "I don't think so we have other plans but thanks for asking."

I was amused by this and Michelle gave me a look that she was amused as well. The two men were visibly put off and after awhile excused themselves to go to the bar.

I said to Garcia after they'd left, "Garcia what's up? Didn't you want those men to wine you and dine you?"

Garcia said, "Hell no! Guys like that are the reasons I don't dress like a girl. Middle aged men in bad suits just don't do it for me."

I said, "I'm middle aged."

Garcia said, "You are another story entirely Nash. In the first place you don't look or act middle aged and in the second place you are sexy and they are not."

Michelle said, "Garcia I couldn't agree more. Oh, I wanted to tell you. A woman invited me to be in a bikini shoot a little while ago. I'm going to do some modeling."

Garcia said, "Chiquita that's wonderful. Oh you are going to look so good. This is great news I'm very happy for you. When will it be?"

Michelle said, "I think this week. I've always wanted to model."

Garcia said. "Excellent, come on let's get some fresh drinks and go explore the boat."

The girls headed towards the bar and I looked around for someone to mingle with. I saw Lene' getting up from the couch and coming towards me in the middle of the salon.

She kissed me on the cheek and putting her arm around me said, "Nash keep these tacky bastards away from me please."

I said, "My pleasure beautiful. Are you getting hit on?"

Lene' said, "Yes but it's more like being propositioned rudely. Those two men I was talking to wanted me to come with them on their yacht and be their sex slave. They really thought I'd spread my legs for a boat ride."

I said, "Not everyone that's rich is tasteful. Garcia just turned down dinner with two men who wanted to go out with you and her."

Lene' said, "I'm glad she did. Where is she anyway?"

I said, "She and Michelle went to explore the boat. Want to go and find them?"

Lene' said, "Sure let's go."

We left the party after getting fresh drinks from the bar and went below looking around. They were nowhere to be seen but the galley, recreation room and staterooms were beautifully appointed. Lene' used the head below while I waited on the couch. When she was done we went topside to the top most flying bridge where we could sit and look at the harbor. We were sitting there in the dark looking at the lights and the boats when we saw Garcia and Michelle stroll onto the large foredeck of the yacht. They went to the bow and Garcia took Michelle into her arms and they started kissing.

Their embrace became more passionate and Lene' turned to me and said, "Nash, let's not be left out."

I turned my face to Lene' and our mouths met lightly. Her tongue found mine and we kissed for a long time. We adjusted our positions on the cushions and were able to hold each other tighter.

We kissed for awhile and Lene' said, "Damn Nash you are really a good kisser. Who taught you how to kiss like that?"

I said, "I can't remember but it was a very long time ago."

Lene' said, "Did anyone teach you what else to do with your tongue."

I said, "Yes I'm good at that too I've been told. Does watching Michelle and Garcia bother you?"

Lene' said, "A little but kissing you makes up for it. What about your seeing the two of them?"

I said, "Not a bother. I like to see them together. I think Michelle needs all of the attention she can get right now. I'm not afraid of loosing Michelle either. I know Garcia too well for that. They're just attracted to each other."

Lene' said, "I agree Michelle does need the attention and I like to watch them too. It's very sexy."

I said, "Michelle got offered some modeling tonight. A woman who saw her wants her in a bikini shoot that's being done here."

Lene' said, "That's great. She'll look fantastic. Wait until they see her with her clothes off. She'll be the star of the shoot. She's so sexy in her bikini she'll melt the lens off of the camera."

I said, "Lene' how did you and Garcia meet?"

Lene' said, "We were sort of in the same business. She was doing business off and on with my boyfriend at our home and seduced me one night when he was away. We saw each other when she would come to where we lived and one day she invited me home with her."

I said, "How long ago was that?"

Lene' said, "Four years ago at the end of this summer. I'd never made love to a woman before Garcia. I'd always been with Hispanic men who paid very little attention to me. They would expect me to be in the mood whenever they wanted me. When they were satisfied if I hadn't finished it was too bad for me. Garcia showed me the real pleasure of sex."

I said, "She can do that all right. I've had some fantastic nights with her. She's a wonderful lover."

Lene' said, "She's that all right. She and I have been together ever since."

I said, "Who was your boyfriend? I might know him."

Lene said, "You know him but I'd rather not say who he is. Talking about him is too uncomfortable for me. We haven't talked for a long time because he didn't like me turning into a lesbian. He still does business with Garcia sometimes though. Nash will you kiss me some more please?"

Lene' and I kissed again and held each other for a long time until we saw Garcia and Michelle leave the foredeck to go back to the party that was raging in the salon below.

Lene' and I walked into the main salon just after Michelle and Garcia did. We met them in the middle of the room and Michelle said, "I'm tired of this can we go home?"

Garcia said, "I'm done. I want to go and get out of this girlie stuff before another man hits on me."

Lene' said, "We're done as well. Let's go."

We went and found our host and thanked him for his hospitality. We invited him to stop by our boat and have cocktails with us and he accepted for the following night. We left the yacht to the dismay of the men who had all been enjoying the girls and walked to the Mo Cuishle.

We boarded and Michelle said, "What will we do with the suite that we rented for the night?"

Garcia said, "Two of us should use it. Who wants to go?"

Michelle said, "You and Lene' go. I want to stay here with Nash. You two can have room service tomorrow morning for breakfast."

Lene' said, "Well you don't have to tell me that twice. Come on Garcia let's go."

The two of them kissed us goodnight and walked off of the boat and headed for the hotel. Michelle and I locked ourselves in the salon and headed for the big bed in the forward stateroom. We undressed each other and slid into bed and started kissing. We were soon making love and Michelle seemed much more passionate than usual.

We were lying there after making love and I said, "Did you have a good time tonight?"

She said, "I had a great time tonight. I spent a lot of it with Garcia."

I said, "I know you did. Lene' and I weren't spying but we saw the two of you on the bow making out."

Michelle said, "Oh, I hope you weren't bothered. We didn't mean to be hiding what we were doing."

I said, "You were fine. Garcia and I talked earlier about you and Lene'. Everything is fine. It seems we're all in love with each other."

She said, "I think so too. Garcia says she's confused. Especially about you."

I said, "She told me that too. She wanted to know if I was still attracted to her."

Michelle said, "I know, she's worried about being older. I can understand why though. She was a lot younger when you two were having a fling. Where did you and Lene' see us from?"

I said, "We were exploring the yacht and saw you two from the flying bridge."

Michelle said, "What did Lene' think?"

I said, "She was OK. It made her want to be kissing someone though."

She said, "Did you two make out?"

I said, "Yes we did. She kisses wonderfully."

Michelle said, "Better than me?"

I said, "Different from you. When I kiss you I can feel it all the way to my toes."

Michelle said, "Same here. I did like kissing Garcia though. I think I'm attracted to her but I'm very much in love with you. More than ever now. I think I really just need attention. I realized when I was being hit on by all of those men at the party. The isolation I went through for all of those years was harder on me than I thought."

I said, "Sometimes it can be all about comfort and being made to feel good about yourself."

Michelle said, "Well I'm feeling better about myself all of the time. It was wonderful when I found out all of you were looking for me when I was kidnapped. I don't think I've felt that loved since I was a little girl."

I said, "What do you want to do about the modeling proposal you got tonight?"

Michelle said, "I'm going to call her in the morning. I really want to do this and the money might be good."

I said, "Great. The three of us will guard you while it's going on. I can't imagine Garcia would miss watching all of those sexy women wearing next to nothing."

She said, "I can't imagine that either. I'm tired now can we go to sleep?"

I reached up and turned off the light next to the bed and after taking Michelle into my arms we fell asleep.

Garcia and Lene' woke us up the next morning coming into the boat carrying the suitcase from the night before. We hopped out of bed and I went straight for the coffee pot and started it brewing. Lene' and Michelle went to put the things that were brought to the hotel away and Garcia stayed with me in the salon while I waited for the coffee to be done.

Garcia said, "Nash vato you have no idea how wonderful it is to dress like myself again. All of that girlie stuff can stay in a drawer for the rest of time."

I said, "Well you looked fantastic for a few hours but I like you just fine in your cut-offs and bikini top."

Garcia said, "Is Chiquita going to call that modeling agent?"

I said, "Yes she is. We'll have to be at the shoots with her. Do you mind?"

She said, "Mind? Me not wanting to see all of those gorgeous girls wearing next to nothing. Nash you must be out of your skull. I can't wait."

CHAPTER TWELVE

The girls came back into the salon and Michelle got on the phone and was told to meet Patricia in front of a hotel that was just down the beach. We dressed for the day and taking our weapons walked there together on the sand. When we arrived Michelle was given to a make-up artist and a hair dresser who went to work on her right there on the beach. We watched as she was transformed into someone who looked like they had just stepped out of a formal gown and put into a bikini. An hour later Michelle went behind a curtain and came out a few minutes later wearing a very tiny bikini which was as sexy as anything I could imagine. She was posed by rocks, trees, surfboards and sand and the three of us thought she looked fantastic. She worked for three hours and we were told the photographs were taken so they could make a decision as to whether or not she was what they were looking for. Michelle was told to come back the next day and we left the site of the shoot. We walked back to the boat stopping at a nice outdoor restaurant along the way.

Garcia said, "So Chiquita how did you like having your picture taken?"

Michelle said, "It was exciting but I can see how it might get boring after awhile. I hope they like the pictures they got today."

I said, "We'll find out tomorrow. What do you three foxes want to do this afternoon?"

Lene' said, "I'm still pretty hung over from last night. I could use some beach time."

Garcia said, "I like that. Doing nothing on the sand would be good."

Michelle said, "I'll go along to the beach. We need to shoot something for dinner anyway."

I said, "Remember we invited our host from last night to cocktail on the boat this afternoon."

Michelle said, "That's right we did. What should we serve for cocktails?"

Garcia said, "How about Margaritas?" Those would be good if we don't want them to stay around long."

Michelle said, "How's that?"

Garcia said, "Because if they're a drag I'll mix them strong and they'll be drunk very soon. Mucho borracho, menudo manana."

Lene' said, "Good idea and I've seen her do this before. Her Margaritas can make a mess out of you."

We finished lunch and went to the beach near the harbor to sun ourselves and relax. Our activities were limited to turning over to get equal sun and dipping in the water to cool off when we got too hot. Just after four Lene' and Michelle put on the snorkeling gear and arming themselves went to find our dinner. They were back in an hour with some lovely trout that we peeled when we got back to the boat and put into the 'fridge until it was time to cook. We rinsed off with the hose on the dock and went below one at a time to change for our cocktail guests. Garcia had just finished making a pitcher of her Margaritas when two couples came up to our boat. They were invited aboard and sat in the cockpit on the cushions while Garcia poured her concoction for them. I re-introduced all of us to our guests and they were two brothers Lawrence and James Builder and their wives Hanna and Mary.

We thanked them again for their hospitality the night before and I asked, "What brings you to St. Croix?"

Lawrence said, "We're here on vacation from Palm Beach, we come here every year and do some island hopping. How about you four?"

Michelle said, "We're just spending the summer cruising and being on vacation. David and I are a couple and Lene' and Garcia are just along for the ride."

James said, "What line of work are you in David?"

I said, "I'm retired from entrepreneurial activities here in the Caribbean. It took me all over the islands for twenty-five years. I used to sell everything from farm implements to X-ray equipment."

Garcia said, "What line of work are you in?"

Lawrence said, "We're in the sugar business. We contract with cane growers in the islands and arrange for their efforts to be shipped to Mexico for processing. It keeps us busy and here in the islands a lot."

Hanna asked Garcia, "And what do you do?"

Garcia said, "We arrange for the movement of different things throughout the Caribbean. It's very much like what David used to do. We know each other because David used to do business with my father."

Hanna said, "How do you get around when you're not sailing?"

Garcia said, "We fly. Lene' is my pilot and business partner. Sailboats are too slow for what we do."

Mary asked, "Michelle what do you do?"

Michelle said, "I've just been traveling with David but I was asked to be in a swimsuit shoot here on the island yesterday. I was asked by Ms. Owens who has the yacht moored next to yours."

She said, "That's wonderful! You're a very lucky girl. Patricia owns a very big modeling agency. She can get you a lot of work."

Michelle said, "That would be wonderful. I'll find out tomorrow if I've been hired or not. I did some test shots this morning."

The conversation went this way and I could tell Garcia was getting bored with our guests. She went below to make another pitcher of Margaritas and I could tell from the look in her eye the next batch would be much stronger than the first. They were nice enough people but had little of interest to talk about. Hanna and Mary were much younger than their husbands and were definitely the trophy wife type. They let their husbands do most of the talking and seemed content to be seen on the men's arms. The second pitcher of margaritas did its job and we watched as they became drunker. Half an hour later they were plastered and excused themselves back to their boat for naps before they went out to dinner.

Our company left us to our own devices and we cooked dinner while we finished Garcia's second pitcher of margaritas. We had a very nice low key dinner and

Garcia and Lene' did the cleanup after we were finished.

Michelle and I were sitting in the cockpit relaxing when they came up saying, "What do you too want to do tonight?"

Michelle said, "Want to go out and find a club or a place where there's a band on the beach?"

Garcia said, "That sounds good but remember Chiquita you have to be in front of the hotel early to see if that woman is going to make you famous."

Michelle said, "Oh, I forgot. I think I'd better stay in so I won't look like shit tomorrow. I've already had a lot to drink."

Lene' said, "Me too. An early night will be good for me."

Garcia said, "That leaves us vato. I want to go out and I want you to come with me and keep the boys off of me."

I said, "Garcia do I have a choice in this?"

Garcia said, "Not at all. Go change your clothes while I brush my hair. We'll leave the lightweights to the boat and the TV."

Garcia and I went below and fixed ourselves up to blend in with the tourists we knew we would be mingling with. We kissed Michelle and Lene' before we left the boat and walked arm and arm down the beach towards the row of hotels that were nearby. We walked for awhile past the shops and restaurants that lined the beach until we came to an outdoor restaurant that had a bar which was right on the beach. It wasn't particularly crowded so we took seats where we could see the ocean.

We ordered drinks and Garcia said, "Tomorrow's going to be a big day for Michelle. I hope she gets hired by this agency."

I said, "I hope so too. I think it would be good for her ego. If she could be financially independent it would help her find herself."

Garcia said, "It surely would help. There's nothing like feeling you can be responsible for yourself. I used to hate living off of my father's money."

I said, "Did you know that Lene' and I saw you and Michelle making out last night?"

Garcia said, "Yes Lene' told me last night when we got to the hotel. Are you OK with that?"

I said, "I am. Actually it was really sexy to watch

Garcia said, "Lene' said the same thing. She said you two made out as well.

Doesn't she kiss great?"

I said, "She does kiss good. You're a lucky woman Garcia."

Garcia said, "We're both lucky. That chiquita of yours is something else."

I said, "We'll really have to be on our guard while she's doing these shoots. Do you want to get some outside personnel?"

Garcia said, "No we should be able to handle it. We'll just have to hang close and be ready if anything should happen. I can't imagine anyone would try to snatch her from the beach. It's too wide open."

I said, "I agree but we can't let our guard down. I don't want a replay of her last kidnapping. She's still freaked by it."

Garcia said, "Vato did you mean it the other day when you said you were still attracted to me?"

I said, "Of course I meant it. I've always been attracted to you. I remember making love to you like it was yesterday."

Garcia said, "I do too. It was always wonderful. You were the only man who really did it for me."

I said, "Garcia what's this all about. This is the second time you've brought this up. What gives?"

Garcia said, "Nothing really. No, it is something really. Here's the deal. I'm getting older and like a regular woman I've got this damn biological clock inside of me. The damn thing is ticking and it's getting louder. It's been making me think about having a kid."

I said, "Garcia, you're thinking about having a child?"

She said, "Yep, I can hardly believe it myself. I really never thought it would happen. Lene says it's happening to her too. It pisses me off really. Sometimes I find myself looking at babies and little kids. I have to slap myself every once in awhile."

I said, "This is a side of you I never thought I'd see."

Garcia said, "You thought you'd never see it? It's definitely a shock to me! I spent all of these years being a rough tough pistol packing lesbian. Having a kid will really screw up my image."

I said, "It might at that. What about raising a child? That's a lot of work."

She said, "I know it is but there are always governesses and tutors and my finca is plenty big enough."

I said, "Don't forget about boarding schools. That might be good when your child gets older."

Garcia said, "Come on Nash, let's dance."

I said, "Dance? Garcia you must be feeling your clock ticking. I've never known you to want to dance."

She said, "Don't give me a hard time vato. I know this thing has got me all twisted around. I want to have a male body next to mine and yours is the only one I like."

We got up from the bar and walked onto the sparsely crowded dance floor where the combo was playing slow dinner music.

Garcia put her arms around me and her head on my shoulder and said, "So what do you think vato? Am I completely crazy?"

I said, "No you're not crazy but I have to adjust to something that's completely unlike you. I have to say I think you'd have a great kid. I'd hope you'd have a beautiful little girl."

She said, "A girl? God if I had a girl I'd go nuts if she was like I was when I was a teenager. I almost put my father in his grave with my running around."

I said, "You might have a boy. It's a fifty fifty shot."

Garcia said, "Can you imagine me having a boy? He'd be dangerous at twelve if he was anything like me. Nash this is really hard for me."

Garcia held me tighter and I said, "Garcia I'm just now feeling there's a reason you're telling me all of this. You'd better spill the beans."

Garcia kissed me on the neck and said, "Vato I'm telling you this because I want you to be the father. I've always loved and admired you and so did my father. I need to borrow some of your sperm."

I said, "Like you're going to give it back someday."

Garcia said, "Nash don't kid me right now. I'm serious; I want you to have a child with me."

I said, "Garcia I'm very flattered but you know I don't like to stay in one place for long. I wouldn't be a very good father."

She said, "I know. I was thinking I'd take care of the raising and you could continue your retirement. You could just come and visit when you wanted or we could fly to meet you places."

I said, "Have you thought about Michelle and what she'd have to say about this?"

She said, "I have thought about it. She's probably having thoughts about having a child with you too. She's head over heels in love with you know. She makes me want to be fifteen years younger."

I said, "Garcia, you don't have to be fifteen years younger. You know I love you. I always have. What does Lene' think?"

She said, "She doesn't know. You're the only one that knows."

I said, "I suppose you'll have a talk with her and Michelle."

Garcia said, "Vato does that mean you'd have a child with me. Is that a yes?"

I said, "I'll help you have a child if you want me to but it means we'd have to have sex a lot and don't get pissed off at me if you have a child with blond hair and blue eyes."

Garcia said, "Blanco I want to have sex with you right now. Do you want to take me to the beach and have me on the sand like we used to do?"

I said, "Garcia that's a very attractive offer but we have two other people to deal with here. I don't want anyone's feelings to get hurt."

She said, "Nash you're sensible. You've always been sensible. I don't want to hurt anyone either. Especially Lene' and I definitely don't want to cause any problems between you and chiquita."

I said, "How about if we have another drink and then go back to the boat. If you offer yourself to me again I might not be so sensible."

We went to the bar and sat having our drinks being close to each other and watching the water. We finished drinking and walked on the sand to the boat holding hands along the way there. The boat was dark when we got there and we tried not to make noise coming aboard and going below. Garcia looked in the forward stateroom and Lene' and Michelle were there together. Garcia pulled me by the sleeve to my bunk in the after stateroom and we got into bed together.

I put my arms around her and before she fell asleep she said, "Thank you Nash. Thank you very much."

We woke up the next morning and I headed to the coffee pot and Garcia went to the head. She was out before Lene' and Michelle got up and they eventually got to the main salon.

I said, "Good morning, who wants coffee?"

Michelle came into the galley and got cups for her and Lene' and said, "What time did you two get back last night?'

Garcia said, "Just after one. You two were sleeping nicely and we didn't want to wake you up."

Michelle said, "Garcia did you borrow my boyfriend last night?"

Garcia said, "I did Chiquita but I only used him for a pillow. Did you sleep well?"

Michelle said, "Yes and I feel wonderful. Let's eat. I have to be on the beach at the hotel at ten."

Lene' joined me in the galley and after giving me a good pinch on the ass began to help me with breakfast. Garcia and Michelle hugged each other and started to get the utensils we'd need for breakfast in the cockpit. It was a typically beautiful island morning and while we were eating Patricia stopped by the boat on her way to the shoot in front of the hotel.

She said, "Good morning. Michelle don't forget ten o'clock. Please don't be late. I had a call this morning and your tests were better than anyone dreamed. You're the new girl and my photo editor wants you in front of the camera all day. I'll have contracts for you to sign when you get there. Congratulations, I think you're going to be very famous."

Patricia walked off down the pier and we all looked at each other. Michelle was stunned and she was hugged by the three of us until she begged for mercy. We finished our breakfast and while Michelle cleaned the galley the rest of us figured out what we would wear to the beach that would cover our weapons. We all walked there together on the sand and on arrival we were taken to the tent that was being used for an office. We looked at the photos in slide form and they were very good. Michelle was very sexy in the shots and was told by the photo editor that she was a natural. Patricia got out the contracts for her to sign and Garcia made sure she went over Michelle's deal with the agency. The contract was for this shoot with options for two more and the money was excellent. I was very proud of her as were the others. When the contracts were signed Michelle was given to the makeup department and we didn't see her again for over an hour. We took up strategic positions near where she was and tried to stay in the shade. We watched as she was dressed in half a dozen bikinis before lunch and two different hairdos.

We got to eat together and during lunch Lene' asked, "What do you think so far Michelle?"

Michelle said, "I like it but it's pretty boring waiting for them to get the light right and waiting for the jet skis to get out of the background. I'm very happy to have a job though. I never was really trained for anything. This is the first job I've had for six or seven years."

Garcia said, "Chiquita you look positively gorgeous out there. The other girls are crying with envy."

She said, "I know. I've seen some of them looking daggers at me. How are you doing? I'm sorry you have to stand around for me."

I said, "We're all right. Its fun watching you look gorgeous. Are you getting creases in your ass from sitting on those rocks?"

Garcia said, "Don't worry Chiquita. We'll send you a bill for our services. I'm having a great time looking at the other cheesecake on the beach."

Michelle said, "Well they're certainly looking at you three. I wonder if they have any idea that you're here on guard and not just stargazing."

Michelle was called from the lunch break and we all went back to work on the beach. Some of the girls were being photographed harnessed up to the Para-sailing boat and Michelle was told it would be her turn for that tomorrow. She was excited by this and said she'd never done it before and was hoping to go up. She was very tired by the end of the day, as we were and we all walked back to the boat to make dinner.

That night was an early night and Michelle and I slept together in my bed leaving Garcia and Lene' their space in the forward stateroom. The next day was a carbon copy of the previous day and in the afternoon Michelle was harnessed to the Para-sailor. When she was all hitched up to the tethered parachute the boat started up and pulled her into the air. The photographer took his shots and then yelled at the boat that was not slowing down. Garcia was the first to see the fright on his face and I then realized this was an attempt to snatch Michelle. As the boat sped away Michelle was helpless thirty feet in the air and I could see her trying to get loose from the harness she was in. Garcia was running with Lene' towards the group of jet-skis parked on the beach and I followed. She was there first and when the guy in charge of them protested her starting one he got a pistol stuck in his face making him back off. Lene' and I left the beach at the same time racing towards the Para-sailing boat that was moving away with Michelle in the air behind it. The men driving the boat were pointing at us and I saw guns being drawn. Garcia already had hers out and as she got closer I saw a muzzle flash. She saw it too and began to zigzag her jet-ski so she would be harder to hit. Lene' and I were being shot at too and we took to the same evasive maneuver that Garcia was using.

We were catching the other boat but slowly. They were headed for the open water where there was most likely another boat waiting to transfer Michelle to it and as we got closer Garcia began to fire at the men running the boat. I shot as well and so did Lene'. I could hear bullets passing close to me and Lene' and I crouched down to be less of a target. We were getting closer and I heard Lene' scream to the left of me. She had been hit in the shoulder but was still on her jet-ski. I looked at her and she waved me on and shut her ski down. Right about this time Garcia shot one of the men on the boat and I watched as he went down. I took aim and emptied the magazine in my .40 hitting the other man who went down with his companion. This left the boat running wild and headed out into the ocean. I steered towards Garcia and we caught up to the runaway boat together. She reached out her knife to me and I took it from her putting it blade up in the back of my shorts. I ran my jet-ski as close to the moving boat as I could and jumped for the rail. I made the grab and pulled myself aboard immediately cutting the tether that was keeping Michelle in the air. Garcia turned back to get her and I went forward to see about shutting the boat down.

One of the men was still very much alive and started to sight his pistol on me. I kicked him as hard as I could and he dropped like a stone onto the deck. I got to the controls and shut the engine down. The boat came to a halt bobbing on the water and I looked around for Garcia. She already had Michelle on the back of her jet-ski and was coming up to the boat.

She said, "Vato! Where's Lene'?"

I said, "She was hit in the shoulder! Go after her!"

Garcia immediately spun her jet-ski around and headed for where mine was bobbing. Michelle bailed out from Garcia's jet-ski and swam to where mine was floating letting Garcia run full speed to where Lene' was limping in to the beach. Michelle headed in after her and I turned the Para-sailing boat around and headed for the beach. As I was turning the boat I saw a larger vessel further out that looked like they might be waiting for the boat I was now driving. I pressed the throttles forward and followed the girls to the beach. They were there before me and I simply grounded the boat on the beach killing the engines and hopping over the side to get to the girls. Garcia was there with Lene' who was still conscious. I saw things weren't bad and ran for my beach bag where there was extra ammo. I scooped it up and ran back to where the girls were and there was a crowd gathering. When I ran up I reached in the bag and passed out the extra ammo to Garcia and Michelle who instantly reloaded. When the crowd saw our guns they backed off quickly.

There was a young man standing near and I said to him, "Dude, give me your T shirt!"

He stripped off his shirt and I used it to wrap Lene''s shoulder that was bleeding pretty badly.

I tied it tight and looked at her. I said, "Did it hit any bones?"

She said, "No it went through. Jesus it hurts like hell though! Chiquita are you OK?"

Michelle said, "I'm OK but you're not."

Lene' said, "I'll live. It's not my first."

Garcia said, "Anyone in that boat alive?"

I said, "One for sure. I kicked him unconscious though."

Garcia said, "Come on Chiquita."

The two of them walked towards the boat after Garcia took her knife back from me. I stayed with Lene' who was pale and shaking but looked all right. A few minutes later I heard Garcia screaming in Spanish and knew what she was doing. There were a few masculine screams and I knew what that was as well. She was back in a few minutes with Michelle who had fire in her eyes.

I asked, "Find out anything?"

Garcia said, "Plenty. He was having trouble hearing until Michelle cut his ear off. He's real talkative right now."

I said, "What's he doing now?"

Michelle said, "Probably trying not to bleed to death the son of a bitch! Let's get Lene' up to the bar and into the shade."

We walked Lene' through the crowd of bystanders to the bar and she sat in a chair. I replaced the T shirt with some clean bar towels and Garcia gave her some whiskey which she gunned down immediately. The paramedics arrived and put some real bandages on her and we all took a trip to the local hospital where we spent the next three hours waiting for her to come out of minor surgery.

While we were waiting the local cops came in and a familiar looking inspector walked up to us and said, "Garcia are you involved in this?"

Garcia said, "Hello Inspector Davis. Yes I'm involved. Sorry about the commotion on the beach."

Davis said, "You mind telling me what this is all about?"

Garcia said, "Kidnapping. The men in the Para-sail boat were trying to kidnap my friend here. We stopped them."

Davis looked at me and said, "Nash is that you after all of these years?"

I said, "Me in the flesh. Long time no see."

Davis said, "Garcia why were they trying to kidnap this girl."

Garcia said, "She has an angry ex boyfriend that won't take no for an answer. This is a second attempt."

The inspector said, "What's your name girl?"

Michelle said, "I'm Michelle Murphy."

Davis said, "Oh the girl from the flyer. We found one on a drug runner we picked up. Garcia what are you doing on the side of law and order?"

Garcia said, "Just helping my friend Michelle. We're all traveling with Nash."

Michelle said, "Are we in trouble?"

Davis said, "Normally yes but you did us a favor. We've been looking for those two bastards for quite awhile. We've got them now thanks to you three. Well we've got one of them. The other is quite dead and what do you think happened to the other one's ear?"

Michelle said, "I couldn't imagine. Maybe he fell down."

Inspector Davis said, "I think it would be a good idea for all of you to be off of the island real soon. Like tomorrow morning."

Garcia said, "Tomorrow it is inspector nice to see you again."

I said, "Likewise."

Davis said, "Garcia I'm amazed I'm not arresting you and Nash. I'm sure there's something in my files that you're guilty of from a few years back. Now get your friend and get off of my island."

I said, "We'll leave at first light. Nice to see you again Inspector."

Davis said, "Don't push it Nash. I don't care if you are retired. I'll still put you behind bars."

The inspector walked off and Michelle said, "Christ are there any cops that don't know you two?"

Garcia said. "No not really Nash and I have met them all I think ".

Michelle said, "Obviously."

The surgeon came out from between the double swinging doors and walked up to us and said, "Your friend is going to be fine. Her shoulder will hurt for awhile though. Do you want to see her?"

We said yes and he took us back to where Lene' was sitting up in bed looking bored and wearing a paper dress.

Michelle said, "Lene' I'm so sorry. Are you in a lot of pain?"

Lene' said, "There's no pain but then again I'm full of morphine. Can you guys get me out of here?"

The doctor said, "I'd really like to keep her here for a couple of days."

Garcia said, "Here's the deal Doc. Inspector Davis wants us off the island by tomorrow morning. Can you fix us up with some pain killers, antibiotics, antiseptic and bandages? I'll make it worth your while?"

The doc said, "Do you three know how to us the stuff?"

I said, "You bet, we're all pretty good at dealing with injuries and I have a great medical book on the boat."

The doc said, "Ok you can take her. Just get her somewhere that can stop an infection if one starts. Let me get what you'll need."

Garcia went with the doctor and Michelle and I helped Lene' get dressed and ready to leave. We took a cab to the harbor and I carried Lene' to the boat where we put her on the cushions in the cockpit which was where she wanted to be. Garcia went for drinks in the galley and poured one for each of us as we sat around on the cushions.

We'd been there for an hour when Patricia Owens walked up and said, "Michelle you run around with a pretty exciting bunch of people. Would you mind telling me what that was all about? It messed up our shoot for the whole afternoon."

Michelle said, "I'm sorry Patricia, can I get you a drink?"

Patricia said, "I'd love one thanks."

Michelle went below and got Patricia a cocktail and said, "Look I'm really sorry about what happened. I have an ex boyfriend in L.A. that is determined to take me back there. What you saw was his second attempt to kidnap me."

Patricia said, "These friends of yours. They went off like a bunch of mercenaries. I thought I was watching a movie."

Michelle said, "They have been hanging around guarding me in case my ex was to try anything. They're not mercenaries I assure you. They just know things. Does this mean you won't want me under contract anymore?"

Patricia said, "Under normal circumstances I'd fire you but my editor is in love with the way you look on film. He wants you back and so do I but without the drama."

Michelle said, "Thanks but we've been asked to leave the island by the cops. They didn't like the problem we caused'.

Patricia said, "I can understand that. Where are you going?"

Michelle said, "We haven't decided yet."

Patricia said, "We're going to be shooting on Martinique in two weeks can you meet us there?"

I said, "Just tell us where to be and we'll meet you there but not a word to anyone that we're going there."

Patricia said, "This is like a movie. OK I won't tell a soul you're coming to meet us. Two weeks from today at the Hilton on the beach near Fort de France."

I said, "Will you be taking your yacht?"

Patricia said, "Yes why?"

I said, "Do you have a single side band radio?"

She said, "Yes we do."

I said, "The name of our boat is Mo Cuishle we'll be on the air every night at ten if you want to contact us or we can be E-mailed or call us on the SAT phone if you need to."

Patricia said she would and after getting web addresses and phone numbers she went to Lene' and said, "I'm sorry you were hurt. You were very brave."

Ms. Owens left the boat and I went to the phone to call the grocers before they closed. I gave them a big order and it was delivered just as it was getting dark.

We worked at putting the order away and when it was done I said, "Garcia, Michelle get the bow lines. We're heading for the fuel dock."

Michelle said, "But we have until tomorrow morning."

I said, "By the time our tanks are full it'll be dark. I want to sail blacked out all night. That other boat will be watching to see if we leave and I don't want them to follow us. I want to be a hundred miles from here when the sun comes up."

Michelle said, "Oh." And went for the lines I'd mentioned.

CHAPTER THIRTEEN

We stocked up with fuel, water and ice and Garcia aimed us for the harbor entrance while Michelle and I scanned the horizon with the night vision glasses. I scanned for over an hour and I could see nothing. We kept all of the electronics off and watched with the night vision glasses all around us.

Garcia had been below and when she came up Michelle said, "Where were you Garcia?"

Garcia said, "I was laying out the weapons and getting ready for a fight. If we're seen we might need them tonight."

Michelle said, "I hope we're not seen. I've had enough excitement today."

Garcia said, "Chiquita you should have seen yourself. You took that guy's ear like a real merc. You should have kept it."

Michelle said, "What's a merc?"

I said, "A mercenary, a professional soldier that hires out to the highest bidder."

Michelle said, "I wasn't planning to do that but I got so pissed off it just happened. Why should I have kept it?"

Garcia said, "A lot of mercs dry them out and wear them around their necks. I've seen old mercs that have a string of them hanging from their webbing."

Michelle said, "Yuck, why do they do that?"

I said, "Think about it. You're the new guy in camp and no one knows you. It tells the men you'll be working with that you're a bad ass."

Michelle said, "Am I a bad ass?"

Garcia said, "You're getting to be one. You handle yourself really well under pressure. You remind me of myself when I'm pissed off. You didn't blink when you took that guy's ear."

Michelle said, "Garcia stop you're scaring me."

Garcia said, "I'm sorry Chiquita. I don't mean to scare you. Let's go below and make some dinner. I'm hungry."

I stayed up in the cockpit sailing the boat with Lene' who'd been quiet during all of this. I looked at her and said, "Lene' how are you feeling?"

She said, "I'm good but I'm whacked out on morphine. I can't feel much and thinking is hard for me."

I said, "Are you hungry?"

She said, "Not much. Morphine really messes with my stomach."

I asked, "What about some soup?"

She said, "Soup would be nice. I could get that down."

I said, "You were really good out there today."

She said, "Thanks Nash but you and Garcia were the heroes. I wish I'd been more help to you."

I said, "I'm just glad you weren't hurt worse. That was pretty close."

She said, "I've had closer. This is my second bullet wound."

I said, "Where was the first?"

She said, "In Colombia. I took one through the ear."

I said, "Damn! You can't even tell."

She said, "The miracle of cosmetic surgery in practice."

I said, "What were you doing there?"

She said, "Trying to get an overloaded plane off of the ground."

I said, "How old were you?"

Lene' said, "Nineteen and stupid."

I said, "Well you must have gotten it off."

She said, "I did but I left the starboard landing gear in a tree at the end of the dirt runway."

I said, "What kind of plane?"

She said, "A clunky C-47 that should have been scrapped ten years before. I ditched it in Belize on the coast north beach of Belize City. We got the dope out and delivered. It was a big score."

I said, "Who owned the plane?"

Lene' said, "I don't know. I stole it with my boyfriend at the time. They're probably still looking for me."

I said, "You were nineteen years old and decided to steal a C-47 full of pot?"

She said, "It wasn't full of pot it was coca. A couple of tons."

I said, "A couple of tons? Jesus Lene' I thought I had a past. That's a lot of money you're talking about."

She said, "A couple of million give or take. I still have most of it invested in European mutual funds. I'm a pretty rich woman. I used to be a pretty bad girl years ago. Are you still in love with me?"

I said, "Yes, I'm still in love with you I just didn't realize you had such a colorful past."

Lene' laughed and said, "Colorful past? That's an understatement if I ever heard of one. Nash I was completely nuts back then. I pulled so much shit you can't imagine. I was tall and blond and had big tits. The Chicanos down there let me get away with murder to get into my pants. There were small wars that were fought over me. It's funny now but I probably should have had my throat slit a dozen times."

I said, "Did you have a different name then?"

She said, "I don't know, you tell me?"

I said, "Did you go by the name La Reina de Nevar, the snow queen?"

Lene' said, "Dammit Nash you have too good a memory. Shit nobody knows that except for Garcia."

I said, "Nice to see you again La Reina. It's been a long time. I'm surprised you're still alive."

She said, "I am too and don't spread it around. I'm still hot."

I said, "Do you remember a little meeting in Barranquilla, Colombia in the Hotel Castillo. Top floor, the presidential suite in about 1980?"

Lene' said, "Nash don't tell me you were there."

I said, "I was there. Think about it. I was thirty-two and trading a shit load of rifles and ammunition for a thousand pounds of coca. I was the guy with the full red beard that had blond hair halfway down his back. You drove a hard bargain."

Lene' said, "That was you! Oh shit! Oh shit! Damn you and your memory Nash. You son of a bitch! Oh god this is terrible. Who put the deal together for you?"

I said, "Esteban Obradores. Remember him?"

She said, "Too well. I don't believe it. Nash it's no wonder I'm in love with you. No one in the world but you would remember La Reina de Nevar."

I said, "I have to admit you were about the best looking woman I'd ever seen. You were really something with your white hair."

She said, "That's what got me the name. It wasn't the coca I moved it was my hair. When I got out of the business I dyed my hair for years. I was all of twenty-three then. This is completely embarrassing."

Just then Garcia came up from below and said, "What are you two talking about?"

Lene' said, "You'll never believe it not in a thousand years."

Garcia said, "What won't I believe? Nash what's up vato?"

I said, "You'll have to get it from Lene'."

Lene' said, "Nash just mentioned La Reina de Nevar."

Garcia said, "That's my vato he knows everybody. Nash how do you know La Reina?"

I said, "You'll have to ask Lene'."

Lene' said, "Nash did business with La Reina years ago and she remembers him."

Garcia said, "No it's not possible. No that isn't right. With Nash anything is possible. Lene' you should know that by now."

Lene' said, "I know that now. What a day. Michelle gets snatched, I get shot, we're told to leave the island and now Nash comes up something about me no one knows. This is beginning to be one hell of a trip."

Garcia said, "Bambina, would you like something to eat?"

Lene' said, "Nash mentioned soup awhile ago. Would you make me some please?"

Garcia kissed Lene' on the forehead and said, "Of course I will. Would you like a cup or a bowl?"

Lene' said, "A cup please thanks."

Michelle brought more food up and said, "How are you Lene'? Do you need any more pain meds?"

Lene' said, "Maybe after I eat something. I'm getting pretty tired but my shoulder isn't too bad."

Michelle disappeared below and brought up the rest of dinner. I set the auto pilot and we sat to eat with just the light from the stars showing us where the food was on the table. Lene' sipped on her cup of soup and before she finished she asked to go to bed. Michelle took the helm and I helped Lene' get below with Garcia. We took her clothes off and put her under the sheets and I kissed her goodnight and left her to Garcia while I went back to the cockpit. I took the helm from Michelle as she raised the night vision glasses and scanned the horizon. Garcia had just come up from the salon and picked up the other pair of night vision glasses and started to scan the horizon as well.

We were all quiet for a good while and Garcia said, "Vato there's a boat on the horizon."

I said, "What's it doing?"

Garcia said, "Heading west. We're headed south south east aren't we?"

I said, "We are. Does that boat have lights on it?"

Michelle said, "Yes its running lights are there and it looks like one of those inter-island freighters."

I said, "Keep an eye on it. I'm going to run away from it. Tell me if it changes course."

I turned the Mo Cuishle in a more easterly direction and the ship stayed its course.

I relaxed when it was out of sight over the horizon and said, "Look we're down a hand. One of you should go and get some sleep for a couple of hours."

Michelle said, "One of us? No way. You get below. Garcia and I will watch things up here. If something starts coming after us I want you rested. We'll wake you in a couple of hours."

I started to complain and Garcia said, "Vato get below. I want you fresh too. Go get some sleep."

I went below and left the two girls in the cockpit watching the horizon through the magic of night vision glasses. I was out as soon as my head hit the pillow and didn't wake up until Michelle shook me just before dawn. Michelle slid into the bed I'd vacated and I went up on deck to find Garcia sipping hot coffee. I poured myself a cup and picked up the night vision glasses.

I asked, "Anything shaking?"

Garcia said, "Nothing at all. I made a course correction a few hours ago and we're back to south south east heading for Martinique. The moon should be rising soon but it's on the wane so it shouldn't be too bright."

I said, "Turn on the GPS and see how far we've gone."

Garcia flipped the switch and said, "We're making good speed. We're a hundred and twenty-five miles from St. Croix ".

I said, "That leaves about one-fifty to go. Another long day on the water should get us there by midnight."

Garcia said, "Yes and two weeks early for Michelle's shoots. I think we should go somewhere else and lay low."

I said, "Might be a good idea where were you thinking of going?"

Garcia said, "Michelle needs better medical care than we can give her here. I want to take her home."

I said, "What's your plan?"

She said, "To stash the boat in Martinique and fly to my island where Lene' can heal up some."

I said, "How will we get the jet?"

Garcia said, "We'll have it flown to Martinique fill it with fuel and take off again. I want her to be comfortable and in her own bed. We'll be completely safe there and can fly back so Michelle can do her shoots and we can look for X."

I said, "You're really worried about her."

She said, "Yes I am. That's my girl down there with a hole in her shoulder. I love her very much despite all of what's going on between Chiquita and you and me."

I said, "Well get on the phone and make it happen. I love her too."

Garcia said, "I'll call in the morning. It can wait until then. Nash I have something I want to talk to you about'.

I said, "Tell me what's up."

Garcia said, "This is strictly between me and you understand."

I said, "I understand tell me what."

Garcia said, "Once we get Lene' and Chiquita to my island you and I are going to L.A.."

I said, "What about Michelle and Lene'?"

She said, "They'll be fine on my island with my army watching over them. I don't want them to know what we're doing. It's dangerous and they'd worry."

I said, "What do you want to do?"

Garcia said, "I'm going to L.A. and kill Wise. When he's dead I'm going to burn his house down too."

I said, "You're right. This is dangerous; neither of us is very welcome in the states. If we get caught it might be jail for us."

Garcia said, "I think we can get in and out OK. That bastard got my girl shot. Now it's personal. I'm going to kill him and bring Michelle his head."

I said, "If that's what you think. We'll get together and work out the plan. You're right too. I don't want Michelle to know about it."

We sailed the boat until dawn when Michelle got up and Garcia went and tucked herself in to bed next to Lene' I went below and made the morning coffee and brought some to Michelle. I began to tell her what the plan was going to be in a limited way.

I said, "Michelle what would you think about taking a jet ride?"

She said, "Sure, where are we going?"

I said, "Garcia is worried about Lene' she wants to take her home where she can get better care and be in her own bed."

Michelle said, "I think that's a good idea. I'm worried about her too."

I said, "So you wouldn't have a problem with that?"

Michelle said, "No problem but I'd still like to do my photo shoots."

I said, "Garcia wants you to do them too. You'll be there for them. Jets are good like that."

She said, "What will we do with the boat?"

I said, "We'll stash it at a friend's boatyard in Martinique. It'll be there when we get back."

Michelle said, "That's fine with me. Would you like some breakfast?"

I said, "Yes I'm getting hungry thank you."

Michelle went below to make us something to eat and brought it to the cockpit and placed it on the table. I set the auto pilot and sat with her to eat. We sailed the boat together until almost noon when Garcia came up and asked if I could help her get Lene' up to the cockpit. I went below and the two of us helped Lene' get to the cushions and propped her up.

Michelle said, "Lene' how are you this morning?"

Lene said, "I'm really stiff and sore. I slept OK but I'm definitely not moving very well."

Garcia said, "Lene' we're going home for two weeks as soon as we get to Martinique. I want you where you can heal better and home is best for that."

Lene' said, "What about Michelle's shoots?"

Garcia said, "I'll fly her back here in two weeks for them. You need to be at home."

Lene' said, "I can't argue with you about that. I hurt pretty badly and I'd love to be home."

I said, "We should be there about midnight tonight."

Garcia said, "I'll have you in your bed by tomorrow morning and Dr. Roda will be there for you'.

Lene said, "Thank you Garcia, I love you very much."

Garcia said, "I love you too. That's why we're going."

Garcia went below and made the necessary calls to her home. The jet would meet us at the airport in Fort de France and the boat would be kept out of sight at David DuMond's boatyard.

After the calls were made and Lene' had eaten something she asked, "Michelle would you mind getting me some meds please. I'd like to stay in the fresh air but I need something for the pain."

Michelle got up immediately and went below bring back the bag of medication that was given to us on St.Croix. The wind picked up some and that assured me we would be in Martinique when I expected.

It was eleven-thirty when I sailed us into the harbor and we tied up at the deep water dock. David was there to meet us and while the girls unloaded all that we would need for the flight to Little Inagua. David understood our situation and said he would cover the boat after it was lifted from the water so it wouldn't be noticed. Garcia and I were just thanking him for his trouble when a large van pulled into the yard to take us to the airport and the waiting jet. Garcia's plane was loaded when we arrived and I helped get Lene' into the most comfortable seat in the rear of the jet.

When we were all loaded Garcia said, "Vato, it's time you learned how to fly. You're in the second seat up front with me."

I went to the flight deck after Garcia and took my place in the second seat. Garcia handed me the headset and I looked over my shoulder into the cabin where Michelle was strapping Lene' in and making her comfortable. The plane had already been turned around and was ready for the flight to Garcia's airstrip on Little Inagua. She pushed the throttles forward and we taxied to the runway. She was very gentle with the takeoff this time climbing out slowly and heading for our altitude at a smooth angle.

When we were at our altitude Garcia said, "Nash why don't you take her?"

I said, "Tell me what to do. I don't want to screw up."

Garcia said, "Put your feet on the pedals and take the yoke in your hands. It's a lot like driving a car. Just test the pedals and the yoke to get a feel for keeping her flat and straight."

I did what she said and was surprised at how easy it was to keep things level.

Garcia said, "See that bubble with the line across it in front of you above the compass?"

I said, "Yes."

She said, "That's your false horizon. Look at the dark grey and light grey bubble that's like the ball on a compass. That's your attitude. Match the line of the two grays with the line on the outer glass and that's level to the ground."

I did what she said and said, "That will keep me from diving into the ocean?"

She said. "You catch on quick vato. If the wings dip from side to side that will tell you as well. Just keep her level and straight and follow the compass heading she's on. I'm going to check on Lene' and bring you back a soda."

Garcia got up out of her seat and I watched the instruments as I was told.

I was keeping things straight and Michelle stuck her head up next to mine and said, "Nash the pilot. You look pretty sexy flying this thing. We're just going to have to get rich enough to buy one."

I said, "I'm not so sure. I think I have the time to sail places."

Michelle said, "Mr. Hedberg I know there's an airplane in your future. I'll just have to make enough money modeling to buy you one."

I said, "That's nice of you. How's Lene?"

Michelle said, "She's OK, she's really happy to be going home though."

Garcia walked up behind Michelle and said, "Hey Chiquita, quit distracting the pilot. He's a rookie."

Michelle laughed and went back to be with Lene'. Garcia took her seat and said, "So vato don't you love my jet?"

I said, "So far so good. Have I done anything wrong yet?"

She said, "Not a thing. Here's your coke. Try not to spill it on my instruments OK?"

I said, "What's our flight time?"

Garcia said, "We should be there in about an hour and a half."

I said, "How do I know how fast we're going?"

Garcia said, "Look at the airspeed indicator. There's one for airspeed and one that shows our speed over the ground. Right now we're going about 450 knots. While you're flying get familiar with all of the instruments. You'll need to know things when we fly to California."

I said, "Do you have a book at home? That would help a lot."

Garcia said, "Hold on I have to call into the Caribbean center and see if there's anything that might hit us."

Garcia made her call and finding there was nothing near us she settled back in her seat and said, "Nothing is near us and we have good weather all of the way."

I asked, "What about the commercial airplanes?"

She said, "They're usually a lot higher than we are. And the prop planes are lower. The only things that can be a bother are the dumb ass drug smugglers that fly where they want and don't talk to the centers because they don't want to be seen."

I said, "I've heard this before."

Garcia said laughing, "Where did you learn about drug smuggling?"

I said, "I saw a program on television about it once. It was very informative."

Garcia laughed again and said, "I'll bet."

Garcia let me have the yoke almost all of the way to Little Inagua and her air strip. She spiraled the jet down from the sky when we were over the island and didn't bother to call the center for landing as there was no tower and it was her private air strip. Her crew were there waiting for us and when we circled the strip the lights were turned on and she lined up for the approach all the while telling me exactly what she was doing. We landed and taxied to the hangar she'd built for the plane and I noticed there was another plane was inside.

I asked, "Garcia do you have two planes?"

She said, "No that one is Lene's. It's a very fast Cessna twin. It's almost as fast as my jet. She likes it because she says it's really fun to fly."

Garcia killed the engines and her crew opened the door of the jet. I felt the warm island air waft into the plane and heard Garcia's crew rattling on in Spanish. Garcia was greeted and she gave instructions to them in Spanish. I helped with Lene' and we had her in a van in no time. All of our things were left in the plane and we were told they would be brought to us at the house.

Garcia's house was completely lit up when we arrived and there were several vehicles in the driveway. Her doctor was there and there were medical technicians waiting for us to arrive. Lene' was immediately taken inside to her bed and everything that would be needed for her recovery was there already. The doctor would be there full time and had a room in another part of the house as did the technicians and the nurses that would never leave Lene''s room or be just outside of the door.

When Lene' was in bed and had been looked at by her doctor we went in and I said, "Are you happy to be home gorgeous?"

Lene' said, "Yes thank you very much Nash. You did an excellent job with the jet on the way here. You're already flying like a pro. Nice and smooth."

I said, "Beginners luck Lene' but I'm ready for some lessons."

Michelle said, "I'm happy you're home. Do you want to sleep?"

Lene' said, "Yes, very much. I've already been given something and thank you for taking care of me on the boat and in the air."

We both kissed our friend goodnight and went down the big staircase to the living room where Garcia met us a few minutes later.

She poured tequila and said, "Now I'm OK. I really couldn't rest until she was here. She'll be all right now."

We drank with Garcia for an hour and we all retired to our beds. Garcia slept next to Lene' and Michelle and I were given the same room we'd occupied before.

We went to bed after our long day on the water and in the air.

Michelle reached for me when we were under the covers and said, "David, I'm a little depressed. Here we are back in Little Inagua and it seems we're no closer to getting rid of the problem with my ex."

I said, "Don't worry, things will pick up in that department real soon."

She said, "How do you know?"

I said, "Garcia and I have to go on a little trip together to finish this thing with your ex. Ever since Lene' was shot Garcia's taking this very personally. Things aren't happening quickly enough so we're going to use the jet to find the people that can make him back off. We want you to stay here with Lene' and take care of her while we're away. We'll most likely meet you at your shoot on Martinique. Lene' should be well enough by then to fly you there. With any luck it will all be over by then."

Michelle said, "Are you sure? That sounds almost too easy."

I said, "Garcia has found out some things and we'll have to go and do them. It will be OK. She and I are used to this kind of thing."

Michelle said, "OK if that's what it takes I'll do it. I'm just tired of having to be on my guard all of the time."

I said, "I couldn't agree more. The law of probabilities says the longer we're in this situation the more chance of something bad happening. That's why it has to be over and done with."

Michelle kissed me and we fell asleep after making love under the clean sheets.

I was up first the next day and Michelle felt like sleeping in. She pulled the sheets back over her beautiful head and I took the hint and went to the kitchen. I was immediately shooed out by the help and went to the dining room as I was instructed. Garcia showed up just after my coffee was served and another cup was brought for her.

She sat with me and said, "Good morning, where's my Chiquita?"

I said, "Staying in bed. She said she wanted to sleep late. How's Lene'?"

Garcia said, "Lene' my love is fine. She woke up hungry and turned on the

TV to watch the news. It's the only thing she does that annoys me. I hate the news especially in the morning. The kitchen help is bringing her breakfast and the doc is going to see her after she eats."

I said, "It's nice to be here. I loved the clean sheets last night and I told Michelle you and I needed to fly away with you and take care of some business. She's OK with that."

Garcia said, "Good, vato what do you say we go to the beach where we can speak privately. We have a lot of details to work out."

I said, "That's fine with me. All I want to do today is lie around and maybe swim in your pool."

We finished our coffee and got into Garcia's Jeep for the drive to the nearest beach. As we planted ourselves on the sand I noticed a patrol boat off shore.

I asked, "Is that ours?"

Garcia said, "Yep that's one third of my navy. No one is getting on my island until I say so."

I said, "So, what's the plan?"

Garcia said, "We'll fly to Bermuda and swap aircraft. I want a plane with U.S. numbers on it so we won't be bothered where we stop. I think it would be best to hop to New Orleans and refuel there and again in Palm Springs. Then we'll fly to L.A. and land at the Santa Monica airport. They park a lot of private jets there so we won't be noticed. I'll have a car waiting for us and a crew so we can be the kidnappers for a change."

I said, "Are you still thinking of dusting Wise?"

She said, "I am. Are you having second thoughts?"

I said, "I am having second thoughts. Can't we take him and bring him to the Caribbean and feed him to the sharks. I'm still pretty hot in the states and it would be bad to get caught with blood on my hands."

She said, "There's your sensible side again. You're probably right. I'll think about it. Maybe there's something else that can be done."

I said, "What about an escape?"

Garcia said, "I thought we'd load that piece of shit in the jet dead or alive and take off. We can come back through Mexico."

I said, "That's sounds about as good an idea as I've got. How long in L.A.?"

Garcia said, "Thirty-six hours at the most. I want to be in and out."

I said, "Good enough. Who's our crew there?"

She said, "It's Hectors connection. They're all reliable and they owe me."

I lay back on the sand and said, "What are you going to tell the girls?"

She said, "I'm going to tell them Hector has made an appointment with us and we have to go and meet him. That should do it."

I said, "When are we leaving?"

Garcia said, "As soon as I'm not worried about Lene' anymore."

I said, "Are you still thinking of having a child with me?"

Garcia said, "Are you having second thoughts about that too?"

I said, "No I just want to be prepared for it. When are you going to talk to Michelle and Lene'?"

She said, "When all of this is done and over. Then I'll have time to think about it."

I said, "Speaking of time how's your clock doing?"

She said, "Ticking like Big Ben. Sometimes I can barely stand it when I look at you. I need a man badly."

I said, "Are you going to seduce me on this trip?"

She said, "I don't know yet. Do you want me to?"

I said, "I don't know. We might not have time."

Garcia said, "We'll have time. There's always the mile high club."

I said, "Who'll fly the plane?"

Garcia said, "That's what auto pilots are for. Michelle says you two are always making love in the cockpit of your boat while you sail."

I said, "She told you that?"

Garcia said, "Of course vato. She tells me everything. I even know how much you like sexy lingerie."

I said, "What do you tell her?"

She said, "Lene' and I tell her everything as well. I have to get her used to the thought of making love to a woman."

Garcia and I went into the water to cool off and we dried each other when we got out. We drove back to the house to find lunch almost ready and Lene' sitting with Michelle at the dining room table.

We walked in and Garcia said, "Lene' my love how are you?"

Lene' said, "I'm much better today. Being home is a dream. Thank you ".

I said, "Hello Lene', hello Michelle, what's for lunch my darlings?"

Michelle said, "Hamburgers or cheeseburgers Mr. Hedberg take your pick."

I said, "I'd like a cheeseburger please and how did you like sleeping late?"

Michelle said, "It was wonderful. I get up so early on the boat it's a delightful change to be able to sleep in."

Garcia said, "Michelle did the nurses help you bring Lene' down for lunch?"

Michelle said, "They did and I really didn't have to lift a finger. They did all of the work."

Lene' said, "They did all of the work but it didn't stop Michelle from holding my hand and being with me."

Michelle said, "Hey, how often do you get to extend your gratitude to someone who may have helped save your life."

Lene' said, "I was there but I didn't do very much except catch a bullet and bleed all over a jet ski."

Garcia said, "Thanks Michelle it makes me very happy you're taking care of Lene' and don't let her get too demanding. Driving and airplanes are out for awhile."

Michelle said, "How about the beach?"

Garcia said, "The beach is in but be sure you take some of my army along with you."

Lene said, "Do they like the beach too?"

Garcia said, "No they don't but make them go anyway. Besides Nash and I have to go and meet Hector. He has a good lead on Wise and Mr. X."

Lene' said, "When are you leaving?"

I said, "In a couple of days when you're better and Garcia won't be so worried about you."

Michelle said, "How long will you two be gone?"

Garcia said. "About a week all together and I might have to borrow Nash as your boyfriend. Would that be all right?"

Michelle said, "As long as I can borrow your girlfriend it'll be all right."

Lene' said, "Good then, Michelle that will give us plenty of time away from these two machos. We can be girls together."

Michelle said, "Is there anywhere to shop?"

Lene' said, "I have catalogues in piles upstairs. We can order one of everything. We'll put the help on vacation and have boys brought in from the big island."

Garcia said, "Fine, fine, fine just don't send the pool cleaner away. That's the most important thing in the house."

Garcia walked over to Lene' and putting her arms around her said, "I'm very glad you're feeling better. I was so worried about you."

Lene' said, "I'll be OK just you and Nash come back safe to us please."

The four of us ate together and the hamburgers were delicious. Lene' wanted to be by the pool in the shade and we placed her there after lunch. All of us spent the day relaxing by the pool until it was cocktail hour and time for dinner. We dressed for dinner as it was Garcia's habit and watched a film afterwards in the living room. Hector was on the phone with us coordinating our venture in L.A. and things were coming together nicely. We planed things for three days while we lived easily at Garcia's finca. During that time I spent quite a few hours with Garcia going over the instruments and the workings of her jet. Not to mention reading all that I could from Lene''s flight instruction manuals.

Lene' was doing much better and her shoulder improved daily. The afternoon of the fourth day I was getting out of the shower when I received a call on my SAT phone that was very important.

I picked up the phone and said, "Nash here."

A voice I hadn't heard in a very long time said, "Nash do you know who this is?"

I said, "I believe so but it's been a long time. How are you?"

The voice said, "I'm fine but you and Garcia have been causing a lot of trouble."

I said, "I know that. We're trying to resolve the problem. We're going to L.A. to finish things."

The voice said, "I know, but things will finish here in the Caribbean. Here's what I want you to do."

I said, "Tell me what you want."

The voice said, "I want Wise. I want you to bring him to me two weeks from Monday at Latitude 15 degrees north and 60 degrees west at twelve hundred hours local time. Got that."

I said, "Yes that L&L is near Martinique."

The voice said, "I know. That's why it was chosen. I want you, Garcia, Lene' and Michelle to be there with Wise. Bring me pictures as well from Michelle's photo shoots. I want to know her."

I said, "We'll be there."

The voice said, "I only want you and Garcia to know about this call understand. And Nash, you've been doing a good job. Keep it up."

The line went dead and I clicked off my phone and looked for the usual number that would have been left on the screen. There was nothing indicating any call had taken place. I thought for a second and went to find Garcia. I went downstairs after dressing and found the three girls poolside in the shade. I was given a drink when I walked up and was invited to sit.

I said, "Garcia we have to go for a drive."

She said, "Now vato? It's almost dinner time."

I said, "Inmediatamente muy importante."

Garcia got up from the table she had been sitting at and I walked her to the parking area and we got into her Jeep. She said, "Nash what is going on?"

I said, "Drive, we have to talk."

She started the Jeep and took off down the road to the beach were we knew we wouldn't be overheard.

When we got there I said, "I just got a phone call from X."

She said, "No shit?"

I said, "No shit. I'm as surprised as you are."

Garcia said, "What did he say?"

I said, "We're to meet him in the middle of the ocean about a hundred miles from Martinique at twelve noon two weeks from Monday. All I have are the L&L coordinates."

She said, "Damn! That's one week after Michelle's photo shoots start."

I said, "I know, seventeen days from today. There's more, he wants Wise. He wants the four of us and Wise to be there. He says he wants to get to know Michelle and wants pictures from her shoots."

Garcia said, "Shit, anything else?"

I said, "Only that you and I are the only ones to know."

Garcia said, "If that's what he wants that's what he'll get. We'll have to change the arrangements."

I said, "I suppose we'll have to."

Garcia kissed me on the cheek and we drove back to her house and changed for dinner not discussing the phone call I'd gotten.

We changed all of the arrangements for L.A. to the annoyance of our contacts and it took quite a bit of doing. Wise was kept under surveillance by Hector's men and we were Emailed pictures of him so we would know what we were looking for.

Preparations were everything and we arranged for Hector to stash Wise after we'd captured him as there would be a week from the time we got him until Michelle's photo shoots were done. We planed on taking Wise to Martinique where one of Hector's contacts would hold him in an old dungeon that was part of his restored Spanish home. This would allow us to be free for guarding Michelle should any further plans for Wise snatching her be in motion before we captured him. The only wild card would be Lene' who would have to fly Michelle in her plane to Martinique for the shoots. Lene' who was feeling better each day was confident she would be able to fly her Cessna to Martinique with Michelle in the second seat. Michelle was pleased to help with the plane and looked forward to getting her first flying lesson.

CHAPTER FOURTEEN

It all began to go down the Monday before Michelle was to begin her shoot on Martinique. Garcia and I took off from Little Inagua after being driven to the airstrip by Michelle and Lene'. We were kissed good bye by our girls and closed to door on the jet. Garcia wound up the engines and we taxied to the end of the runway where we could see the girls watching for us to take off.

Garcia said, "This is it vato. Want to take her off?"

I said, "I'll try, just back me up."

Garcia put the wing flaps down and told me to push the throttles forward. I did as she said and the jet started down the runway. It sped up faster than I expected and before I knew it Garcia was telling me to pull back on the yoke. I did so and the jet rotated up and lifted off of the runway.

I asked, "So how am I doing?"

Garcia said, "You're doing fine. Just keep her straight and climbing. Level off at fifteen thousand feet so I can call the center and get into the traffic pattern for Nassau where we'll swap planes.

Garcia checked with the center and then instructed me to climb to twenty thousand feet.

Almost as soon as I reached the altitude she said, "Nash I'll take her now. We have to get into the landing pattern."

Garcia took over for me and after swinging in a huge circle to the west she began to descend as she spoke to the tower at the airport. Thirty minutes later we were touching wheels to asphalt and taxiing to the terminal for private planes of all sorts. Garcia parked the jet in the row of others and while I unloaded our things she went inside to deal with the paper work concerning the jet we were to fly to the west coast. We were in the leased jet an hour later and taxied to the runway in a line with the other planes that were waiting for take off. When our turn came she pushed the throttles forward and we ran down the runway until we were airborne.

She climbed to twenty-five thousand feet and after fitting into the air traffic for New Orleans she set the auto pilot and said, "Nash be a dear and get me something to drink."

I said, "What do we have?"

She said, "I don't know. I told them to stock the plane so find me a soda or something. We've about three hours to kill and I'm thirsty."

I went to the small galley and found two sodas and brought them to the flight deck where I settled back into my seat.

Garcia opened our sodas and I said, "I like flying it's no wonder you like it so much. How long will we be on the ground in New Orleans?"

Garcia said, "About an hour and then its back up there. We'll sleep in shifts so we're both fresh when we get to Palm Springs. We'll contact Hector's men from there in case Wise is on the move."

I said, "Do you still want to walk up to Wise and bust him?"

Garcia said, "I think so. He won't be expecting that at all. It's much better than hitting him at home when he's guarded. I don't want to get into a fire fight if we don't have to."

I said, "Agreed and where are the stewardesses on this flight."

She said, "I don't know maybe you should have hired some. What do you want? A bag of those crappy peanuts?"

I said, "I want a pillow and a blanket and cocktails thank you."

Garcia said, "Vato if you want that you should have bought a ticket on Delta or one of those other cattle cars."

I said, "No thanks I've suffered enough airline abuse in the past. This is just fine thanks."

We chatted about the instruments in the plane and Garcia turned off the auto pilot so I could fly the jet and get more hours behind the yoke. She gave me some good explanation about speaking to the air traffic controllers at the centers while we enjoyed the scenery below us. The hours passed quickly to New Orleans and we were on the ground there before I expected. The private jet terminal had us turned around in another hour and we took off for Palm Springs as it was getting into the middle of the afternoon. I took the controls from Garcia as we flew towards the setting sun and she got some sleep in the cabin behind the flight deck. I was comfortable flying our course and I woke Garcia a few hours later when I got hungry. She got into our stores and found some really great sandwiches that had been made for us. She set the auto pilot and we ate together in the cabin. We washed the sliced corned beef down with cold soda and I missed not being able to drink beer while I ate. Garcia took over the plane and I got some sleep in the cabin for a couple of hours. I gave her a bathroom break when I woke up and took over the plane which I flew for another hour until she took over the airplane again and after talking to the nearest center brought us down into the desert heat. I opened the door when the plane was stopped and the heat came in like a furnace. It was hot as hell and dryer that I could imagine. It was nothing at all like the tropical heat and humidity that we both lived in. It was seven o'clock and the sun was still up. We had been in the air or refueling for twelve hours but the time differential made it three hours earlier. The crews from the private jet terminal were around us doing their job of refueling our plane and Garcia got on her cell phone. I heard her curse in Spanish and knew something was up or had changed.

She came to me in the air conditioned terminal and said, "Wise has moved. We have a new destination."

I said, "Where's that?"

Garcia said, "Las Vegas. Wise got on a commercial jet for there at about noon L.A. time. He's lost Hector's tail and now we have to find him there. Will you call Michelle and find out what games he likes and what his favorite hotel is?"

I took the SAT phone from Garcia and dialed the number at her finca. It was eleven o'clock there and the phone was answered by one of the soldiers Garcia had guarding the girls. I told her who I was and asked to speak to Michelle.

She was on the phone a few minutes later and I said, "Hello my love have you fired the help yet?"

She said, "Not yet, Lene' and I didn't want to exert ourselves so we're waiting for tomorrow when we're rested. Where are you two?"

I said, "We're in Palm Springs re-fueling the plane. We just found out Wise left Los Angeles and has gone to Las Vegas. What do you know about his habits there?"

Michelle said, "He mostly left me at home when he would go there but he had some of those tacky satin jackets from Caesars Palace that he would wear from time to time around the house. And sometimes he would leave casino dice on top of the dresser. Does that help?"

I said, "Yes it does. It helps very much. What are you two up to?"

Michelle said, "We've got one of the flat screen TVs out by the pool and we're watching a film in the hot tub. Lene' is feeling much better but that might just be the Sangria."

I said, "Is she seducing you?"

Michelle said, "Not really. We're just watching TV and drinking. She's been telling me all about her ex boyfriends. I imagine you two are going to Las Vegas and will be staying at Caesars Palace?"

I said, "That we are. We'll be flying there very soon."

Michelle said, "David, please be careful. Oh there's one other thing. I heard him talking once at a party about an escort agency there called Prom Queens. He might use their girls."

I said we would be careful and after a few intimate words we hung up the phones and I went to where Garcia was waiting. I said,

"Time to get on the jet. We're leaving."

I walked to the jet with Garcia and we climbed the steps and shut the door. She asked, "Where is he?"

I said, "Most likely Caesars palace. Michelle says he plays craps and might use an escort agency called Prom Queens if he wants company."

Garcia had the jet wound up and we were taxiing to the runway waiting in line with the other planes when she said, "Las Vegas is just a hop from here. What are the girls doing?"

I said, "They've got a TV out by the hot tub and they're drinking Sangria while La Reina is telling her all about her ex boyfriends."

Garcia said, "That could take a couple of days. How's Lene' feeling?"

I said, "Michelle said Lene"s feeling better but it could be the Sangria."

Garcia said, "They really are being girls together. Is my girl seducing your girl?"

I said, "I asked her that and she said they were just hanging out together and being girls."

It was our turn on the runway and Garcia spoke to the tower while I listened in on the headset. She was the pilot on the way to Las Vegas as there was quite a lot of air traffic and controllers to deal with in the hour it took to fly there. We touched down at Mc Laren field after circling a city that we could see the glow from almost as soon as we were airborne from Palm Springs. It was incredibly bright and seemed to be made of lights. We taxied to the private terminal and shut the plane down. I got onto the phone while the car was coming for us and Caesars had a suite with Garcia's name was held for us. The car drove us through the gaudy streets and I was amazed at seeing what Las Vegas had turned into over the years. There were sinking pirate ships and volcanos that belched real fire not to mention families out on the streets. I was glad for the lifestyle I had chosen and Garcia said the same thing as I did. The car dropped us off in the front of the hotel / casino and men in strange attire took our bags while we went to the VIP check in. We were shown to our suite and it was decorated with Greek columns and silver wallpaper and mirrors on the ceiling above the round bed. I laughed after we were inside and had tipped the bell hop out.

Garcia said, "This is so weird. There's nothing like Las Vegas. I'm starving, do you want to eat?"

I said, "Yes I'm really hungry. Are we going down stairs?"

Garcia said, "Not tonight vato. We don't have the clothes for it and we'd attract too much attention wearing what we brought. Tonight we're having room service and staying in."

I said, "That's fine with me. I'm tired and need to be horizontal. The front seats in your jet are hard."

She said, "Hard is good. They make them like that so you won't get too comfortable and fall asleep while you're flying."

I picked up the phone and said, "Starving woman what do you want to eat?"

Garcia said, "Steak, Lobster. Tequila, red wine, Mexican hot sauce, bottled water, and salad with Blue Cheese dressing, good cognac and whatever you can think of. I'm going to take a shower and get a dozen limes for the Tequila."

Garcia began to take off her clothes as she walked to the shower as I spoke to room service. The food was delivered at the same time she got out of the shower and the bell man put it all onto our dining room table. I signed for the check and Garcia sat down to eat wearing a big terry cloth bathrobe that had the hotel's logo embroidered on it. I sat with her and we ate looking at the incredible amount of lights that ran down the strip.

We finished with our dinner and put away all of the things I'd ordered which we wanted to keep in the suite. Garcia called room service to take the rest of it away while I undressed and got into the shower that was in the middle of a very large tub. As the tub filled I lay down in the hot water to ease my aching back which was sore from the seats on the flight deck.

I was ready to get out when Garcia called to me and said, "Vato there's a call for you."

I dried myself quickly and went into the living room wearing the other bathrobe and took the phone from Garcia.

The voice on the other end of the line said, "Mr. Hedberg my love there's something I want you to do."

I said, "What's that Mrs. Hedberg?"

Michelle said, "I want you to make love to Garcia tonight."

I said, "Are you sure you want this to happen?"

She said, "Yes I do. I've been talking to her and she needs this badly. She's saved my life twice and I want this for her. I want you to know this will in no way be a problem with our relationship. I know all about her biological clock and I know she wants to have a child with you and I don't mind. I love Garcia very much and I want her to have what she needs. Is this OK with you?"

I said, "Yes it's fine with me. I've been mostly worried about you and what you'd think."

Michelle said, "Then is it OK if I make love with Lene'?"

I said, "Yes go ahead. I see no reason for you not to do that. Remember I love you very much."

Michelle said, "I know that. Be as sweet to her as you know how and please remember to be careful while you're in Las Vegas. My ex can be very mean."

I hung up the phone and turned to find Garcia posed sexily on the round bed with a glass of red wine in her hand with her jet black hair down and over her shoulders.

She said, "Vato, is this going to be OK?"

I said, "Yes its fine and you look beautiful. I've been thinking about this for a long time."

She said, "I have too. Why don't you get a glass of wine and come and join me."

I got a glass and brought the bottle to the night stand. I filled my glass and slid onto the bed next to my old lover and we put our arms around each other and started kissing. I could feel Garcia letting the soft side of her go and we were soon making love and it was wonderful. She was just as I remembered her and we spent a very long time making love while we took turns watching each other in the mirrors on the ceiling.

We woke up the next morning wrapped around each other and slowly began to move around. Garcia looked very different to me that morning and she was definitely looking at me differently. We had breakfast in our room and while we were eating

I said, "So how's that clock of yours? Is it banging away still?"

Garcia said, "Not any more. I feel as soft as a young girl that just lost it on prom night. Nash I haven't been with a man for more than ten years and you're still the best lover I've ever had. I think I never should have let you get away."

I said, "You're still the wonderful lover you always were. When you let your softness out you're like a different person. I love you both ways."

She said, "I love you too. I wonder how Michelle liked making love to Lene'."

I said, "I guess we'll have to call and find out."

Garcia said, "We'll do that later. We have to go shopping this morning. I need a couple of outfits to wear and so do you."

I said, "You obviously have a plan. What is it?"

She said, "I'm going to dress like a girl and see if I can seduce Wise into taking me to my room thinking he's going to get lucky. When I get him here I'm going to dose the shit out of him. While he's unconscious we'll take him to the jet and fly his ass out of here."

I said, "Good plan. The hard part will be finding him."

Garcia said, "I don't think that will be too hard. I have friends here in Vegas who will help. One of them owns a fancy escort service and she knows every bell captain in the city. We should find him in a couple of days at the most."

I said, "Well today is Tuesday. That gives us until Friday at the latest to get Wise. I think we should be in Martinique by Saturday at the latest to stash Wise in the dungeon. I'll get the boat back in the water on Saturday so the girls will have a place to stay when they arrive on Sunday."

Garcia said, "I think that will work. Let's go shopping."

I said, "I have to go?"

Garcia said, "Yes you have to go. I need you there to tell me when I look sexy. If I'm right I'll have to look like a five thousand dollar hooker."

I said, "OK I can help with that."

She said, "You need a couple of suits so you'll look like a high roller that rented me for the evening if he should see us together. Don't worry; I'll pick them out for you so you won't have to think."

I called room service to pick up the remains of our breakfast while Garcia dressed to go out. I put myself together and we took the elevator to the lobby where the promenade was which was lined with shops. We went into two men's stores and Garcia liked neither of them. We continued along the promenade and went into another that she liked the clothing in. My suits were picked out and while I stood on the pedestal having the cloth marked for alterations Garcia walked around selecting shirts, ties, socks and boxers for me. I was done with the fittings and met her at the sales desk where she was with the pile of things she'd selected for me. She was adamant that my suits be ready by the afternoon and delivered to our suite. She paid for the lot in cash and we walked to a store so I could get some shoes and belts. She picked out what she liked and I was dreading wearing shoes.

I said, "Damn Garcia I can't wear shoes. I haven't worn shoes for a few years now. Do you have any idea how uncomfortable this will be?"

She said, "Shut up Nash. Do you have any idea how uncomfortable I'm going to be wearing a bra? If I can do it you can do it. We have to look right around here. You can't look like you just walked off of your boat. Maybe you'll attract a rich bitch that will want to keep you."

I said, "I already have one or two of those thanks."

Garcia said, "You do at that don't you. Oh well a couple of more can't hurt."

She paid for my accessories and we left the store. Garcia began to seriously look for outfits for herself and she tried on several things in different stores but none of them were right. She finally went into a store that was very expensive but the dresses were exactly what she was looking for. She started with three in the dressing room not to mention piles of lingerie. I was consulted on all of it and she finally had one outfit together that was perfect. She looked as sexy as I could imagine and very rich as well. One down and one to go I thought as more dresses and lingerie were brought to her. I had to admire her patience as the first outfit had taken two hours. The next one went quicker and when she was satisfied and I had voiced my approval it was well past lunch time. The delivery was arranged and we went to the coffee shop near the keno area for lunch.

We ordered and I said, "Garcia you have the patience of a saint. My feet are killing me from standing around waiting."

She said, "Mine are killing me too and I'm not looking forward to wearing heels. I'd better not drink because if I do I might break an ankle."

I said, "How do you want to work things tonight?"

She said, "We'll cruise the casino looking for him. We'll probably do some gambling as well to fit in. That's something you'll have to teach me. I know shit about it. Is craps hard to learn?"

I said, "Not really. I used to do some in the islands when I was younger. I can show you what to do."

She said, "When did you used to gamble?"

I said, "When I was young and had too much money for my own good. There was nothing like a pile of hundred dollar chips in front of you to attract the ladies. I actually made some money sometimes too."

We finished lunch and went up to our suite where Garcia proceeded to call her friend who owned the escort agency. The situation was explained and she said she would make some calls to find out what she could. We would hear from her later that afternoon. While Garcia was speaking to her friend the purchases we'd made began to be delivered and I accepted them at the door. We spent the afternoon putting things on hangers and getting used to the roles we would have to play that night.

We finished with our chore and Garcia said, "Vato, I'm going to wash up. Will you make us a reservation somewhere to eat tonight? Make it for about ten between the shows in the theatre."

I got us a reservation at ten-thirty at the best restaurant in the hotel and when Garcia came out of the bathroom she put her arms around me and said, "Sex slave will you make love to me again before we nap?"

I said, "That all depends."

She said, "Depends on what?"

I said, "On who gets the mirror view first. I liked that very much."

She said, "I liked it too. Maybe you should mirror the overhead in the stateroom of your boat."

I said, "I don't think so."

She said, "Then you can have the mirrors first this afternoon if you undress me."

I said, "That will work. Want to start now?"

She said, "Right now. That damn clock of mine is ticking again."

We undressed each other and made love until we fell asleep napping through the sunset. There were still streaks in the sky when we woke up and the lights of the city were beginning to come on. Garcia was first to stretch and leave the bed. She got up slowly and went to where our food supplies were, coming back with water and crackers and cheese. I sat up and took the water from her and she lay next to me and began cutting pieces of cheese and placing them on the crackers for us. We snacked for awhile sharing the bottled water and watching the lights of the city come on below us.

Garcia finally said, "I'm beginning to think that maybe I'm not a lesbian'.

I said, "What makes you say that. You've been having women for lovers for almost as long as I can remember."

She said, "That's true, but making love to them is nothing like making love to you."

I said, "Of course not. I'm a man, I'm different."

Garcia said, "I know you're a man but you're not like any other man I've had sex with."

I said, "Every one is different. Maybe I'm just sensitive."

She said, "Maybe it's because I've been in love with you since I was a girl."

I said, "Maybe so. We certainly have great chemistry together."

She said, "I'll say, you do things to me that just don't happen with anyone else. What's it like making love to Michelle?"

I said, "Great but different. Why don't you call her? You can find out if she's stolen your girlfriend from you."

Garcia said, "Shut up vato. I'm calling her right now. You men are all the same in one sense."

I said, "What's that?"

She said, "You all get more dominant and sarcastic after you make love to a woman. Girls don't do that. Making love softens us. It makes us vulnerable."

I said, "Perhaps that's the reason you choose women for lovers?"

Garcia said, "Perhaps that's it."

Garcia dialed the phone and called her finca. The help answered and there were a minute or two while the phone was taken to the girls. I didn't want to be in the room so I went to the living room where there was another TV and turned it on. I sat there with a cold beer and watched a replay of the nightly news while Garcia talked on the phone in the bedroom. The news was almost over when she came into the living room and handed me the phone after kissing me on the face.

I put it to my ear and said, "Hi there what's up?"

Michelle said, "I'm feeling wonderful thanks to you."

I said, "Did you have a good time with Lene'?"

She said, "Yes, making love to a woman is wonderful. It's completely different from making love to a man."

I said, "Garcia and I were just speaking about that same thing."

Michelle said, "I know she told me everything. She said you're turning her brain into pudding."

I said, "Well she didn't exactly put it that way to me but I'll take your word for it."

She said, "Well it's nothing you haven't done to me. I haven't been able to think straight since you made love to me at Hector's house."

I said, "Is that why you keep following me around?"

Michelle said, "I think so. You've turned me into something I never thought I could ever be and I love you for it."

I said, "That's good. Garcia has been making me shop with her for most of the day. She's been buying girlie clothes and I had to help."

Michelle said, "I heard. She said you have good taste."

I said, "What are you doing tonight? More hot tub and TV?"

Michelle said, "Most likely but I want you to remember I can't stop thinking about you. Garcia told me what you two are doing tonight and I want both of you to be careful."

I said, "We will. How's Lene'?"

Michelle said, "Lene' is fine. Do you want to talk to her?"

I said, "Not right now. I think Garcia should talk to her though."

Michelle said, "I think so too. Remember I love you and be careful."

I handed the phone to Garcia who went back to the bedroom with it.

She was back in half an hour and said, "Well we've got two very happy girl-friends in the islands. That's good. No one is jealous and I think we should get ready for this evening. Do you want to share the shower with me?"

I said, "Sure that sounds like fun. Afterwards you can tell me which socks to wear."

She said, "Only if you help me pick out my lingerie for the evening."

I said she had a deal and we took off what we were wearing and went to the shower together where we would begin our evening.

Garcia and I headed for the shower and had great fun soaping each other. When we were clean we went into the bedroom and Garcia lay on the bed while she dried her hair. I turned on the TV setting it to the channel that gave twenty four hour gamming instruction. She watched the program on craps and with a bit of instruction from me about which bets were for suckers she said she understood. We began to get dressed and Garcia started with her lingerie. It was added piece by piece and with a few suggestions from me she was as sexy as one could imagine when she was done. She added her robe and sat in front of the vanity to apply her makeup. I took much less time dressing and sat watching TV until she was done.

She came into the living room and said, "So how do I look?"

I said, "You look positively gorgeous and completely sexy. Garcia you dress up really well."

She said, "Will Wise want to get into my pants?"

I said, "Everyone will want to get into your pants starting with me."

She said, "You I want in them but you'll have to wait and you look positively fantastic in your suit. All of the women will want you."

It was just after ten so we took the elevator downstairs and went to the restaurant I'd chosen. We were seated immediately and I loved looking at all of the men who were eyeballing Garcia. I scanned the restaurant for Wise but he was no where to be seen. We had a wonderful dinner and after finishing we went to the casino to cruise and look for our target. We played craps and Garcia won some and said she liked winning. We searched for a couple of hours but saw nothing of wise. Garcia pulled out her phone in one of the bars and called her friend who ran the escort company.

She said when she rang off, "Wise is definitely here at Caesars but he's been keeping company with a whore from that Prom Queens agency. He's booked her for the second night and from what my friend said they have stayed in their room."

I said, "That's something we haven't thought of. How will we get them out?"

Garcia said, "I don't know. The hotel here says he hasn't booked tickets for any shows and he hasn't signed any markers for chips."

I said, "Anything else?"

Garcia said, "One thing. He's playing golf tomorrow. My friend knows the owner of the escort service he uses and says she'll find out more for us from the girl he's screwing",

I said, "What do you want to do now?"

Garcia said, "Well we should stay in the casino on the off chance he comes out of his hole. Let's go gamble and have fun and maybe we can make some money."

We spent the rest of the night until about four in the morning playing games and did pretty well at them. Garcia had a knack for rolling the dice and I had a knack for putting our money in the right places. We played until we were tired and cashed in our chips. We had made a few thousand and as we were leaving the cashiers cage I saw Wise walking in the casino with the girl he had rented. He went to a horseshoe shaped bar and Garcia and I went and took seats opposite him and his escort to observe. He didn't take long to notice Garcia and he looked her over obviously enjoying what he was seeing. The girl he was with didn't seem to have much interest in him but she definitely looked expensive. Garcia played her part well even winking at him once. I gave Wise plenty of opportunity by taking two trips to the bathroom hoping he would go and talk to her. He seemed satisfied with the girl he was with and Garcia was only able to make eye contact with him. They went and played craps for awhile and we watched from the bar. He seemed good at loosing and they didn't play for long. They disappeared from the casino floor and we called it a night and went to our suite.

We were both tired when I opened the door and we went inside.

The sun was streaking the sky outside and Garcia put her arms around me and said, "How would you like to take all of my clothes off?"

I said, "That would be nice. Are you going to take advantage of me when I'm done?"

She said, "I certainly am. My clock is ticking again and I've been excited ever since I put on all of this lingerie. It's pretty sexy when you get used to it."

I said, "Well removing it will be my pleasure."

I began to undress her and she started with my clothes at the same time. We fell into bed and had a wonderful time making love until the sun was coming over the mountains. I got up and closed the drapes blacking out the room so we could sleep and we passed out until one in the afternoon.

I was first up and we dressed for brunch downstairs in the coffee shop. When we went back to our suite Garcia called her friend at the escort service and spoke for a long time.

When she was finished she came into the bedroom where I was reading and said, "It seems that Wise is a pretty bad boy."

I said, "I already knew that."

She said, "He's worse than we thought. My friend says he's had a different girl almost each night since he's been here and the girls will only see him once. Apparently he's pretty rough with them and they don't like it much. Word has gotten around about him and he has to pay more and more for their company. He's booked for tonight but my friend is going to send me to him Thursday night. Her friend who owns Prom Queens is definitely pissed at him for being rough with her girls and wants to get back at him."

I said, "You're going to be his escort?"

Garcia said, "I am. He likes to stay in his room and drink with the girls and that will be the perfect opportunity to get close enough to slip something nasty in his drink."

I said, "What will you give him?"

Garcia said, "A good old fashioned Mickey Finn, Chloral Hydrate exactly. It'll be good for sixteen hours out and a very bad headache later when he wakes up."

I said, "That's pretty dangerous don't you think?"

Garcia said, "A little but you'll be in the next room. She's going to arrange it with the hotel for you to be in that room should I need a rescue. Besides I'd love to Kung Fu his sorry ass if he gets rough with me."

I said, "I'm sure Michelle would like that too."

Garcia said, "Today we need to buy a good sized steamer trunk to put him in for the ride to the airport. We can't exactly put him on a luggage cart and wheel him unconscious through the lobby can we?"

I said, "OK but I want to be close and have a key to the room if you should need me."

She said, "You'll have it. He's playing golf today and we can find the trunk we'll need. Tonight we'll do as we did last night and watch the casino again. Who knows? He might come looking for me there. If he does we'll bag him tonight and be out of here."

Garcia and I left the hotel and went shopping for an appropriate trunk for our target. It was delivered that afternoon and our plan seemed to be coming together. We dressed and ate in the sushi bar that night and played the games of chance on the casino floor. Garcia was again good at rolling the dice and we did well for our efforts. We saw Wise again that night and watched him from a distance. He was with another girl and she seemed no more pleased with him than the girl from the night before. This night he did come and speak with Garcia while I was in the bathroom and she told him she was for hire and told him how to make arrangements for her services the following night.

He was just walking away when I was coming back to our places at the bar and as I sat down Garcia said, "What a scum bag. I'd almost rather not dose him. That man needs a good ass beating. This is going to be a pleasure to take him down. I still think we should take him out to the dessert and leave him there."

I said, "Except for the fact that X wants him."

Garcia said, "I've been wondering about that. Why is X so interested in him? He's just a small timer that needs a lesson or two."

I said, "It's not for us to decide. If X wants him he'll have him. It's what has to be done."

We finished our drinks and went to our suite where I took care of Garcia's clock and we slept until well after dawn. Garcia called her friend after noon and Wise had already called and requested her for the evening. A key to the room next to his was delivered to us before cocktail hour and I checked the room before dinner. The key was right and there was an extra key that would let me into his room if trouble was to start. I felt confident that if Garcia were to have trouble I would be able to come to the rescue and our plan was officially in motion. Garcia dressed the part for her rendezvous with Wise and she went to his door at nine. I walked with her and took my place in the next room where I got out the cheap stethoscope which would help me listen to what was happening through the wall. I put myself in a comfortable position and listened as Garcia knocked on his door.

Wise answered the door and I listened as they spoke as she entered the room. The cash was settled on and once that was over I heard drinks being poured and they settled into small talk which was mostly about what a rich person he was. I could tell he was trying to get comfortable with her and Garcia kept the conversation light and professional. More drinks were poured and I could hear Garcia preparing them at the bar. I knew he was being dosed and during the second drink he began to try and take her clothes from her. She was being adamant that things should go slow and he didn't like what she was telling her.

He got more and more forceful and just when I was getting nervous and prepared myself to go and take him down I heard Garcia say, "Oh fuck it! Your ass is mine!"

I heard a hard blow and then a body hit the floor. I straightened up immediately and went to the door of the room I was in. I opened it and looked out just as Garcia did the same thing. I closed the door to my room and went to his. He was there on the floor with blood coming from his nose.

I asked, "What did you hit him with?"

Garcia said, "The palm of my hand at the wrist. Takes them right out. He'll sleep now and I hope he bleeds to death. What an ass hole."

I said, "You'll get no argument from me on that one. I wish I had hit him."

She said, "Have at him if you want or you can wait until later. Let's get the trunk in here and pack up the rest of his things. He's checking out tonight."

We got the trunk and jammed him inside of it. Garcia called the airport and had them get the jet ready. She called her friend and told her the mission was accomplished while I went through the room collecting his clothes and things. I opened a drawer and under a few shirts there was about a hundred thousand dollars in hundreds all wrapped up and waiting to be put into a suitcase. Garcia looked at the pile of cash and whistled.

She said, "Good we can use some of this to pay for things and tip our friends that helped. The rest can go to Michelle and buy jet fuel."

I dragged the trunk and the suitcases to the next room and Garcia made sure we left no trail that could be followed. She went back and cleaned out our suite while I waited. An hour passed before she returned and I was glad she did. I called for a bellman and one with a cart showed up shortly. I helped the bellman with the luggage and we took the whole pile to the van that was waiting to take us to the airport. The whole thing had gone down smoothly and the jet was ready when we pulled up next to it on the tarmac. I loaded our things into the tail of the plane and the trunk came in the cabin with us. I strapped it in place as Garcia taxied down the ramp to the runway where we waited to get our instructions from the tower. They came quick enough and Garcia pushed the throttles forward and the jet bolted down the runway. When we were airborne and headed south for Mexican airspace I looked at my watch and it was a little after one am. I went to the flight deck and we kissed and shook hands for a job done well.

I said, "Good job my love. Your first job as an escort and you stole your client and his money."

She said, "That bastard, he had it coming. Paid for or not he's got a bad way with women. No wonder he had to keep Michelle hostage. You'd better let him out so he doesn't suffocate. Tie him to the couch and make sure he doesn't bleed on it please."

I went to the cabin and took Wise from the trunk. I stretched his greasy ass out and used the seatbelts to secure him tightly. I tied his hands with some straps I'd bought for that purpose and he stayed where I tied him.

I went back to the flight deck and said, "He's secure and definitely not going anywhere."

Garcia said, "Good, I don't want him to be waking up and giving us any trouble."

I said, "By the way how much did he pay for you?"

Garcia said, "Why vato are you going to buy me sometime?"

I said, "Nope, I was just curious."

Garcia said, "Ten grand to stay until morning. I think he'll get more than his money's worth."

I said, "Not bad, not bad."

She said, "Would you pay ten grand for me?"

I said, "I don't have that kind of money. Are you going to start charging me?"

She said, "No I'm not but as soon as this jet is at altitude in Mexican air space there's something I want you to do."

I said, "Clock ticking again?"

She said, "Not at all. I just want to make love to you."

I said, "My pleasure. By the way where are we going on the way to Martinique?"

She said. "We'll stop in Monterrey to refuel and again in Kingston. That will put us into Martinique at about five or six PM Martinique time. We'll give the scumbag to Hector's people and fly to the Bahamas to get my plane back. Lene' and Michelle will have to take Lene's turbo prop plane to Martinique to be there on Sunday. We'd be able to get them but we can't fly 24/7 because we'll have to rest."

Garcia was true to her word and as soon as the jet was at altitude and pointed towards Monterrey she set the automatic pilot and after throwing a couple of blankets over Wise we made passionate love in the cabin of the jet.

I flew most of the way to Monterrey and was really getting to enjoy being at the controls. Garcia was there with me and it made for a lot of conversation. She eventually napped while I flew the jet and we switched off after she had the plane over the Gulf heading for Kingston. Calls were made to all concerned and they were all happy our mission had been a success.

We were about an hour from Martinique when I went to the galley to get some cold drinks for us and saw Wise had his eyes open and was looking around the plane with fear on his face.

I called to Garcia and she came back to the cabin and looking at Wise said, "Hello scumbag remember me?"

Wise just looked at her with fright and I said, "I'm David Nash and if you believe in god you should start praying. This is Garcia. We told you to leave Michelle alone but you weren't smart enough for that. Now you're on a plane ride and it's most likely your last one. How does it feel to be kidnapped?"

Garcia ripped off his gag harshly and said, "Wise you fucked with the wrong people. You should have known when we sent your man back to you with his hand in a jar. That was just a warning. Now your life has just turned to shit."

Wise said, "I have money, lots of it."

Garcia said, "We took what you had in Vegas. You're buying the fuel for this flight."

He said, "No I have millions. I'll pay you to let me go. Anything you want."

I said, "Sorry money won't work in this situation. Have you got anything else to trade?"

Garcia said, "Sure what else do you have?"

I got a pencil and paper and began to write down the accounts and holdings Wise was telling us about. It was substantial and I hoped we could get it all into Michelle's hands.

He finished with his list and Garcia said, "I don't think that will be enough. There's the X factor involved here."

Wise said, "What's that?"

Garcia said, "Our friend Mr. X. You might have heard of him."

Wise said, "The Mr. X. That person is just a myth."

I looked at Garcia and said,

"Get that Garcia, he thinks X is a myth."

Garcia said, "X will love this. Look you stupid shit there are powers you don't understand at play here. I assure you X is real and he doesn't much like cowboys like you fucking with his territory which is most of this hemisphere. Whatever you've heard is wrong and now you've pissed him off. We would have just killed you and been done with it but now you have to talk to the man and he won't be very nice."

Wise said, "Please no, I'll do anything you want. I've made a mistake please help me."

Garcia said, "And there's the Garcia factor. One of your men shot my girl-friend. That's really bad."

I said, "Don't forget the Nash factor. My boat needs a lot of repairs from your men shooting at me before Michelle blew it out of the water."

He said, "Michelle did that?"

I said, "Yes she did. She's become very proficient with weapons lately."

Garcia said, "Yes she's definitely not shy either. She took my knife from me just the other day and sliced the ear off of one of your men who tried to Para-sail her off of St Croix. She'd love to see you dead but there's Mr. X and we always do what he wants."

Wise was really frightened by now and Garcia and I headed to the flight deck to prepare for landing the jet on the island of Martinique. We were on the ground soon enough and Hector's men were there waiting for us with a van. They took custody of Wise and we went in a car to the hotel where we would stay for Michelle's shoots. We were only going to get some sleep and we woke early the next morning to go back to the airport and fly up the chain of islands to Nassau where we would change planes again. It was Saturday and while we were flying we knew Lene' and Michelle would be on their way to Martinique. Garcia and I were both excited to see our girlfriends and we would have a great reunion that night on Martinique.

We arrived in Nassau on schedule and put ourselves into Garcia's plane for the trip back to Martinique. It had been a very long day when we finally landed in Martinique again and we found our girls in the bar at the hotel waiting for us. They were on their feet when we walked in and Michelle leapt into my arms kissing me all over my face while Lene' and Garcia were locked into a very tight embrace. We all went to our suite and the girls had prepared for our arrival by stocking the bar and having food already there for us. We began to eat and drink being happy our trip was over. There were a thousand questions about what went on and we patiently answered them all.

CHAPTER FIFTEEN

Michelle first asked, "Do you have my ex?"

I said, "We do, he's being held in a dungeon here on the island and being fed bread and water."

Lene said, "How did you capture him finally?"

Garcia said, "I dressed up to be his nightly whore and dosed his drink to put him out."

I said, "Not before getting tired of his shit and knocking him cold."

Michelle said, "How'd you do that?"

Garcia said, "I turned around and Kung Fu'd him and he was out for twelve hours. When he woke up all he could do was lie there and beg for us to let him go. He offered us the world and Nash wrote it down so now we know where all of his money is."

Michelle said, "Can I go where he is being held? I want a piece of him myself."

I said, "I think that could be arranged. Just don't hurt your hands for the shoots and remember X wants him in one piece."

She said, "X wants him?"

I said, "Yes you weren't supposed to know but X called me and we're to bring

Wise to him a week from tomorrow. He wants to meet you too Michelle. In fact he's adamant about meeting you."

Garcia said, "Enough. I've been flying for two days and I'm tired and I want to go to bed and make love to my girl."

She took Lene' by the hand and they went to their bedroom and Michelle and I turned off the lights and went to our room where we undressed and got into bed.

Michelle said, "I've missed you terribly Mr. Hedberg."

I said, "I've missed you too Mrs. Hedberg."

She said, "Do you still want to make love to me after Garcia?"

I said, "Of course I do. You're my girl remember."

Michelle said, "I remember. I had a wonderful time with Lene' but she was no substitute for you. I thought about you all of the time you were away."

I said, "I thought about you all of the time too. I really missed you. Will you make love to me now?"

Michelle and I began to kiss and we made love for a very long time.

I knew I was really missed the next morning when instead of getting out of bed Michelle grabbed me and had her way with me again. It was Sunday morning and I needed to go and see if the boat was put back in the water per instructions. Lene' and Garcia declined the invitation to go along so Michelle and I went together. All was well with the boat so we sailed it around to where we had reserved a slip for it so we could live on it during the shoots. Michelle wanted to go and see her ex so I made a call and drove her there but not before she piled all of her weapons into a bag and took them with us. We found Hector's friends and they took us into the old Spanish house they lived in. Michelle dressed in her mercenary gear for the meeting with her ex. I understood what she was up to and didn't object. We were walked to the dungeon and before we went inside the lights were turned on. Wise was there on the floor and looked up as we came into the stone room. He was chained to the dirty floor and looked like he'd spent the night in hell which I'm very sure ran a close second to where he was being kept.

Michelle walked up to him and said, "What do you think about me now you evil piece of shit?"

Wise looked at her hardly believing what he was seeing.

Michelle said, "Nash can I kill him?"

Wise turned white and I said, "No you'd better not. X wants him remember. Besides you don't want him to have it go quickly. I think he should suffer before he swims with the sharks."

Michelle said, "You're right. What was I thinking? A long slow death would be much better. How about a few of Garcia's S&M lesbians going to work on him with a propane torch and some vise grips?"

Wise cleared his throat and said, "Please Michelle. Don't let them kill me. I love you."

Michelle went off saying, "Oh I forgot, you did this all because you love me! That explains it! I'm clear now! Nash when you love something you smother it and scare it half to death by telling it you'll kill it unless it does what you want! I'm glad that's cleared up. Wise you son of a bitch! If X didn't want you I'd open you up right here like a can of beans and let you die trying to stuff your guts back inside of yourself!"

Michelle pulled her Japanese Oyabun knife from her belt and started for Wise brandishing it menacingly. Wise's eyes got big when he saw the fire in her eyes and I wondered if I'd be able to get Wise to X intact.

Wise said, "Please don't kill me Michelle. Please don't kill me. Please let me live."

Michelle got close to him and said, "I'm not going to kill you, you filthy bastard. I'm your worst nightmare come to life in front of you and if I have anything to say about it you'll live the rest of your soon to be very short life in horrible pain. I'll have you eaten by rats from your feet up you son of a bitch! Remember this is what you turned me into. I was a nice girl before you met me. What do you think now?"

Wise was pissing in his pants by now and Michelle was looking pleased with herself for accomplishing the reaction she wanted. As Wise lay on the floor whimpering Michelle put her knife under his nose and lifted his head with the razor sharp point. Wise looked at her as she put the tip of her knife into his nostril and flicked it up and out. His nostril came open for about an inch and he screamed in pain.

He held his bleeding nose between his hands and Michelle said, "That's for having me kidnapped by those bastards and for having your friend shoot Lene'. You're lucky I'm busy this week because I'm enjoying what I'm doing. You stay here and think about it. If it wasn't for X I'd make a jewelry bag from your ball sack."

Michelle got up and after spitting on Wise she and I left the room and the iron door closed behind us. When we got upstairs I told Hector's men to make sure he didn't bleed to death and Michelle and I walked to the car while she took off her webbing.

She got into the car and said, "Nash my love I feel a whole lot better. It's a nice afternoon and I want some ice cream. Let's go get Garcia and Lene' and get some. Then we can hunt for dinner and cook on the rail of the boat after cocktails."

I said, "That sounds like just the thing. I've been missing cooking with you and I'm in the mood for some fresh flounder."

We drove to the hotel and found Lene' and Garcia who were relaxing in the living room of the suite. We asked them about ice cream and they thought it would be a great idea. There was a stand near the harbor and we went there to choose the flavors we wished. We wandered to the boat after being served and the question of accommodations came up while we sat in the cockpit eating our ice cream. It was agreed we would all move back to the boat and continue living as we had done when we were looking for our friend X. We finished our snacks and went back to the hotel for our things to move them to the boat. When we were all moved in it was time to hunt for dinner and Lene' and I went to do that chore while Garcia and Michelle worked on the rest of the meal in the galley.

We were eating our grilled fish and veggies when Michelle said, "I went and saw my ex today."

Garcia said, "Did you kill him?"

Michelle said, "No I just went to scare him. I thought it was fair for all of the years I lived in fear of him."

Lene' said, "What did you do?"

Michelle said, "I dressed in my webbing to show him who I was now. It scared the hell out of him. He was pissing in his pants when I left."

I said, "Not to mention holding his nose together."

Garcia said, "You cut him up?"

Michelle said, "I split his nose open for getting me kidnapped and Lene' shot.

It should leave a good scar if he manages to live."

Just then Patricia Owens walked up on the dock and after saying hello to us handed Michelle a catalogue of the swimwear she had previously modeled. Her picture was on the cover of the new catalogue and she looked every bit the sexy model in the picture.

I said, "Michelle you look fantastic, this is great!"

Garcia got up and hugged Michelle saying, "That's my Chiquita. She's the sexiest bitch on the planet."

Lene' got up and hugged Michelle and Patricia said, "Michelle we're getting unbelievable response to your photographs. I'd like to represent you professionally. Will you sign with my agency for a year?"

Michelle said, "You'll have to speak with my business manager."

Patricia said, "And that would be?"

Michelle said, "Garcia of course. Would that be all right Garcia?"

Garcia said, "Of course Chiquita. It would be my pleasure. Patricia can we talk terms during this shoot?"

Patricia said, "I'll be happy to Garcia. How about lunch on Tuesday?"

Garcia nodded that it would be fine and Patricia got up from the cockpit and left the boat. I said, "Garcia it looks like you're going into a legitimate line of work. Will you have time for it?"

Garcia said, "I'll make time vato. Anything for Chiquita. I'm going to make her very rich."

Michelle said, "Thank you Garcia and you don't have to make me rich. I just need enough money to keep Nash from paying all of the bills."

Lene' said, "Michelle I'm so proud of you. I know you're going to be a big deal in the modeling world, congratulations."

I said, "Yes congratulations. Hold on I'll be right back."

I got up and went below where I reached into the back of the fridge and grabbed the bottle of cold champagne I kept for special occasions. I got four glasses and headed back to the cockpit where I opened the bottle and poured our glasses full. I passed them around and said, "To Michelle Murphy. A very beautiful and extremely dangerous woman. Cheers."

Garcia stood and said, "To the sexiest merc I've ever known, may the cover of Soldier of Fortune Magazine fall to you."

Lene' said, "Por La Reina de Caribe. May you rule well my sister."

Michelle said, "This has been the best day I've ever had and I owe it all to you. Thank you very much and does this get me out of helping with the dishes?"

We all laughed and I said, "Tonight only then it's back to work for you."

Michelle said, "Work, shit I have to sit on the sand and look pretty tomorrow. I need to stop drinking and get to bed early."

We all laughed and finished our champagne together before Garcia and I took the dishes to the galley and started our cleanup.

I was washing and she was drying and I said, "It's nice that things are working out for Michelle. It's easy to see she's very happy."

Garcia said, "It certainly is vato. What about you? Are you happy?"

I said, "I'm very happy. Just don't book her too many shoots. I need some quality ocean time with her."

Garcia said, "Vato, I think you should marry this girl and have children with her."

I said, "Do you really think that Garcia? Don't you think I'm too old for having a family?"

Garcia said, "I just want the one I'm going to have with you to have some family. I might be pregnant."

I said, "Garcia are you? How do you know?"

She said, "I should have gotten my period and I didn't. I'm also feeling really weird inside and my clock has stopped ticking. My female parts are talking to me vato."

I said, "Damn, that didn't take much. We only had sex a few times."

Garcia said, "All it takes is once vato. Remember I haven't had sex with a man for years. You just might have stirred things up enough to get me pregnant."

I said, "Are you OK with this?"

She said, "I am. I want this very much. And I want my baby to have blond hair and blue eyes vato."

I said, "Garcia you must be pregnant. I've never heard you talk this way."

Garcia and I kissed as we finished the dishes and went back to the cockpit where Lene' and Michelle were enjoying the evening. We sat on the cushions with them and Michelle said, "Nash I'm going to bed will you join me?"

I smiled and Michelle stood up and taking me by the hand we went below to our stateroom where we undressed and got into bed.

We held each other and Michelle said, "I want you to know I think meeting you was the best thing that could have ever happened to me. If anyone has ever been saved it's definitely me. Ever since I met you my life has been exciting and wonderful."

I kissed her and said, "Even when you were kidnapped?"

Michelle said, "Well that wasn't too much fun but it was exciting and it will give me a great story to tell our children."

I said, "Do you really want to have children with me Michelle?"

She said, "Yes I do. I can't think of a better person to be the father than you. If I have children that are half as wonderful as you are I'll be completely happy."

I said, "Even if they are as wild as I was?"

Michelle said, "Especially if they're as wild as you were. I'm pretty wild myself. I've turned into someone I never thought I could be. I used to be afraid of things but I'm not anymore."

I said, "You certainly aren't. You get a look in your eye sometimes that scares me. You had it today when you confronted your ex."

She said, "I know I did. It was fantastic to get some payback."

I said, "Well you certainly deserved it. I don't feel sorry for him in the least."

Michelle said, "I don't either. He's going to get everything he deserves. Mr. Hedberg?"

I said, "Yes?"

She said, "Will you make love to me now? I don't want to talk any more."

We made love and went to sleep to get up the next morning and go let Michelle have her picture taken on the beach. Garcia was up first the following morning and had already made the coffee for the rest of us. We ate together in the cockpit of the boat and cleaned up to go with Michelle to her shoot. It was the same as before and we watched her back while she posed endlessly for the camera. We went with her every day and watched for trouble but there was none.

Garcia cut a very respectable deal for Michelle with Patricia and it was promised that Michelle would be able to pick and choose the shoots she wished to do. Hector came to the Island at the end of the week and we got ready for our rendezvous with Mr. X. It was decided Hector's men would transport Wise to the coordinates and Hector would sail there with us. I prepped the boat for our sail to the spot and we left the afternoon before we were supposed to be there. The watches were split between all of us and we were at the L&L before dawn. When we arrived I woke everyone up and Michelle and Lene' made breakfast for all of us. We ate while we waited for Mr. X and watched the sun come up together. Hector's men were there as well and when it got light we could see the boat Wise was on bobbing near us on the water. It was just after six when we saw a very large vintage flying boat coming towards us from the west and we watched as it circled our two boats and landed on the water. The flying boat was magnificent and looked completely restored. I had never seen one like it except in old movies and we all admired the way our friend X had chosen to travel. Hector's men put a boat over the side to transport us from our boat to Mr. X and we were all excited to say the least. I went in the second load and once inside of the amphibious plane I sat in a beautiful living room and was given coffee by one of the two lovely female attendants. We sat together as they left the room and X came in from the rear of the aircraft and we all stood up. He smiled when he saw us and Hector was the first to speak.

He said, "X old friend it's wonderful to see you."

X said, "Hector it's nice to see you as well. Garcia you look beautiful as always."

Garcia said, "Thank you X, you remember Nash of course?"

I said, "X its been a long time. It's nice to see you again."

X said, "Nash you look great. How's the retirement."

I said, "Wonderful. It'll be nice to get back to it."

X laughed and said, "And this of course must be Michelle. You are very, very beautiful. You realize you've turned the whole Caribbean upside down don't you?"

Michelle said, "It's nice to meet you and I'm sorry for the trouble I've caused."

X said, "It's not your fault. Wise has had to go for a long time. Thank you for giving me an excuse to get rid of him."

They finished shaking hands and Lene' walked up to X and putting her arms around his neck and kissing him on the cheek said, "Hello daddy, it's wonderful to see you. I wish you'd visit more often."

X said, "Hello my beautiful daughter. How's your shoulder?"

217

I said loudly, "Daddy? Lene', you're X's daughter?"

Garcia said, "This is a surprise! Lene' is there anything else I should know about you?"

Hector said, "X old man I never knew you had a daughter."

X said, "No one did. It's been kept a secret since she was born. It just would have been too dangerous for her. Especially when she was young."

I said, "La Reina I can't believe this. All of these years and no one knew."

Michelle said, "Who is La Reina?"

Garcia said, "La Reina de Navar Michelle. That's who Lene' was years ago."

Michelle said, "What does it mean?"

Lene' said, "It means the snow queen. Daddy gave me that nickname when I was a child because of my white hair. Every one knew me by that when I was moving odd things around the Caribbean. Nash remembered me from when I was a teenager. Now there are only five people who know me by that name."

X said, "And there are only four people in this room who know Garcia's first name. Garcia would you like to make it five?"

Garcia said, "No I wouldn't X. Damn you!"

X said, "Garcia it's only fair. I insist."

Michelle said. "Garcia am I going to find out your first name?"

Garcia said, "Yes but if you tell anyone you're dead meat Chiquita."

I said, "Go on Garcia you'd better tell her and get it over with."

Garcia said, "Shut up vato! Michelle, my first name is Estrella. It means Star in Spanish."

Michelle said, "Garcia that's a beautiful name. I'm proud to know it."

Garcia said, "You can have it Chiquita. It's just so not me."

I said, "X what about the Wise situation."

X said, "Michelle what do you want me to do with him?"

Michelle said, "I don't know. What do you suggest?"

X said, "A slow death would be good. The sharks are always hungry."

Michelle said, "He does deserve it but I've got enough bodies on my conscious already. What else could we do with him?"

X said, "I was already going to give you his money for some compensation. What if we drop him in the jungle and let him fight his way out. If he makes it out I'll make sure he never works in the business again."

Michelle said, "I wouldn't mind having his money and thank you. What if we put him on an island which has food and water where there are no people for him to torment? I don't think he should stay there forever but it should be long enough for him to learn a good lesson."

X said, "Not a bad idea. Michelle you're a much more benevolent person than I am. I would have just fed him to the sharks."

Michelle said, "Then it's the island for him. He kept me for five years so I think five years would be good for him."

X said, "Five years it is. I know just the place to put him. No one goes there because it used to be a leper colony. Isolation will be good for the bastard."

Garcia said, "Good choice Chiquita, let the bastard live on bananas for a few years."

X said, "Hector can we rely on your men to take him there?"

Hector said, "Sure. I know the place you're talking about. He'll be on his way before lunch."

X said, "Good this has been a great meeting. I'm sorry to say I have to go but there are at least five governments looking for me."

I said, "Only five? X are you mellowing out in your old age?"

X said, "No more than you are Nash. I suggest you marry this girl before you get too old."

I said, "I will if you'll come to the wedding."

X said, "Michelle did you hear that? It sounded a lot like a proposal to me what do you think?"

Michelle said, "X does that mean you'll come to the wedding?"

X said, "I'd be pleased to stand with Nash at your wedding. What do you say?"

Michelle said, "Then I say yes if Garcia and Lene' will stand with me."

I said, "What just happened here?"

Michelle said, "Mr. Hedberg, you just proposed to me and I just accepted."

Garcia said, "Vato you're going to get married that's what just happened, con-gratulations you've become engaged."

I moved towards Michelle and took her into my arms and kissed her while our friends hugged us and applauded.

X said, "Time to go. I can smell the coast guard coming. Lene' my lovely daughter give me a kiss and I'll see you at the wedding."

Lene' said, "Goodbye daddy, I love you very much."

X left the room and we all were shuttled back to the Mo Cuishle where we settled in. Hector gave his men the name of the island Wise was to be taken to and we watched as they motored away from us. The big flying boat started its motors and turned into the wind and was airborne in a few more minutes. When the plane was out of sight I let the sails out and we headed back to Martinique.

Once the boat was sailing nicely and we were all in the cockpit with the drinks in our hands Hector and Garcia had made for us I said, "Lene' my dear is there anything else you'd like to tell us about yourself?"

Garcia said, "Girl that was a serious surprise. I'm with Nash is there anything else?"

Lene' said, "No there's nothing else but I love you all very much. Actually I'm surprised daddy would allow you to know. It's a secret I've had to keep all of my life."

Michelle said, "Well your secret is safe with us La Reina."

Hector said, "Too bad we have to keep it a secret. Maria would love to know."

Garcia said, "Michelle now that you're a rich woman what are you going to do?"

Michelle said, "I think I'd like to invest all of the money from Wise and keep modeling until I get tired of the attention."

I said, "Anything else?"

Michelle said, "Yes there is Mr. Hedberg. I want to buy you a bigger sailboat to replace this one. The next one has to be large enough to have children grow up on it."

I said, "Children eh? Garcia was telling me a few days ago I should have children with you."

Michelle said, "That's what she told me too. I thought it was a good idea seeing that she's probably pregnant by you."

I said, "She told you?"

Michelle said, "Of course she told me. Garcia tells me everything. You should get used to that Nash."

Hector said, "Ay yi, yi. This is getting to be like a soap opera on the TV. Garcia are you really pregnant?"

Garcia said, "I think so Hector and you can tell Maria but that's as far as it goes OK?"

I said, "Mrs. Hedberg when do I get my new boat?"

Michelle said, "As soon as I get my money and we decide what to buy my love. Can you wait that long?"

I said, "I can if we can be on vacation for awhile."

Michelle said, "I'd love a vacation. Can we go back to the island where we met and start from there?"

I said, "I'd like that. We did leave on short notice and you have a wedding to plan."

Michelle said, "I do at that and you have a family to plan. I don't want Garcia to get too much ahead of me. I want my children to know their steps."

It was a long beat to the wind to get back to Martinique. Michelle and I steered us through the entrance to the harbor the next morning and we were happy her ordeal was finally over. Garcia and Lene' gathered their things and took a taxi to the airport to fly back to the finca on Little Inagua. Hector went to the airport with them as well to catch a flight back to Miami and his ride to Key West. There were too many hugs and kisses goodbye but our friends had their lives to go back to and we had a life to start. We would spend the night together on the boat alone for the first time in what seemed like a year. Michelle and I would then sail the twelve hundred miles north north west to the islands that made up Bimini starting in a couple of days and we went to dinner together that night for the first time without our guns.

We had drinks at the bar and were just seated at our table when I said, "Michelle that was quite an adventure. I'm going to enjoy going back to being retired but will you be able to stand it?"

Michelle said, "I'm very ready for it. I've had enough excitement for awhile thanks."

I said, "Do you want to stop anywhere along the way?"

She said, "No, I just want to be with you. I've disrupted peoples lives for too long and I think its time we left them alone for a bit."

I said, "When do you want to leave here?"

She said, "What if we provision the boat tomorrow and sail the following day after we go to the fuel dock?"

I said, "That's fine with me. Let's decide what we're having for dinner."

We perused our menus and made our choices. We danced after dinner and staggered back to the boat to make love and get up the next morning. I was the first up and made the coffee for us. It was interesting waking up not on my guard and I liked the casualness of it. So many weeks of sleeping with my pistol under my pillow had been tiring and I began to settle back into my retirement. I had nothing to do that day except some basic maintenance and the provisioning of the boat. I would do both with Michelle and I hoped the mechanics of the engine and generator would come easily to her. There was also the water maker which needed a new membrane and I would have to look at that as well.

Michelle was awake in another hour and when she came up to the cockpit with a cup of coffee she said, "Good morning my love. Thank you for letting me sleep in."

I said, "Not at all gorgeous. I was just thinking about the chores we need to do on the boat today."

She said, "What are those?"

I said, "First I'd like to make breakfast and eat with you here in the cockpit. Second we need to do some maintenance on the generator and the diesel and the water maker. After that it will most likely be lunch time. Would you like to go for a nice lunch on land?"

She said, "Lunch sounds nice but you'll have to teach me about the other things. I'm afraid I don't know much about motors and water makers but I'm willing to learn."

I said, "Good for you. There's not much to it. Really it's just changing the oil and the oil filters. The water maker needs a new membrane."

Michelle said, "What does the membrane do?"

I said, "That's what takes the salt out of the sea water making it fresh for us to drink."

She asked, "Where do we get one?"

I said, "I always carry a couple of spares because they're so important. This is the last one so we'll have to order two more."

Michelle said, "What do you want for breakfast my soon to be husband?"

I said, "Do you really want to marry me?"

She said, "Yes I do. I think you'll be the perfect husband. When I get tired of you I'll send you off sailing by yourself and I'll stay with Garcia and Lene'."

I said, "Good thinking. My regular life might be to boring for you. You saw the way I was living on the island. It's romantic but pretty much the same each day."

Michelle said, "Well I'll just have to make your life a little more exciting then unless you really like the boys at the pub for company all of the time."

I said, "I like that all right but I have always wanted a woman to sail with and you have your shoots to run off to. I think it'll work out."

Michelle said, "Good, now answer my question. What do you want for breakfast?'

I said, "Sorry, how about bacon and eggs? We can make them together."

Michelle kissed me and we went below to cook what was in the 'fridge. I went about pulling out what we wanted and Michelle began to make a list of what we had on board while I began to fry the bacon.

Michelle said, "We need to go to the store for provisions after lunch. Do you want to sail tomorrow?"

I said, "Tomorrow will be OK unless you want to stay another day."

She said, "Not necessary, I'm tired of this island and I want to be on the water headed for Bimini."

I said, "Then we'll sail with the morning tide after we get fuel and water. I'm looking forward to having someone to share the watch with."

The bacon was done and Michelle took over the pan to scramble our eggs while I blotted the excess grease from the cooked bacon. It was all done in another minute and we set the cockpit table to eat from."

We sat to eat and she said, "Would you mind terribly if I buy some things for the boat?"

I said, "What kind of things?"

She said, "We could use some new napkins and some place mats would be nice."

I said, "Sure the ones I have are pretty old. What about some new towels and sheets?"

Michelle said, "I'd like that. You don't mind do you? I've not had a say in what my surroundings were like for a long time. Everything was always to my ex's taste."

I said, "You go right ahead and make the boat comfortable for you. I've been living like a bachelor for far too long. I don't mind if you nest just don't make the boat too frilly."

She said, "I won't I promise. Do you want to go with me?"

I said, "No why don't you go on your own after we go to the grocery. You can surprise me with what you get. Do you need my credit card or money?"

She said, "No I still have money from my ex and Garcia gave me what was left from his hotel room after she took out for the jet and the fuel."

I said, "How much do you have?"

She said. "About eighty grand all together. It's a lot of money to have on the boat."

I said, "What do you want to do with it?"

She said, "I don't know. How do you handle your money?"

I said, "I use American Express. My interest is deposited in my account and I draw on that. My account is pretty big."

She said, "How big?"

I said, "I usually have about seventy or eighty grand in it. When it gets to a hundred I have the extra recycled into my funds by buying more. You might want to open an account for yourself with what you have. Remember you'll be getting the funds from your ex's accounts from Mr. X."

She asked, "How much does he have? Do you know?"

I said, "Garcia and I got that out of him on the plane when he was trying to buy his life from us. He said it was a few million."

Michelle said, "A few million! Damn! I knew he had money but I never knew how much."

I said, "Now you know. How does it feel to be a wealthy woman?"

Michelle said, "I didn't know I was wealthy. This will take some time to get used to. How much will our new boat cost?"

I said, "It depends on how big of a boat we buy. They are sort of priced by the foot."

She said, "What do you suggest?"

I said, "Something about seventy feet if you want lots of space. Alden 72's are nice. There are other boats that are plusher and others that are more austere. Cushy interiors are expensive but nice wood is wonderful. This boat and half a million should buy what we want."

She said, "Where should we look. Are there boat lots like car lots?"

I said, "Sort of. There are brokerages that are on the internet. You should log in tonight and see what you'd like."

She said, "I will but you'll need to tell me which are the most seaworthy and I want our boat to be fast."

I said, "That will be my pleasure. You look for what you like and I'll take care of the rest."

Michelle said, "This is exciting. I've never shopped for a boat before."

We finished breakfast and went below to do the dishes and clean up our mess. When it was done I set about the tasks on the boat with Michelle on my elbow. She had some mechanical sense and I instructed her on much of the work and let her do what was necessary. We were done just before lunch and we changed to go and find a nice place to eat. We walked there holding hands and found a great place on the beach near where her shoots were done. We were near the end of our meal when a young girl of about thirteen came up to our table and holding out a copy of the swimsuit catalogue Michelle was on the cover of asked, "Miss is this you on the cover of this catalogue?"

Michelle said, "Sure, that's me."

The girl said, "May I have your autograph please?"

Michelle looked at me and I said, "Sure you can young lady. What's your name?"

The girl said, "Stacy."

Michelle took a pen from her purse and wrote the to and from on the cover and signed her name. The girl said, "Thank you I've never met a movie star before."

Michelle looked at me and said, "Mr. Hedberg what just happened?"

I said, "You just signed your first autograph. How does it feel to be famous Mrs. Hedberg?"

Michelle said, "That was weird. Why did she think I was a movie star?"

I said, "Because she's young and doesn't know. She'll remember this for a long time. You made her day."

Michelle said, "I guess I did. This is something I'll have to get used to."

I said, "Think what will happen if Patricia gets you into one of the major magazines. That was just a swimsuit catalogue. You'll have the Paparazzi after you whenever we're in port."

She said, "Do you think?"

I said, "I'm sure of it. We all know you're going to be famous. That's good because you're already rich."

Michelle smiled and said, "I guess I am. How about that? I might have to call my family and tell them."

I said, "They might like seeing you on a catalogue cover. They can show it to their friends. You might like to tell them about me when you call. They might also like to know you're not with Wise any more."

Michelle said, "You're right I need to call them tonight. I've gotten so used to not talking to them I've gotten out of the habit. My poor mother only heard from me once or twice a year. She was always great to me when I was growing up and I need to get to know her again."

We finished our lunch and Michelle paid cash for it out of the thousands in her bag. We went to an American express office and she opened a new account using most of the money she had. When the paper work was done she asked that her card be sent to the island we were going to and we walked away to the grocers. We both shopped and picked out what we wanted to eat at sea. Our tastes were similar and I was pleased we liked the same things. I went with the groceries when we were done and Michelle went to one of the department stores on the island. I put the stores away after I got them to the boat and waited in the cockpit reading for Michelle to return from her shopping trip. She was back at the start of cocktail hour and I made drinks for us below while she showed me the things she'd bought for the boat. I liked her choices and she used them that night to set the table in the cockpit while I cooked the fresh steaks on the grill. We went to bed early that night and Michelle set the alarm to wake up in the middle of the night and call home. I felt her get out of bed after midnight and went back to sleep while she made her call.

CHAPTER SIXTEEN

We woke up at dawn the next morning and went to the fuel dock to fill our tanks. When we were done I untied the bow as Michelle got the stern lines. She motored us out of the harbor just as the sun was fully up and I stayed on the bow to let the jib out when there was enough room to maneuver the boat. When we were sailing I heard her cut the diesel and I went back to the cockpit to join her. She was somewhat quiet this morning and went below after saying she wanted to make breakfast for us. I stayed at the helm sipping coffee waiting for her to be done with breakfast. Michelle came up with plates of French toast and went below again to get the pot of coffee.

We started to eat silently and were about halfway through our breakfast when she said, "I'm glad I called home last night. My mom was really happy to hear from me."

I said, "How was it, what did you tell her?"

She said, "I told her everything. The call took over an hour and I'll give you the money for it."

I said, "Don't worry about that. What did she say?"

Michelle said, "She cried the whole time while I was telling her what happened to me for the last five years. I told her about escaping and you rescuing me.

I told her I have started to model and that I'm rich now and she doesn't have to worry about me anymore."

I said, "That's a lot to drop on someone all at once. Did you speak with your dad?"

She said, "He was on the extension listening while I spilled my guts. He wants to meet you and said to thank you for rescuing me."

I said, "Tell him the pleasure was mine."

Michelle said, "That bastard of an ex of mine never gave me the messages that they would call. They've been thinking I didn't love them for all of these years. I feel so badly for what's happened. They were so worried and I never knew it."

I said, "Michelle why don't you have them come to the island when we get there. They can stay in the hotel and I'll get to meet them."

She said, "Would that be OK?"

I said, "Of course it will. You have to remember you can do as you like from now on. You don't have to ask me just do it."

Michelle said, "I'm sorry I forget that I'm with you and you're wonderful. I'll call them back when we're a couple of days from the island and they can make arrangement to meet us there. I want to pay for their tickets too so my dad won't have to spend his money to get here."

I said, "Now you're talking. Pay their way here and for their hotel. We'll take them sailing and you can show them the catalogue you're in and the pictures of you in your merc stuff."

Michelle said, "I didn't tell them I'd killed people."

I said, "That couldn't have been helped. It was them or us and you don't have to tell them ever."

She said, "I told them I was in love with you and you had proposed to me."

I said, "Did you tell them you accepted."

She said, "I did. My dad was very happy. So was my mom, she wants to be at the wedding for me. Do you think it would be OK with Garcia?"

I said, "What would Garcia have to do with it?"

Michelle said, "Garcia wants us to get married at her finca. Will that be Ok with you?"

I said, "Of course. We'll have to have it somewhere that is secure for X. You can be sure there will be incredible security for him. It will be fine; you don't have to tell them you've fallen in with a bunch of gun running ex drug dealers. Tell me what are their names?"

She said, "Gerald and Sarah."

I said, "Wow like the book?"

Michelle said, "What book?"

I said, "There was a book written called Living Well is the Best Revenge by Gerald and Sarah Murphy. It's an account of the turn of the century in Paris when they hung out with Picasso and Gertrude Stein and Hemmingway. It's a famous book and it's really good."

She said, "I didn't know about it. I'll have to read it."

I said, "You can probably download it from the 'net."

Michelle said. Thank you David. I should have known you'd be so understanding about all of this. It will be so nice to see them. What about your parents or relatives you've never said anything about them?"

I said, "There's not much to say. My parents figured out what I was up to when I was a teenager. Needless to say they weren't pleased that I was running whatever I could around the Caribbean. They found twenty grand in my drawer once and it was difficult to explain my sailboats which were expensive. The cash they found was more than my dad made in a year. I heard they died in a car wreck when I was about forty."

Michelle said, "I'm sorry, do you have any other family?"

I said, "Not really, I have some cousins I talk to every couple of years. Garcia and Hector and the others are my real family. X was like a father to me on many occasions. He's gotten me out of more than a few jams."

She said, "So that's why he's coming to stand up with you."

I said, "That's it. I knew he would come if I said that. I wanted him to be there when I proposed to you."

Michelle said, "So proposing to me was no accident?"

I said, "No it wasn't. I've been in love with you since our second sail. I hope you don't mind."

She said, "David, I don't mind at all. I'm really happy you love me. I was falling in love with you too on the way to see Hector. I thought you were beautiful the first time I saw you coming out of the water with a fish on a spear. That's why I chartered your boat. I wanted to get to know you. It seemed so romantic, a great guy living on his boat in a beautiful place. It's like a film or a book."

I said, "So I didn't have to rescue you to get you to fall for me?"

Michelle said, "Of course you did. I needed a knight in shining armor or in your case fiberglass. It was just the right thing."

Michelle got up and cleared the cockpit table to the galley. I heard her put the plates in the sink and the next thing I knew she was standing naked in the companionway beckoning me to our stateroom.

Our sail back to the island took thirteen days and they were wonderful. We had two good squalls to contend with and they both kept us hunkered us down in the cockpit for wild rides while they beat on us. It was great to have someone there to help with the boat and we took turns cooking. Michelle did a lot of gut spilling to me and I let her talk getting the baggage out of her system She called her parents three days from the island and told them where to come and meet us. I called and made reservations for them at the hotel on the island and Michelle told me later they would be there four days after we'd landed.

It was Monday at eleven when we motored into the harbor on the island. Michelle got the lines as I backed the Mo Cuishle into the slip I was usually given and when the boat was tied and the engine cut she came to the cockpit and kissed me. It had been a very long time from the day we'd left and it felt great to be back. We began to clean the boat up and we opened beers early that morning to celebrate completing our voyage.

We were drinking our beers and hosing the decks when Dennis walked up from the fuel dock and said, "Mr. Nash welcome back to the island. How was your trip?"

I said, "You're joking right?"

Dennis said, "Yep, I've heard a few things. The whole Caribbean has been talking about you two on the SSB every night. I'm glad you're all right."

I said, "We had some close calls. Did those guys that came to the island come back here?"

Dennis said, "One of them did and he asked a lot of questions. The boys in the bar ganged up on him one night and beat the crap out of him. He left the next day."

I said, "I'm glad he didn't give you any problems."

Dennis said, "One man I can handle."

Michelle said, "I'm Michelle and I want to thank you for helping me get out of here."

Dennis said, "Not a problem Michelle we don't much like it when the bad guys come to our island anyway. I'm happy you're all right and your problem is over."

Michelle said, "Thanks Dennis I am too."

I said, "I at least owe you lunch."

Dennis said, "Now you're talking. How about a roast beef sandwich tomorrow? It's Tuesday and Ben will be slicing."

I said, "That will be great. We really came back here for one of his sandwiches. Michelle hasn't had one yet."

Dennis laughed and walked back to his office and Michelle and I continued putting the boat right for port living. We were done two hours later and went for a late lunch at the hotel. People seemed happy I was back and I introduced Michelle to everyone. After lunch we picked up the mail and Michelle bought fresh vegetables for the galley. We walked back to the boat and I settled in at the cockpit table to go through all of the mail I had accumulated while I was away. There was some for Michelle from American Express and she was pleased to get her card which gave her access to her new line of credit. There was really nothing new in mine and I threw most of it out except for the monthly financial statements regarding my funds. Michelle did more clean up below while I went through the mail and when she was done she came on deck outfitted for spear fishing.

She said, "Want to help get dinner?"

I said, "Sure, just give me a minute to get my gear."

I was back in a minute and we went to the nearby beach where we could hunt. We floated for ten or fifteen minutes until Michelle saw a nice Puppy Drum and nailed it to the sand below us. We left it there and snorkeled for awhile longer floating on the surface holding hands. When we got out of the water we walked back to the boat and I cleaned our dinner in one of the troughs. I stepped onto the boat just as Michelle was coming up with the afternoon cocktails and she poured one for me while I went below and put the cleaned fish into the sink.

I went up on deck and she said, "This is good. I'm enjoying being back here."

I said, "I am too. I'm beginning to feel retired again. What would you like to do tonight?"

She said, "How about drinking in the pub after dinner. I need to thank Harry for keeping the guys off of me that time. I'd also like to see those guys try that with me now."

I said, "I'm sure they won't. Once Harry lays down the law to them they tend to remember."

Michelle said, "I was just kidding about that but it does feel good to know I can take care of myself."

I said, "OK but try not to have any drama tonight. I've had enough for the whole year. I'm retired remember."

Michelle said, "I remember and I'm on vacation. I'd like to get quietly drunk now that I have no responsibilities for awhile. No bad guys, no sails no radar no squalls. Just decent whiskey and good sex."

I said, "I like that. We'll get drunk and stagger back here to the boat. I'll make love to you until we pass out."

We finished our cocktails and cooked our dinner together. We ate watching the satellite news while the sun was going down in the west. I cleaned up the galley and we took turns showering on the dock. When we were both ready we strolled to the pub and took seats at the end of the bar.

Harry was working and came up to us and said, "Hello David, Ms. Murphy. It's nice to have you back."

I said, "It's nice to be back Harry. How about some drinks?"

Harry took our order and came back with what we wanted and said,

"I heard you two had quite an adventure out there."

Michelle said, "We did but all is well now thanks to Nash here."

Harry said, "I heard you were pretty good yourself out there Michelle."

Michelle said, "I took care of my share and thanks for taking care of me in here before I left."

Harry said, "Not at all. You were OK but the boys just aren't used to seeing single women in here. They just got too revved up and out of line with you."

232

I said, "Well they'd better get used to it because we'll be here for awhile. I'm retired again and Michelle is on vacation."

Michelle said, "David, I'm going to play some pool."

I said, "Win if you can I'm staying right here."

Michelle went to put her money up on the table rail and I sat with Harry, who said, "Nash that's one beautiful woman. I heard you're getting married is that true?"

I said, "It's true. There's no date set but we'll get hitched soon enough. Her parents are coming in a few days and I suppose I'll have to ask for her."

Harry said, "That's nice but I don't think anyone does that anymore. I think her family would be happy she's latched on to a rich bastard like you."

I said, "Rich like me? Harry she's the rich one and I'd be careful if I were you. She might just buy this pub and fire you. You old goat."

Harry said, "OK I'll be nice. I'm just jealous."

I sat back and watched Michelle play pool as I chatted with Harry between the drinks he made. I was on my fifth or sixth cocktail when I heard a loud voice come from the pool table.

It said, "Get your hand off of my ass and don't touch me again!"

Harry said, "Nash do you want me to take care of this?"

I said, "Nope, they have to learn not to fool with her. She can take care of herself."

I went back to my drink and heard a few minutes later,

"I said, don't touch me dammit!"

I turned and watched the local reach for Michelle's ass again while she was bent over shooting. She made the shot and turned around and cracked the guy across the head with her cue and he went down. The guy's friends lifted him up and splashed water on his face after sitting him in a chair. Michelle calmly began to rack the pool balls and another guy took the others place.

I felt Michelle was doing fine and went back to my conversation with Harry, who said, "You're right Nash; she's got quite the attitude."

I said, "He's lucky she wasn't armed. She pulled on some guys in Jamaica who were trying to rob us. It scared the hell out of them."

Harry said, "Well she'll get into the pecking order here soon enough. I'm pretty sure they'll leave her alone now that she's proven to be dangerous."

Michelle came over to where I was at the bar after another hour and said, "Mr. Hedberg, Mrs. Hedberg is drunk and would like you to take her home and have your way with her please."

I said goodnight to Harry and Michelle and I staggered back to the boat where we fell onto the couch pulling at each others clothing. We were naked soon enough and made love until we both passed out in our bed.

We woke up the next morning with bad hangovers and Michelle spent most of the day on the beach getting rid of hers. We had lunch at the bar with Dennis and after I stayed with my book on the boat while Michelle went back to the beach. By cocktail hour my hangover was gone so I headed for the beach to spear fish for dinner and Michelle was there asleep on the sand. I didn't disturb her and waited until I had the night's dinner in hand and was headed back to the boat.

I walked up to where she was sleeping and gently nudged her; she woke up and said, "Hi there is it time for dinner yet?"

I said, "Almost, come and clean up. I've bagged dinner and you've been asleep all afternoon."

She said, "I know, it was wonderful not having to do anything. What have you been doing all day?"

I said, "I've been reading in the shade on the boat after we took Dennis to the pub for lunch. Come on let's go and eat dinner. I want to watch a film tonight."

Michelle said, "I'd love that. I'm very tired from overdoing it last night. I can't wait until tomorrow night after I've had a normal day."

We went to bed after watching the film that night and woke up early. Michelle went to explore the island and I took to the pub in the afternoon to play chess with Ben. I met up with Michelle at cocktail hour and we talked about the day we each had. I was pleased she liked to go and find something to do on her own and leave me to my own devices.

We lived this way on the island for two more days while we waited for Michelle's parents to arrive. Each day Michelle became more and more excited about her parents coming. This went on until the morning they arrived and we walked to the end of the pier where the seaplane float was and waited for their plane. We watched as the plane landed on the water and taxied to the float. Michelle was almost shaking with anticipation as the plane cut its motors and coasted to the float. The door opened and out stepped a very hansom couple who were about a dozen years older than I was. Michelle hugged her mother and father for a long time before I was introduced to them. I instructed the boys on the dock to take their luggage to the hotel and we walked her parents to the boat. We sat them on the cushions and Michelle went below to bring up the iced tea she'd made the night before. I waited for Michelle to sit and begin the conversation.

When she was seated she said, "I'm so happy you're finally here. I've been as nervous as a cat waiting for this day."

Her mother said, "Honey I'm very glad to be here. This is a lovely little island. It's so small and has no big hotels on it. It's charming."

Michelle said, "This is where I met David. I came here because it was so small and I could be anonymous."

Her dad said, "That was a good day and David thank you for helping Michelle get away from her ex. I'm indebted to you."

I said, "Not at all. It was my pleasure and the time was exciting for us."

Sarah said, "Yes thank you very much. I've missed her terribly. Each time we called they told us she didn't wish to speak to us."

Gerald said, "If I'd only known I would have gone and gotten her myself. I was a United States Marine and we know how to kick ass."

I said, "That's what it would have taken. Those guys were pretty mean."

Sarah said, "David your boat is beautiful. I think your retirement is wonderful. Imagine just sailing from place to place whenever you want to. Have you ever sailed to Europe?"

I said, "I have. I've been in the Med several times. It's wonderful there."

Michelle said, "When can we leave?"

I said, "After you do some shoots for Patricia and get your new career off of the ground."

Michelle got up and went below to get her pictures and I said, "Wait until you see how great Michelle looks on film. You won't believe it, she photographs really well."

Gerald said, "She always did. I brought her family pictures with us to show you what she was like when she was growing up."

Michelle was back and said, "These are the pictures that were taken of me on St. Croix and Martinique. Look I'm on the cover of the new catalogue."

Her parents perused all of the photographs and her dad stopped at the one of her and Garcia dressed as mercenaries. He asked, "Michelle what is this one?"

Michelle said, "That's Garcia, she's my best girlfriend and we're getting married at her finca."

Sarah said, "What's a finca?"

I said, "That's the Spanish word for estate. She lives on Little Inagua."

Gerald said, "You two are dressed like mercenaries. Is that real?"

Michelle said, "Garcia taught me all about weapons. I needed to learn because of the men who were after me. I had to protect myself while we were trying to find a solution to my problem."

Gerald said, "I understand. Garcia is really beautiful. What's her first name?"

Michelle said, "I can't tell you. She doesn't like it and goes only by her last name. I only found out three weeks ago and I was sworn to secrecy."

Sarah said, "How does she know about weapons?"

I said, "She was in the military for awhile and she has to protect her finca."

Michelle said, "Come on, get up and let's walk you to the hotel. What would you like to do this afternoon? There's the beach or we could go sailing or we can get a car and see the island. What would you like to do?"

Sarah said, "Michelle you know I love the beach. I want to swim in this beautiful water."

Michelle and I walked her parents to the hotel where they changed to their beach wear from their traveling clothes. Michelle and I waited in the bar for them to come down.

I said, "Michelle I like your parents, they're very nice."

She said, "I'm really happy they're here. I have a lot of catching up to do."

I said, "What else are you going to do with them?"

She said, "I guess we'll just sail and hang on the beach. I'll get them some snorkeling gear so they can enjoy the lagoon. My dad would probably like to spear some fish with us."

I said, "You didn't tell me he was an ex marine."

She said, "I guess I forgot. He fought in Korea I think. Do you think he'd like to shoot guns with us?"

I said, "I don't know. You should ask him."

Michelle's parents came downstairs to join us and we went to the beach and put our towels on the sand. They both had tans and admitted to spending time in the sun where they lived. I excused myself from the group after awhile and went back to the boat to get our snorkeling gear and met them back on the beach. They both knew what to do with the masks and fins and took to the water while Michelle and I waited on the beach. They were back in another hour and Michelle went to get my Hawaiian sling so we could shoot something for dinner. She went with her dad and they came back with two nice Flounder to cook that night. They hosed down with us on the dock while I cleaned our dinner. Michelle took them to the cockpit to dry off and made drinks for her and her mother. Her dad preferred beer and I stayed with what he was drinking. We had a great time watching the sun go down and I loved hearing about Michelle's teen age years. She had been a good athlete as I expected and very active in her high school social life. She had been good looking and her dad complained about all of the boys that constantly came and went from their house.

They helped us cook on the grill and we had a wonderful dinner together. I sat with her dad while the girls did the cleanup and we sipped beer as we talked.

He said, "David, I'm very happy Michelle and you are getting married."

I said, "I'm happy too but I worry about being so much older than she is."

He said, "Don't worry about it. I think it's good for a man to be older than the woman. I don't think men get their act together until they are at least forty."

I said, "You might be right. I will tell you I'll take good care of her."

He said, "Anything would be better than what she was doing before you met her. Make sure she takes good care of you. I always taught her a man needs to be cared for as well."

I said, "I'll give her plenty to do. Everyone has always said I've needed some-one to take care of me and she's already started doing that. Just a few weeks ago she bought new towels and sheets for the boat."

Gerald said, "Just make sure she calls home regularly. The last few years have been very hard on her mother."

I said, "I'm sure they have. Hard on you as well."

He said, "Yes but men expect their daughters to marry and go away. A girl and her mom are forever. Sarah has really missed her."

The girls came up from below and Sarah said, "Gerry, I'm tired and want to go to the hotel. We'll see these two tomorrow."

Michelle's mom and dad got up and after saying their thanks went to their room to get some sleep.

We spent the time Michelle's parents were on the island sailing, snorkeling and just lying on the beach. Michelle and her mother would get involved in long conversations and her dad and I would go to the pub in the afternoons. Gerald loved to play chess and he fit right in on the island. The eight days they stayed went quickly and all too soon Michelle was saying goodbye to her parents at the float. We watched and waved as the seaplane taxied into position to take off into the wind. I stood with Michelle and we waited for it to be out of sight before we went back to the boat to begin our decompression from her parents' visit to us. It took two weeks for Michelle to get used to being back in touch with her parents and I could see she was pleased. She planed to call home each week and she seemed to enjoy speaking with her mother. I was getting used to being retired again and Michelle loved being on her permanent vacation. She read everything I had on board and took to reading in the afternoons in the lobby of the hotel which had hundreds of books on the shelves lining the walls. We were enjoying life on the island and were very comfortable until one day when the SAT phone rang in the afternoon and there was a text message on the screen.

It said, "Tomorrow noon be ready. La Reina."

CHAPTER SEVENTEEN

I said to Michelle, "Shit something's up and I'll bet it's not good."

Michelle said, "What could it be?"

I said, "I don't know but I'm going to call Hector and see what he knows."

I spoke to Hector and he knew of nothing but wanted me to call if there was trouble. Michelle and I spent that afternoon with the weapons and our mercenary gear putting it all together to be ready as Lene' had requested. I managed to call a few other friends but no one knew what might be up. Both Michelle and I were worried and we waited pensively for the next day at noon. Michelle was much more worried than I was as Garcia was her new friend and I had known her for years also knowing she was pretty good at getting herself out of trouble.

We ate on the boat that night with one ear on the radio and the SAT phone and went to bed early in anticipation of what we would undoubtedly find out the next day. We tried to sleep in but it was difficult so we both got up and made breakfast to pass the time. I was cleaning the boat and Michelle was doing her best to read when at about eleven thirty a PBY Catalina passed overhead and circled to land on the water and taxi into the big float.

When we saw the plane Michelle said, "That's weird what is Lene' doing in that plane? That belongs to Crazy Larry."

I said, "I don't know but we'll find out in a few minutes."

The plane landed on as it taxied towards us Michelle said, "Look it's been all shot up. There are big chunks missing from the tail and the left wing."

She was right as there was evidence the Catalina had been in a pretty good fire-fight and I began to get nervous about the outcome. The Catalina cut its engines as it got to the float and I watched Lene' leave the cockpit to exit the plane.

She got off onto the float and grabbed both of us and said, "We have to go to your boat and talk."

We walked the short distance to the Mo Cuishle and went below where she said, "Garcia's been captured and we have to go rescue her. Here's the story. We were making a run to an island off of the Gulf of San Blas in Panama with a shit load of new laser guided rockets and weapons. We used the PBY because it was about three thousand plus pounds of stuff and there's no airport there. It all went down perfectly until the end. Our delivery was to an outlaw group who were going to get the weapons into Colombia and use them against one of the cartels there. Just when the money had changed hands another group, some kind of contras hit us to steal the shipment. I'm sure they weren't with the cartel because they didn't look like it. I think it was a new group trying to get some weapons for themselves. Anyway when they hit us Garcia was headed back to the plane with the suitcase full of money and they opened up on us. Crazy Larry went down right away and his head was gone so I know he's dead. Jose Cruze was there and he was hit but managed to make it into the plane through the port blister. Garcia was right there and managed to get the money into the plane and I saw her go down as she yelled for me to get out of there. She was wounded but the last I saw of her she was killing them in bunches from the dock. She was fighting like a maniac and when she ran out of ammo I saw them grab her and drag her off of the dock. I was airborne by then but had been taking fire from the guys who were after Garcia. The Catalina's a mess but she still flies and we need to patch her up before we go back for Garcia."

I said, "Where's Cruze?"

Lene' said, "He's on Jamaica. I stopped there and dumped him off to Desmond. He's shot up pretty bad but I think he'll live. I couldn't bring him here because he wouldn't have made it."

240

I said, "What's first on the list?"

Lene said. "Patch the plane. It's really a mess and very hard to fly. It's just because the wings and tail are so shot up. I practically killed myself keeping her level and straight. We need to get the damage fiber glassed which will be a good temporary patch. We need weapons and aviation fuel and food. I'm bloody exhausted and I need a couple of drinks and food and some rest. I've been flying for twenty-eight hours and I'm seriously tired."

I said. "Michelle take care of her. I'm going to see to the Catalina."

Michelle was already getting a drink for Lene' and I left the boat heading for the float.

Dennis was already there inspecting the damage and I said, "Dennis get out the fiber glass. We've got to patch this bitch and get her back into the air."

He said, "That's a lot of holes. It looks like about six hours of work."

I said, "Get your boys on it. It's an emergency. How much aviation fuel do you have?"

He said, "Just a couple of hundred gallons. I have to keep some for the daily planes."

I said, "Can we have a hundred gallons? We just have to get to the keys."

He said, "You've got it."

I said, "Tell your boys they're on double pay and there's a bonus for them to get it done fast and right. Put on as many guys as you can find. I'm paying for it."

He asked, "What's wrong? Is it big trouble?"

I said, "It is, Garcia's been taken prisoner and we have to get back down there. I'll help with the 'glass. We need to get this done."

Dennis nodded and began to bark orders to his crew. I went back to the boat and Lene' who was stretched out on the couch with her drink as Michelle was cooking for her and the two of us.

I said, "Lene' my love will a hundred gallons get us to Sugarloaf Key?"

She said, "Yes it will are we going to refuel there?"

I said, "Yes. We don't have enough fuel here and we need Hector and more arms. Where's the money?"

She said, "In the plane. You'd better get it off of there."

I said, "How much is in the suitcase?"

She said, "A couple of million. Laser weapons are really expensive."

I got up and kissed Lene' on the forehead heading for the float and the suitcase. The inside of the Catalina was definitely a mess with blood everywhere. I asked Dennis to get a couple of hands on the interior to clean it up and took the suitcase back to the boat and put it under the bunk in the main salon. Michelle was already wearing her .45 and Lene' had one of the forties next to her on the couch.

I said, "I'm going to call Hector. We have to arrange the fuel."

I picked up the SAT phone and dialed. Hector picked up the other end and I said, "Amigo it's bad. A small conta group has Garcia on the little island in the Gulf of San Blas in Panama. We need to get back down there before they move her. Lene"'s sure she's wounded but not too badly."

He said, "I know the place. It's the little harbor with the big villa just off of the dock. There's almost nothing else there but the villa and the pier."

I said, "Here's what we'll need. One thousand gallons of hi-test aviation gas, rubber boats. Parachutes of the sport chute variety. A couple of fifty caliber machine guns, Two thirty caliber machine guns, night vision glasses, radios, climbing gear. Your sniper rig and all of the trimmings and any nasty hardware you can put together. We're in Larry's Catalina and it will hold a lot."

Hector said, "Where's Larry?"

I said, "Lene' said he never made it off of the dock."

Hector said, "Consider it done. Do I need to bring personnel?"

I said, "Sure, two of your best if you can."

Hector said, "How about our old MASH surgeon Peter?"

I said, "The Scottish guy?"

Hector said, "Yes he's retired but I can get him to come."

I said, "Great and bring some Kevlar and anything else you can think of especially food and drinks."

Hector said, "When will you be here?"

I said, "How about Chaz's marina at three A.M. tomorrow?"

Hector said, "We'll be there."

I said, "I'd like to be airborne at dawn if it's possible."

Hector said, "Dawn it is, see you there."

I put the phone down and said, "Lene' I know you're tired but we need a drawing of the island and the villa that's there. We're meeting Hector at three AM in the keys. I have to go and fix the Catalina. Can I take ten grand for Dennis and his crew?"

She said, "Take what you need we have to get back down there."

I grabbed the cash from the suitcase and headed for the float. I pulled Dennis into his office and handed him the cash. I said,

I said, "Will this take care of it?"

Dennis smiled and said, "That'll do it. Let me get back out to the plane. I've got to keep these guys moving."

I went with him and began to help with the more difficult of the patches on the tail. It was going well and we were making good progress and were halfway done by six that night. As soon as it was dark we let Lene' sleep and moved all of our firepower to the Catalina. I woke Lene' up at eleven thirty and she went to the plane to inspect what we'd fixed. She was pleased with the patches and when the fuel was put in the tanks we loaded ourselves into the Catalina and Lene' started the twin twelve hundred horsepower engines. I got into the second seat and she taxied to the harbor entrance pulling the throttles back when we were clear and taking the plane off.

We climbed to altitude and she said, "Good job on the flight surfaces. She handles like new. It was a bitch to fly her here. I was struggling with the plane since I left Panama."

I said, "How long to the keys?"

She said, "A couple of hours. Get me the GPS map there."

I did as she asked and she had me fly the twin engine plane there. It was nothing like the jet but I enjoyed flying a piece of history and it became more fun as I got used to it. We landed at just before three and the gear began to come onto the plane. The fueling was taking place and Lene' had the crew checking the other vital fluids as well. When we were loaded and Carlos and Danny were on board Lene' took off and we began to plan our attack of the island and the villa. It was decided that Hector and Carlos would climb into the hills on either side of the villa and take their positions with the sniper rifles they brought with them. Between the two of them they could cover most of the villa and its compound. I would parachute in with Michelle and do a slither up to the villa and ascertain where Garcia was being held. Peter and Danny were to stay with the plane manning the machine guns that were now mounted in the places that were designed to hold them. Lene' had control of the fifty in the nose and peter would stay with the plane and be prepared to receive any wounded especially Garcia.

The waiting was difficult for us but Catalina's were never a fast airplane. They would fly for twenty-four hours and cover about twenty-five hundred miles in this time. It would take about ten hours to get there and I wanted to arrive just after dark.

The time came and Lene' landed us a few miles from the coast of the island. Getting as close as possible we put Hector and Carlos into one of the rubber boats with their gear so they could get to their positions in the hills that rose on each side of the villa. We headed back out to sea and waited for them to radio us that they were in position. I talked with Michelle about what we were going to do when they called.

I said, "Are you ready for a parachute ride?"

She said, "No not really. I've never done that before but it's for Garcia and I guess it has to be done."

I said, "No worries. It will be a low level drop and there will be a static line to open your 'chute. There won't be much time before you hit the ground so you'll have to be ready for it. When we get to the ground we'll hide the 'chutes and get ready. I'm going in first and see where Garcia is. I'll leave all of my gear except a pistol so I can move easily. When I know where she is I'll come back to get ready with you and plan how we're going in. Hector and Carlos will be in the hills watching our backs. They can hit anything they see with those rifles and the night vision scopes that are on them. It'll be like long distance."

Michelle said, "Long distance?"

I said, "Sure, reach out and touch someone, zap your dead."

Michelle said, "What do you want me to carry?"

I said, "An M-16, two Uzis and all of the extra magazines and frags you can carry. I want you to be throwing bombs all over the place and killing whatever moves. Don't get weird if someone should fall in front of you. That'll be Hector or Carlos tagging them from the hills. Are you scared?"

Michelle said, "You're damn right I'm scared. Give me some of that rum."

I said, "Me too. I'm scared but all you have to do is keep your head. Those guys will not be expecting us and they'll be the ones who are confused."

We both continued checking our gear and in another hour Hector radioed they were in position. Lene' went to the cockpit and lifted the Catalina off of the water. When we were airborne she set our course to fly away from the island and come in from the south. This would allow Michelle and me to drop into the flat acreage behind the compound and not be seen. I could tell by Michelle's eyes she was nervous but the flight was short and she didn't have time for much anxiety. Lene' throttled back the motors and I opened the port blister. Peter and Danny helped us onto the rail and when I saw the drop zone we hopped off. Michelle went first and I went second. I saw her 'chute open and heard her scream "OH SHIT!!!" as the nylon came out of its pack. I heard my own 'chute pop and the two of us decended into the darkness as Lene' hit the throttles and veered away from the compound to land on the water and wait until we were ready. The drop was a short one and I heard Michelle hit the dirt below us with a good thud and I hit two seconds later. I pulled my 'chute in and crawled to where I thought she was.

I found her as she was gathering her 'chute and when I got to her she said, "That was completely terrifying! But I want to do it again sometime."

I said, "Are you OK? Are all of your limbs working?"

She said, "They are but my ass will never be the same. I hit on it pretty hard after my feet hit the ground."

I said, "Stay here with the gear. I'll be back in a couple of hours."

I took off all of my webbing and with only my forty and a few magazines I started crawling towards the compound. Hector talked to me on the radio and through my ear piece I was told there were two sentries at the front of the villa and one on the dock. There were two more on guard at a small building at the back of the villa and I hoped Garcia was there. I silently crawled to the back wall and using a nearby tree climbed up and got onto the wall to reconnoiter. It was pretty quiet and I could hear the sentries speaking Spanish between themselves. The roof of the back building was close to the wall and I climbed onto it being careful not to break any of the ceramic tiles it was covered with. I climbed to the skylight and carefully looked over the edge. We were in luck and Garcia was inside. She was out and lying on a small bed and I could see she had bandages over her shoulder and around her chest. I checked the skylight and it would open easily from the bottom. The distance to the floor was fifteen feet and I felt I could drop a rope in and rappel down to the floor with a minimum of noise at the same time Michelle was taking out the guards. I made sure the skylight was unlocked and re-traced my steps to the wall and the tree and to the ground.

I crawled back to where Michelle was waiting and when I got there I said, "Good news, Garcia is in the back building with two guards on the only door. I'm going in on a rope and to the floor. I want you to take the guards out and check the door. If it's locked put a grenade on it and get out of the way. As soon as it blows head for the villa and start throwing frags in through the windows. Throw all you can because we want to make a lot of noise and scare hell out of them. Toss a half dozen and get back to the shack. I'll be coming out and Garcia might be on my shoulder. If she is I'll only have one free hand and you'll have to light the place up. Most of the opposition will be coming from the front of the building but still watch the windows OK?"

Michelle said, "I will, David be careful."

I said, "Mrs. Hedberg I certainly will, you too. Are you scared?"

She said, "Not now, I'm locked and loaded and ready. Let's go kick some ass Mr. Hedberg."

I put on my gear and we crawled to the edge of the compound and went up the tree to the top of the wall. I silently motioned to Michelle to crawl past the rear house and be ready for me to disappear through the skylight. We put ourselves into position and I opened the skylight listening to Hector telling me I was OK and no one was coming for us. I dropped to the floor and grabbed Garcia who was out.

She woke up and said, "Is that you vato? What took you so damn long?"

I rolled her bed over to use for protection from the grenade that was most likely to blow the door from its hinges and then I heard Michelle's Uzi go off in two bursts. I heard the sentries drop and Michelle shook the door.

A minute later she yelled, "Fire in the hole!"

I held Garcia tight and the door blew into tiny pieces. I picked up Garcia and she groaned from her wounds and said, "OW! Take it easy!"

I said, "Shit lose some weight bitch!"

I tossed her onto my shoulder and she made her discomfort known to me. I came out of the door as Michelle was tossing grenades into the windows along the house and they began to explode. I saw two men coming towards us from the front of the villa and I watched them drop from Hector and Carlos's bullets. With Michelle in front leading the way I turned around to watch our six and we moved up the side of the burning building. I could hear voices screaming in Spanish and the voices were full of commotion and excitement. Two men came from around the back and I took them out with my Uzi. I quickly reloaded as Michelle was dropping three more that came from the front. I felt bullets pass my head and I turned to watch another man fall from Hector's sniper fire. A second later three more came from around the front corner of the villa and Michelle burned them down as if she'd been doing this all of her life. Hector spoke to me on the radio and said there were a dozen in the front courtyard who were organizing to come for us. Michelle heard the same thing and I saw her reload her two Uzi's and pull two more frags from her belt. These she lobbed over the roof and I heard screams just before they went off.

The next thing I heard was Lene' saying, "Hold your position Nash; I'm on a strafing run."

I heard the Catalina's motors and the front of the villa exploded from machine gun fire. Michelle went around the corner of the building and I heard her Uzi talk to the ones who were left. I went to cover her and saw another drop from Hector's rifle. Michelle was reloading and I did the same. Two more came from the villa and I got one and Carlos dropped the other as I headed out of the compound with Garcia on my shoulder. Things were quiet now and I humped Garcia to the end of the dock where I laid her out on the planks. I reloaded and took out my M-16 and started to the compound. Michelle came with me after telling Lene over the radio that we had taken the dock. There were dead or wounded all over the courtyard and Michelle and I carefully went into the villa. There was no one inside and we searched the building finding only three very frightened women hiding in the pantry. I spoke to Lene on the radio and she said she was coming in and would be at the dock in a few minutes. Michelle and I stood guard in the compound and we waited for Hector and Carlos to come from their positions in the hills. That took quite awhile and Lene' was there before they were. I stayed on guard and Michelle went to the dock were Garcia was being loaded into the plane for Peter to check out.

When she came back to me I looked at her and seeing a dark wet spot on her upper arm said, "Mrs. Hedberg, did you spill something on your shirt?"

Michelle looked at her arm and said, "Damn, I've been hit!"

I went to her and ripped the sleeve from her shirt revealing a nice crease that was made by a bullet grazing her arm and taking the meat with it.

I said, "You OK?"

She said, "I'm OK. I didn't even feel it. By the way Mr. Hedberg check your ear. There's a piece missing."

I felt my right ear and there was blood coming from a nick where my ear got too close to a bullet. I took off the black rag I had on my forehead and blotted the blood from the wound and passed the rag to Michelle who pressed it to her arm. Michelle suddenly raised her Uzi up quickly and pointed it in the direction a familiar large shape was coming from.

I said, "Don't shoot. It's Hector."

Hector walked up to us and said, "Not bad, not bad. Carlos and I got eleven in all. Let's see what you two did."

Michelle and Hector went off and started checking bodies and I watched as Michelle took out her Oyabun and started to collect ears from the ones she remembered killing. I was surprised but turned to see Carlos coming towards me in the light of the burning building.

He walked up and I said. "Amigo, esta bien?"

He said, "Si amigo esta bien. Uno grande pavo disparar."

I said, "A turkey shoot?"

He said, "Si, It was easy. Are you OK?"

I said, "I've got a nick in my ear and Michelle's got a new crease in her arm. Will you stay here while I go check on Garcia?"

Carlos took my Uzi from me and I went to the plane where Dr. Pete was working on Garcia. I stuck my head in the blister where Danny and Lene' were helping. I said. "Is she all right?"

The doc said, "She'll be OK. Her wound opened up when she was on your shoulder but that couldn't be helped. I'm running some plasma into her now and I gave her a shot to put her out. We won't hear any more from her tonight."

I said, "Danny, bring me four cold beers please."

Danny brought me the beer and I went back to where Carlos was guarding the compound. I gave him one which he opened with his knife and said, "Gracias amigo."

I said, "De nada," and went to find Garcia and Michelle.

They were in the villa and Hector had uncovered all of the laser rockets Garcia had sold the faction and after I handed them both a beer he said, "Nash, we need to get this all to the plane. It's ours again and it's too valuable to leave here."

I agreed with him and went to get the others. Garcia was stable by this time so together we loaded all of the re-captured weapons into the plane and made preparations to take off into what was now becoming dawn. I settled into the second seat next to Lene' and she started the twin engines. She taxied the plane away from the dock while Peter was tending to Michelle's arm.

We were airborne in five more minutes and Lene' turned to me and said, "Nash, thank you for saving my love. You are my true hero and I'll never be able to repay you."

I said, "Anything for you La Reina. Make sure you thank Michelle. I couldn't have done it without her and your strafing was perfect."

I asked, "Where are we going, by the way?"

Lene' said. "To Garcia's finca. The med staff will be there and waiting for us. The flight will take about ten hours. I'm OK to fly and Garcia's out so why don't you go back and get drunk with the others. You certainly deserve it."

I said, "Thanks doll, I surely do need a drink. Call me if you want to take a break."

I left the flight deck and went back where the others were sitting on piles of expensive laser guided munitions. Hector and Carlos were smoking big cigars and I was handed the bottle of black rum immediately. I toasted a successful raid and sat next to Michelle who said, "Mr. Hedberg, here's to you. You are the most bad ass merc in the Caribbean."

I said, "Next to you my love. How many ears did you get?"

Michelle smiled and said, "I have seven. I'm going to hang them on my webbing so everyone will know I'm a dangerous bitch."

I said, "Planning on doing this again?"

Michelle said, "You bet your ass. That was a rush and a half. I'm beginning to like the devil girl I turn into."

I said, "Well you certainly have the head for it. You stayed really clear back there. I'm proud of you and you saved my ass two or three times."

Michelle said, "I know, you saved mine as well. That was great team work."

We flew through the whole day and Lene' put the Catalina down near Garcia's harbor on Little Inagua and we taxied to the pier and she cut the engines. We gave Garcia to the medics and Peter went with her. The plane was left at the pier and Garcia's men took their positions nearby. We grabbed two jeeps and drove to the finca where champagne was ordered from the kitchen and we relaxed in the air conditioning. We drank many toasts to each other and when we were just drunk enough Hector and Carlos picked me up and took me out to the pool where I was thrown through the air into the water. The rest of them followed suit and we were all in the water soaking wet and getting rid of our clothes while the help brought bottle after bottle of cold champagne and black rum and tequila. We played until we were very drunk and went to bed. Lene' stayed with Garcia and the doctor stayed as well. Michelle and I finally got to bed and made love like maniacs until we passed out together.

We woke up the next morning and went downstairs to eat breakfast. The others came down one by one and when we finished Lene' came to the dining room to tell us Garcia was awake and wanted to see us all in her room. We filed up the stairs and stood around her bed.

I was the first to speak and said, "How are you this morning?"

She said, "I'm OK. I hurt like hell but that's what morphine is for."

Hector said, "Garcia you have to stop this drama. I'm entirely too old for this kind of thing."

Garcia said, "Lene' said you're still a great shot. She said you and Carlos got eleven."

Hector said, "Michelle was wonderful in the fight. She's got seven ears for her webbing and a parachute drop to boot."

Garcia said, "Chiquita you jumped out of an airplane for me?"

Michelle said, "I certainly did and I found out I like throwing hand grenades at people."

I said, "Lene was the real hero. She flew all of the way here in a broken airplane to get us and all of the way back to get you."

Garcia said, "That's my girl. She's much more than a good piece of ass."

I said, "She certainly is. By the way, we got your money and the weapons back. You can sell them again."

Garcia said, "Nash you bastard, you said I was fat."

I said, "I did not. I said you should loose some weight. Having you on my shoulder was hard work."

Garcia said, "Can you knuckle heads take me down to the pool. I hate being in here."

Peter said, "OK but carefully. I don't want you to start bleeding again",

Michelle and Lene' went downstairs to make a bed for Garcia by the pool and with the help of a stretcher we moved Garcia to poolside. When she was there she said, "Where's Cruze?"

Lene' said, "He's on Jamaica in a hospital. I called Des this morning and he's going to live."

Garcia said, "And Crazy Larry?"

Lene' said, "He died on the dock down there. Do you know if he has any family?"

Garcia said, "Shit, I hate that. No he has no one. Does his plane still fly?"

Lene' said, "It flies well. It got us back here OK."

Garcia said, "Chiquita how'd you like to own a PBY Catalina? Lene' will teach you how to fly it. You need something to get around the islands that's faster than vato's boats. What do you say?"

Michelle said, "Yes, yes, yes, I'd love it. Thank you very much."

Garcia said, "Lene' said you enjoyed yourself out there. Do you want to be my partner and play with us on a regular basis?"

Michelle said, "Yes I would Garcia. I said to Nash last night I was beginning to like the devil girl inside of me."

Hector said, "Garcia she's as good as I've ever seen. A real gato infierno."

I said, "There goes my retirement."

Michelle said, "Nash you stay retired. I'm going to marry you and have your children. I have an airplane and we'll spend plenty of time together. This will leave you to your friends at the bar and your chess games. When you get bored you can come and rescue me."

I said, "Michelle I love you and you go ahead and do what you need to. Just keep modeling so I can brag to my friends about you."

Garcia said, "Michelle Murphy, the mercenary model. I told you you'll be on the cover of Soldier of Fortune magazine. I'll bet they've heard already and are looking for you."

Hector said, "If they're not I'll call them. They owe me anyway."

I said, "This is good. I get my retirement and Michelle gets the life she wants. Do I still get a new boat?"

Michelle said, "Yes you still get a new boat. I can't fly all of the time and I happen to like traveling on your boat. Lene' can I start my flight training today?"

Lene said, "I see no reason why not. I'll give you the basic books. You'd better read them with Nash so you both can learn. When you've got it down I'll help you get your jet rating."

Michelle said, "Do you think I'll ever be able to afford a jet?"

Garcia said, "Chiquita a few runs together and you'll have your jet. If you can't afford one I'll steal you one."

We spent the afternoon around the pool getting drunk while Garcia ate her morphine. She mustered up the strength to have dinner with us in the dining room and I had to admit she was one tough chick.

We had gone to bed when I said to Michelle, "Going to be a mercenary huh?"

She said, "I'm sorry Nash. This is something I have to do. Are you disappointed in me?"

I said, "It's all right. I like the way I live but you'd better come and see me from time to time. I know my lifestyle would eventually be boring for you. You just have to promise me that I won't have to read about you in the newspaper."

She said, "I promise you won't. Can I still come and make love to you anytime I want?"

I said, "Of course you can and if you don't I'll be coming to find you. I said I wasn't going to let you get away and I meant it. Whether you live with me or not you're still my girl."

We went to bed and fell asleep after making love and Michelle and I began our flight training the next day. We went through the instruction together while we helped Garcia get better. One month later Garcia was getting around pretty well and Michelle and I had both soloed in the Catalina. We were both officially pilots and we took the Catalina back to my island where I could retire again and Michelle could be on vacation.

CHAPTER EIGHTEEN

Michelle landed the plane and we went to the boat and opened her up and put our things below. I had missed my home and it felt great to be back. Michelle liked it too but I knew she would miss the crazy life with Garcia and Lene' before long. It wasn't a long wait as Patricia called to tell her about a shoot she was wanted on. Michelle accepted the job and made the preparations to fly there and live on her plane which she had named Amnesia Castle. I stayed on the island for those two weeks and I did miss her company and warm body next to mine at night. I was pleased she had chosen the same life I once had and I looked forward to seeing the Catalina circling the harbor before landing and taxiing to the float we had built for it. That day came soon enough and hearing the plane's motors I looked to the sky and saw my love making the last of her approach and setting down on the water. She taxied up to the new float and I went to greet her. When the engines were shut down she came out through the port blister and stepped onto the dock and into my arms. We kissed for a long time and holding hands we walked to the boat and sat on the cockpit cushions.

She said, "Mr. Hedberg, I've missed you terribly. What have you been up to while I was away?"

I said, "My usual, of course. I play chess and chase down my dinner every night. I'm comfortable but I do miss you terribly when you're gone."

She said, "I miss you too and I have a present for you."

I said, "What's that?"

Michelle said, "Your new boat my love. It's all paid for and you can sell this one and keep the money if you'd like."

I said, "What kind of boat is it?"

She said, "It's an Oyster 82 with all of the trimmings. Garcia helped me find it and it's beautiful. It's like a Rolls Royce or maybe a five star hotel on the water. It has lots of beautiful wood and the interior is just magnificent. I hope you'll love it."

I said, "Damn girl that's one hell of an expensive boat. Where did you get it?"

Michelle said, "Garcia found it at an auction of conficiscated property seized in a raid of a drug lord's finca. The government took it and I bought it for about the price of your Beneteau."

I said, "That sounds great. Where is it?"

She said, "It's moored in the British Virgin Islands. We can take it any time we want to."

I said, "Thank you Michelle. I guess I'll be living in style from now on."

She said, "That's we'll be living in style unless you don't want me any more."

I said, "Not at all. You're still my girl and you will never have to worry about that."

She said, "Good, then our relationship is working."

I said, "So far so good."

She said, "I got my money from Wise while I was gone and I want you to know I owe it all to you."

I said, "How much?"

She said, "After X took a small cut it amounted to about three million and change. I bought your boat with the change and I want you to sell your boat and keep the money. Put it in your account and live on it. Mine will be yours and yours will be mine when we're married anyway."

I said, "You still want to marry me?"

She said, "I most certainly do. Garcia is pregnant enough to be more than just showing and I want to have a child with you next year if you don't mind."

I said, "I don't mind. You tell me when you want this to happen and we'll make it happen."

Michelle said, "How about if we start making things happen right now. Will you take me to bed and make love to me?"

I said I would and Michelle pulled me by my sleeve to our bunk where we spent most of the afternoon.

We finally got out of bed and went to the restaurant where everyone was pleased to see Michelle again.

We drank in the bar after dinner and Michelle said, "Mr. Hedberg, when would you like to go and get your boat?"

I said, "Any time will be fine with me. I'll have a lot to do to it to make it the way I like things. It will probably take about a month."

She said, "What if you and I fly there and have your boat sailed to the BVI so you can take what you want from it. I'm happy to help you do the change over. When it's done we can sail it back here and you can continue your retirement."

I said, "That sounds fine with me. When do you want to leave?"

She said, "How about tomorrow morning. We can put all of your stuff into the Catalina and fly it there. Can Dennis find someone to sail your boat down?"

I said, "I'm sure he can. I'll tell him after we load and before we go."

We spent the next morning transferring all of my things to the Catalina and Dennis said that sailing my boat to the BVI wouldn't be a problem. Michelle and I took off just after noon for the flight there. She had redone the interior of the Catalina and it was very comfortable inside. She had built a small galley and a stateroom and a living area that was wonderfully comfortable. She said she was the envy of all of the other girls she modeled with and who could blame them. Her plane was beautiful and I enjoyed helping her fly the restored relic south.

It took nine hours to fly the distance to the BVI from the island in the Bimini group. Michelle landed the Catalina expertly just after dark and we tied up to a buoy in the less populated part of the harbor which served Road Town on the island of Tortola.

We shut the plane down and Michelle said, "Mr. Hedberg would you like something to eat?"

I said, "Sure what have you got? Do you want to go out?"

Michelle said, "Let's stay here and have a quiet dinner together. I've been really enjoying my airplane. It's the home I never had until now."

We looked in the 'fridge together and it was well stocked. We settled on steak for dinner and I cooked the vegetables as Michelle made the salad. She had a grill attached to the rail of the starboard blister and when the accompaniments were finished I grilled the steaks on the rail. We ate in the living area and the food was good. When we were done Michelle asked me to follow her and we went out of the port blister and climbed to the top of the wing where it was attached to the plane. She'd had this area reinforced and it was lovely to sit there with our drinks and look at the stars.

We looked silently for a long time and then Michelle said, "David, how do you like the way I'm living?"

I said, "I think it's great. You're very lucky to have a life this nice. It must be quite a turnaround from when you left L.A.."

She said, "It is wonderful but I miss you very much. Would it be all right if I sailed with you on the new boat back to your island?"

I said, "Of course you can. I'd love the company and we'll be living in the height of luxury on the way there. Oysters are wonderful boats and they sail beautifully. Would you like to stop on the way and see how Garcia's doing?"

She said, "Yes I would. I was there two weeks ago but I missed having you there with me. The four of us together was wonderful and you need to see the future mother of your child."

I said, "Why hasn't Garcia called me?"

She said, "Because she didn't want you to feel you needed to be a part of her pregnancy and that wasn't part of the deal. Garcia loves you very much and she wants you to have your freedom. That's very important to her."

I said, "I guess I should have called her but I get very complacent when I'm on my island. The days click by and I get lost in my retirement. Have you thought about getting married to me?"

Michelle said, "I have and I've wanted to speak to you about it. Would you like to marry me in the spring? Garcia will have had your child by then and it would be a good time for everyone to come to Little Inagua for the wedding."

I said, "That sounds fine with me. Are we going to have a big deal or do you want to keep it small?"

Michelle said, "I've been thinking I want to have a traditional Spanish wedding. It will go beautifully with the finca and I love Spanish wedding dresses. I want to wear white lace and I'd like for you to be in a white linen suit. I just want to have my parents and our friends from the Caribbean there. Most likely a hundred people in all. Will that be OK?"

I said, "That sounds fine with me. I'll go along with what you want as long as I'm married to you at the end of the ceremony. Where would you like to go for a honeymoon?"

Michelle said, "What if we borrow Garcia's jet and fly to Europe? I'll be rated for it by then. We could go to Rome and eat spaghetti."

I said, "I like pasta but I want to take a few trains around the country and see the sights."

Michelle said, "That sounds good. We'll book the whole thing first class and eat nothing but room service. There's one other thing though."

I said, "What's that my love?"

She said, "I want to quit my birth control before our wedding so you can make me pregnant. I want to have your child before I get too old."

I said, "You do what you want to. I told you I'd let you decide and that's what I want to do. I'm happy to help you be pregnant and have this child and I want you to know I'm always there for you."

Michelle said, "Thank you David. That's really all I want."

We finished our drinks and went below where we made love for a long time before we fell asleep. We woke the next morning and Michelle ran up the flag that alerted the harbor boat we wanted to go ashore. She hailed a taxi and we went to the big harbor where my new yacht was moored. Michelle got the keys from the harbor master and we went aboard the vessel. It was incredible inside and out. It had Teak decks, a fully equipped cockpit and electric winches to help handle the sails. Down below was better than my wildest dreams. I really could not imagine such luxury. Everything was done perfectly and I couldn't believe all of the space everywhere. There was truly plenty of room to stretch out and the master stateroom was a lot like a five star hotel. I went to work seeing what needed to be done to put the Oyster the way I liked a boat to be. Other than the single side band radio and my big flat screens to see the weather and navigation on I was pretty happy with my gift.

We spent the month changing the interior to my taste and I asked Michelle to buy all of the upholstery and linens for the boat. The Mo Cuishle showed up half way through the process and I placed the screens where I wanted them and installed the SSB radio. When she was done I had her repainted and named Amnesia Castle which was my original name for the Beneteau. The local broker took possession of the Beneteau and it was sold in a week. I transferred the funds it brought me into my account and my monthly income got larger. We left for points north the week following the completion of the new Amnesia Castle and it was a pleasure to sail her. She was a great boat and the trip to Little Inagua was easy and very comfortable.

Garcia's harbor was on the horizon before noon of our fifth day and I was impressed with the speed the Oyster made. We tied her up and taking one of the Jeeps we drove to Garcia's finca. She was there in the living room speaking on the phone when we walked inside.

She immediately dropped the phone and screamed, "Vato, you son of a bitch! Why didn't you call before you came to me?"

I said, "Hello Garcia. I didn't call because I was trying to give you a heart attack. Where's the booze or have you quit drinking?"

She said, "I quit drinking because of this devil you made inside of me. It's the most difficult thing I've ever had to do."

Garcia was up and went straight to Michelle kissing her on the lips and saying,

"Welcome back my love did vato like his present?"

I said, "I did at that. She's a wonderful boat. Now I get to live like the rich people."

Lene' walked into the room and said, "Nash my darling how are you? Look at what you've done to Garcia. Isn't she beautiful?"

I said, "She certainly is. Garcia pregnancy really makes you glow. You're a very beautiful woman as always."

Garcia said, "Oh bullshit vato. How can you say that? I don't even have a waist any more and I look ridiculous on the beach. Something like a beached whale and it's all your fault."

I said, "Well maybe you lesbians should look into birth control."

Lene' said, "Or maybe keep our knees together."

Michelle said, "You two leave Nash alone. He hasn't been in the same room with this many women for a long time. Please don't chase him back to his boat."

We all laughed and did a group hug in the middle of the room. Lene' rang for sangria and we all drank with the exception of Garcia who was noticeably annoyed at not drinking.

Garcia said, "Vato how long can you stay?"

I said, "Long enough to be with the woman who carries my child for awhile. I wish you'd called me. I do want to share some of this with you."

Garcia said, "Vato you can do the whole thing if you want to and if you want to share something share the fat with me. I'm not taking to being a fat girl very well."

I stayed for a week spending a lot of time with Garcia and listening to the plans she had been making for our offspring. Michelle listened with me and I felt Garcia had a good plan for raising the child. Michelle and I left a week to the day afterwards and sailed for my island. We arrived in five more days of good sailing and it was nice to be home. Michelle stayed with me for another week before she got into her seaplane and flew off early one morning.

Dennis visited me after she'd left and said, "Nash you must be the luckiest bastard on earth. I'd give almost anything to be in your shoes."

I said, "Dennis all I'm trying to do is be retired. Things keep coming up and I have to deal with them from time to time."

He said, "When will Michelle be back?"

I said, "I'm not really sure about that. She said she was flying to St. Croix to have her picture taken and from there she said she has business to do for Garcia. What that might be I'd rather not know."

Dennis said, "I think that would be the best thing. It's pretty early but how about going to the pub and doing some early drinking?"

I said that would be fine and we headed for the pub and the beer we knew would be inside.

That winter wasn't like most winters. I had regular visits from Michelle and we went on a couple of long blue water trips together. She would decide I needed to visit Garcia from time to time at her finca to be a part of her pregnancy and would come and fly me there. I live as I liked for the most part and I loved being retired.

I got a SAT phone call one morning and Michelle was on the other end of the phone.

She said, "Pack a bag Nash. I'll be there in one hour. Garcia's going to have your child tomorrow. Hopefully not before we get back."

I packed a bag and left my keys with Dennis to look after for me. Michelle landed and picked me up and we took off immediately.

We flew straight to the island and I went to Garcia's bedroom where she was in labor she said, "Vato you bastard! I should never have gone soft for you. Look at what I have to do. Shit this is painful!"

I said, "Don't blame me! It was all about your clock that was ticking. What can I do for you?"

Garcia said, "You can put a knife in your eye for starters. That's about how painful this shit is. While you're getting the knife I could use some ice to suck on."

I said, "Sorry Garcia, I know you're hurting but what do you think we're having?"

She said, "I don't know but it's got spikes all over it. Don't let Michelle see me like this or she'll never reproduce ever."

I said, "I meant boy or girl?"

She said, "I know, I know. I think it'll be a girl. My worst nightmare. I need another bitch in the house getting PMS like I need a hole in the head. It's bad enough with Michelle and Lene' and me. The middle of the month is like a train wreck. A very bad train wreck."

Just then she had another contraction and the doctor said, "Good girl Garcia, one or two more of those and you'll be out of the woods. It's almost over."

Garcia said, "Caramba! Doc one more of those and I'll never walk again. Christ this is like shitting a watermelon!"

Garcia had another big contraction and the doctor said, "Good girl Garcia you've just had a beautiful baby girl congratulations."

Garcia said, "We'll impose roles on it later doc does it have all of its fingers and toes?"

The doc said, "Yes she's perfect. She's got blond hair and blue eyes just like Nash there."

Garcia said, "Oh no las perra blanca. Damn you Nash I not only have a girl but she looks just like you. Doc, tell me does she have white skin too?"

The doc said, "Nope she's got light olive skin just for you."

Garcia said, "Good then, she'll do well at the beach. Nash look at her please is she beautiful?"

I took a look at the child as they were washing her for presentation and turned to Garcia and said, "Garcia she's really beautiful. Good job."

Garcia said, "Is she really Nash? She's really beautiful?"

I said, "Yes she's gorgeous. She has your face with blond hair and deep blue eyes. She'll torture all of the boys when she gets older."

The doctor handed the baby to Garcia who took her and held her close.

She looked at her and tears came from her eyes. She said, "Damn vato she is beautiful. She's just gorgeous. Hello my bambina I'm Garcia and this is your father."

I picked up my daughter and held her as Garcia cried silently watching us.

I kissed her on the forehead for the first time and handed her back to Garcia saying, "Well Garcia what do you want to name her?"

Garcia said, "I must be having a weak emotional moment here but I want to name her Estrella. My father would have liked that. It was his mothers name and if anyone asks I'm saying I was drugged and you talked me into it vato."

I said, "I think it's a beautiful name and I'll take the blame for it if you want me to."

The Doc had let in the rest of our family and they all came to the bedside to see Garcia and her offspring. I was complimented as well and I have to say I was very proud of Garcia and my child.

That evening was wonderful at the finca. Champagne flowed and Garcia let everyone in to meet our daughter. The word got around fast and the SAT phones went off continually as our friends from afar called in their congratulations. Michelle was thrilled at Estrella and couldn't get over how beautiful she was.

When things died down in the house Michelle came and sat with me by the pool and said, "David I have to say I'm really impressed with Estrella. I never dreamed a baby could be so beautiful. Do you think ours will be as wonderful?"

I said, "I do, you and I should have a great child and the probability of us having a baby with blond hair and blue eyes is much higher."

She said, "I'd like that. I've always wanted a blond daughter."

I said, "What about a blond son?"

Michelle said, "That would be good too but I've never really envisioned myself with a son. My fantasies were always about having a daughter."

I said, "How long is it until our wedding?"

Michelle said, "June thirtieth is the date I want to get married on. It will work out for my parents and Lene' says it will be good for X. I'm looking forward to getting married. Are you?"

I said, "I am and I'm also looking forward to having a child with you. Estrella has really impressed me. I'm really going to like teaching my daughter how to sail."

Michelle said, "I'm glad this has been a good day for you. I wondered if it would be when I was flying to pick you up."

I said, "Garcia's been a wonderful friend to me over the years. I'm happy to have helped her have a child and I like having a legacy to keep my blood line going."

Michelle said, "I want to quit my birth control at the first of May. I'm pretty sure I don't have any shoots to do then and Garcia has been saying she's not moving anything until Estrella is weaned."

I said, "Good I'll look forward to spending more time with you. Would you want to sail to Europe with me during that time?"

Michelle said, "That's a good idea. A long ocean voyage should be good for lots of sex. We can make love all of the way there and hopefully I'll come back pregnant.

I said, "That will work for me."

Michelle flew me back to my island a week later and we planed to sail to Europe in another month. I had made all of the preparations for the trip and one afternoon the Catalina circled the harbor to land. I met Michelle at the big float and she hugged me long and hard when she got out of the plane.

The two of us carried her things to the boat and she said, "My love are we ready to go?"

I said, "All we have to do is get fuel and water and you might go to the store and see if there's any special food you want for the trip. Once we leave here we won't stop until we reach Bermuda."

Michelle said, "I'd love to go to Bermuda. Garcia says it's wonderful there."

I said, "Speaking of Garcia, how's my Estrella doing?"

She said, "She's wonderful and getting more beautiful each day. She's growing like a little weed and is incredibly alert."

I said, "Do you still want to get pregnant on our voyage?"

Michelle said, "I certainly do. I stopped taking my birth control last month and I should be fertile very soon."

I said, "Would you like to leave in the morning?"

Michelle said, "Yes, let's leave after we fill the tanks and point her north. I've been dying to get some blue water under me. Will Dennis watch the Catalina for me?"

I said, "I've already spoken to him about that. He's up to the task and will make sure it's perfect for you when we get back here."

We went to the pub that night and had a great time with Harry and Dennis. Michelle played pool with no incidences and all of the regulars treated her with great respect.

CHAPTER NINETEEN

We woke up at just after dawn the next day and motored to the fuel dock to fill the tanks. When they were full we shook hands with Dennis and cast off our lines and set our course for Bermuda which was a thousand miles to the north east. We made the trip in nine days and cleared customs at noon of that day. We settled into living on the tiny island that was almost halfway across the Atlantic. Michelle loved the island and we went somewhere different for dinner each night. We stayed for a week and after filling our tanks we set our course for ninety degrees east and aimed for the sun that was rising in front of us. I calculated we would arrive in the Canary Islands in about fifteen days depending on the wind and the currents. It was a wonderful voyage and other than eat and sleep and sail the boat we made love constantly. Michelle was very serious about coming home pregnant and I was having a bit of a hard time keeping up with her lust. We sailed into the harbor on the Canaries sixteen days after leaving Bermuda and we only had two small storms to contend with. The Oyster had a helm station below and it was nice to keep her sailing and not have to be wet up on deck. Michelle wanted to keep moving and we sailed for Casablanca a week after we arrived in the Canaries. Michelle didn't care for it there so we upped anchor and sailed for the Spanish city of Valencia were we saw the sights before going to Mallorca. We loved it there and Michelle especially like the myriad of languages that were spoken in the most popular vacation spot in the

Mediterranean. I had been there before but enjoyed being there with Michelle who was continually excited at everything she saw. From there we went to Barcelona and visited all of the Gaudi architecture and the beaches full of tourists. From there we spent a month exploring the French and Italian Rivera's and Michelle decided she would like to retire there eventually. We were half way to the Greek islands to see if we could get lost in them forever when Michelle came to me in the cockpit where I was sailing the Castle around the Italian peninsula.

The sun was setting and she said, "Mr. Hedberg, you are a very viral man."

I said, "How's that my love?"

She said, "I'm two weeks late on my period. I think I'm knocked up."

I said, "Well congratulations to us. Are you sure about this?"

Michelle said, "I've never been late a day in my life and I feel like I'm pregnant. I'm very happy."

Michelle came and kissed me and we cuddled on the plush cushions in the cockpit. She was all smiles from that day on and from that day on she started to glow from within. I was very pleased and very happy for her as I knew she wanted this very much.

We stayed for another month in the Greek islands and when Michelle said it was time we sailed out of the Med. We sailed back through the Gibraltar straights and headed for Trinidad using the lower half of the great circle route. It was a long time on the water but we arrived there twenty five days later. Michelle missed her period once more and she was sure she was pregnant. She quit drinking and I did as well other than a few beers late at night when I was alone in the cockpit at the helm. One week in Trinidad was enough and Michelle was anxious to get home to the finca on Little Inagua. We took a different route back to my island and the Catalina by sailing for Cosumel and then crossing the Gulf south of the Florida Keys. We were back on my island a month to the day before our wedding and after two days of cleaning the Castle Michelle flew back to the finca to begin the preparations for our wedding.

I went back to being retired and settled in to the routine I loved for three more weeks. I sailed the Amnesia Castle to Little Inagua for the wedding and I have to say I was very excited to be getting married.

The guests began to arrive two days before and I loved seeing so many of my friends from the past. Garcia had bought me a new linen suite that complimented Michelle's wedding dress and at ten in the morning on the thirtieth of June we were lined up to walk down the Isle.

X walked into the room at almost the exact time the Mexican wedding march began to play and he stood where he would be just to my right side. Lene' and Garcia stood with Michelle and I have to admit my bride looked more beautiful than I'd ever seen her. The ceremony was short and very beautiful and Michelle and I exchanged vows in front of our friends. When it came to our rings I surprised her with a beautiful platinum wedding band with a matching diamond engagement ring as we had never officially become engaged. There were tears in our eyes when the ceremony was over and we kissed in front of our friends. Garcia let out a yell when it was over and there were champagne corks popping all over the inside of the villa. It was a wonderful event and we both felt closer to each other that we ever had before.

We flew away the following night to Paris in Garcia's jet and stayed for a whole week barely leaving our suite at the George V. We flew back to the finca and I spent the next several months getting regular visits from Michelle on my island and I was very interested in taking part in her pregnancy. Lene' came and got me two days before Michelle was to give birth and I was with her in her room at the finca while she was in labor. She was having a decent time with the trauma of birthing and I said, "Michelle, are you hurting a lot?"

She said, "Not really, it's only when I have the contractions. They're bad but nothing like Garcia described to me."

I said, "That's good because she was cussing like a sailor the whole time."

Just then Michelle crushed my hand with hers and gritted her teeth until it was over. I put the cold towel on her forehead and the doctor said, "Michelle can you do that again we're almost done here."

Michelle gritted her teeth and crushed my hand again grunting from the pain and the effort. She repeated the effort once more and sighed a sigh of relief as the doctor pulled our child the rest of the way from her. Michelle held my hand as the doctor handed the child to the nurses and they began the cleaning.

He said, "Nice job Michelle. You've had a very beautiful baby boy."

Michelle said, "Nash that was just for you. You need a son and Estrella needs a brother to protect her."

I said, "Thank you my darling." As the doctor placed our son into Michelle's waiting arms. Michelle looked at her baby and began to cry as she said, "My god he's just beautiful. David he's got your eyes."

I said, "He does and he's got your face and hair. Blond and handsome, Michelle you've done wonderfully. He's the perfect compliment to his sister Estrella."

The doctor let all of our family into the room and Garcia said, "He's beautiful Chiquita. What are you going to name him?"

Michelle said, "His name is David, like his father. Another David Nash for the world to love."

I said, "I'm pleased at that. After all of these years I have a son and I'm really excited."

Michelle admitted to being very tired and we left her to sleep with my son while we all went to the living room to drink and speak of how beautiful my name sake was. It was late when we went to bed and Michelle was able to move around the villa some the next day. I stayed for the rest of the month and went back to my retirement leaving the girls to raise their offspring. I had regular visits from all of them and I loved hearing the motors of the Catalina. As the children got older I would go to Garcia's finca and take care of the kids as Michelle and Garcia worked at their vocation of moving difficult to get items all over the Caribbean. I loved being with my children and being a part time father to them. As they grew older I knew I would be spending more time with them when the girls would go on their adventures. I looked forward to the kids growing up and hoped they would like sailing. Michelle said she would make sure of this and we sailed with the kids on a regular basis. The beach was part of their lives and so were the tutors who were brought to the finca when the kids were barely old enough.

It was a good relationship between the girls and me. I was happy to stay out of the loop and Lene' was like a third mother to the kids and everyone had plenty of space for themselves due to the help at Garcia's finca.

I heard the Catalina motors a few months later months and expected Michelle and Garcia to be visiting me on my island.

I was wrong as it was Lene' who got off of the plane and said, "Nash my love we have a situation. The girls went down hard and are stuck on an island near St. Kitts. They're in a dangerous situation because of the factions there and we have to go and do a rescue."

I was packed and ready to go in another hour and Lene' and I took off heading south to find the girls.

To be continued...

David Nash was born in New Orleans, Louisiana in the middle of the Twentieth Century. He was born of educated parents and attended private school. His family raised him modestly between New Orleans and the Gulf Coast of Mississippi until 1963 when he moved to Southern California and the small town of Huntington Beach.

He was raised on the water and was a proficient sailor throughout his youth. After moving to Huntington Beach he became a surfer / skateboarder / skier who also loved hot rods, motorcycles and rock and roll. He discovered art on the Gulf Coast eventually earning both a bachelors and masters degree in fine art in Southern California after working with extremely notable artists for more than twenty years in the entertainment industry. Still dabbling in music production Nash taught sculpture and ceramics at university level for eleven years before retiring to yacht and his home restoration business in New Orleans. He has worked in twenty-seven countries and began his writing career in the year 2000. Of all of his hobbies and interests he loves sailing the best and is active in the sport as well as cruising.

David Nash has always enjoyed life in the fast lane and has no intention of living any other way. He is unmarried with no children and still enjoys sailing, surfing, hot rods, high powered weapons and beautiful women.

He is currently organizing his effort to completely retire to his yacht, The Amnesia Castle in the islands. He plans to live out his life sailing from place to place as it pleases him until he runs out of places to visit or the authorities won't allow him to return.

It has always been his wish that his death should come from the cold kiss of the sea unless the Jamaican pirates should happen to take him first.

www.ingramcontent.com/pod-product-compliance
Lightning Source LLC
Chambersburg PA
CBHW031829090426
42741CB00005B/183